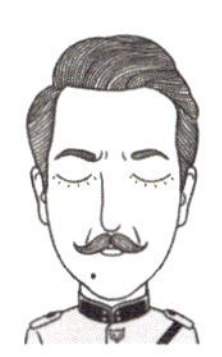
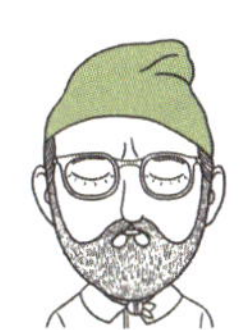
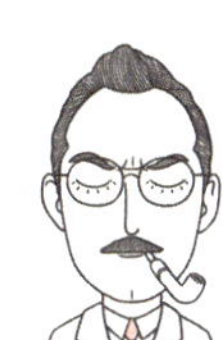
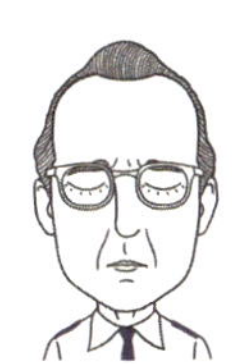

AF597829
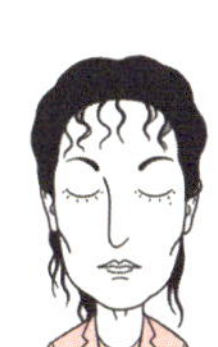
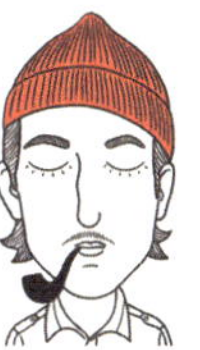
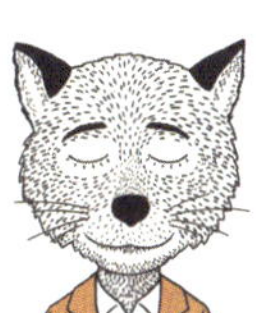
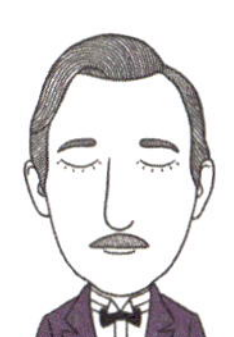
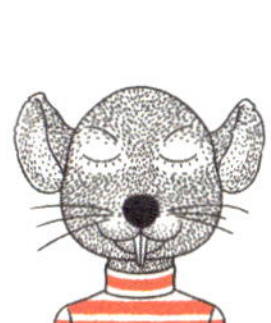
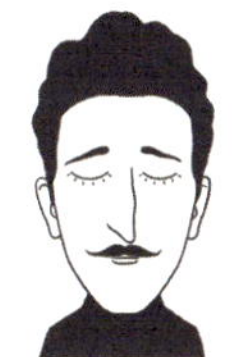
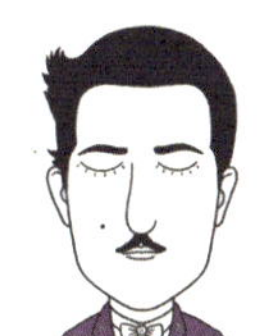
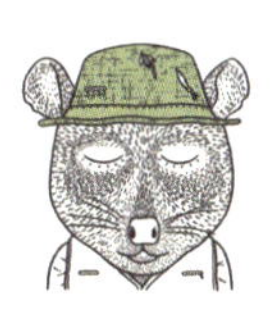
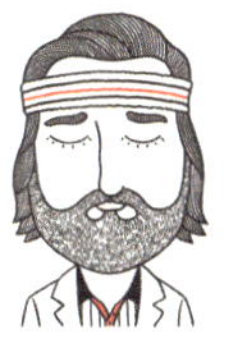
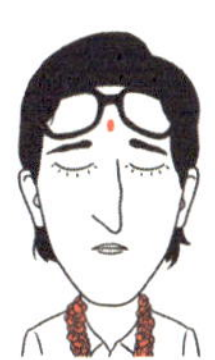
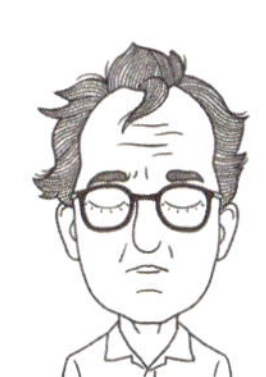
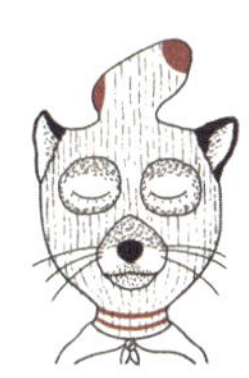
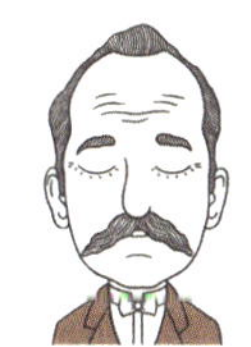
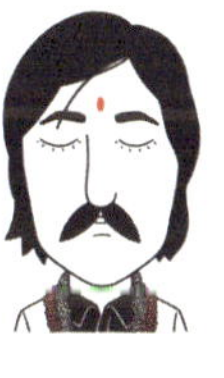
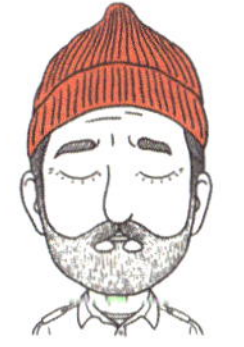
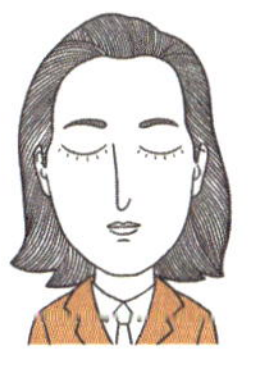
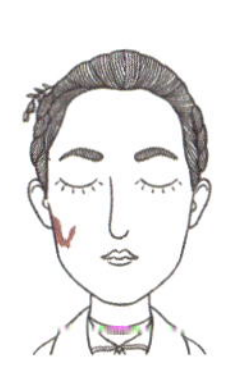
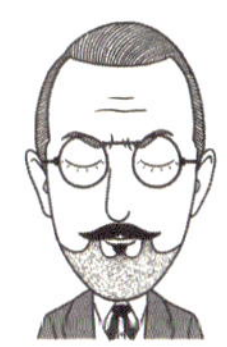
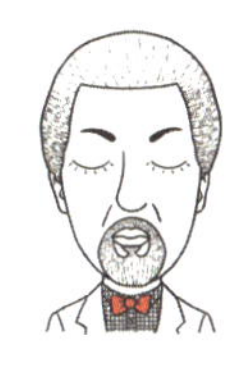
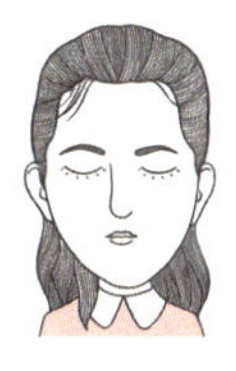
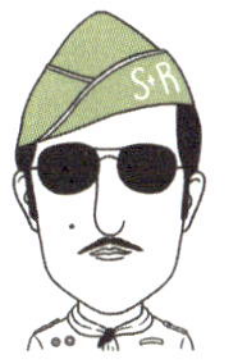
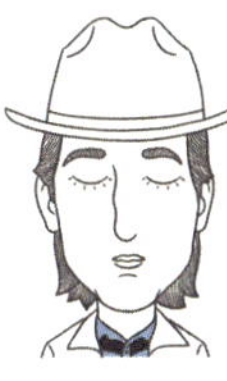
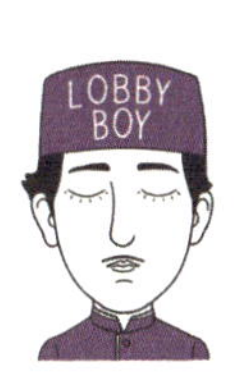
LOBBY
BOY
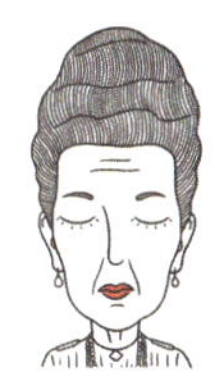
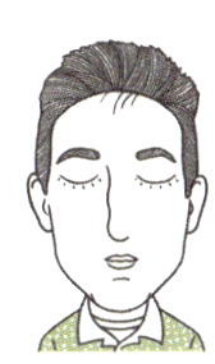
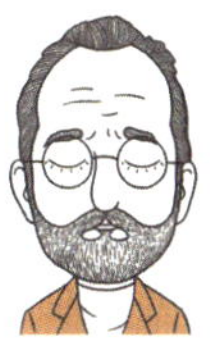
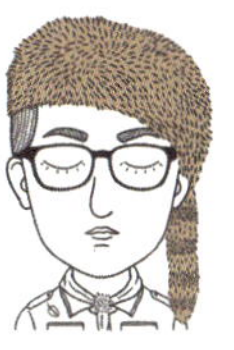
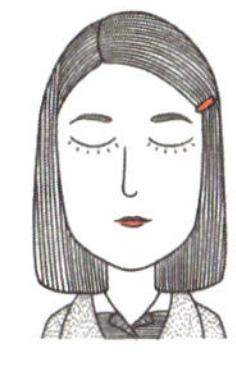
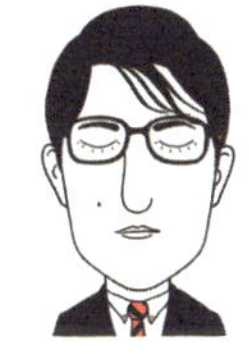
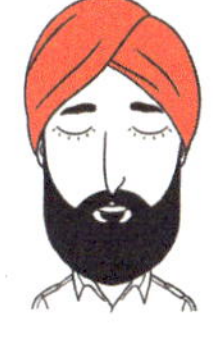
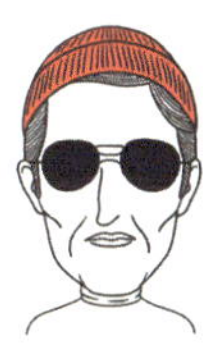
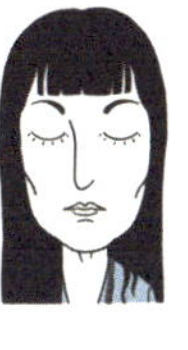
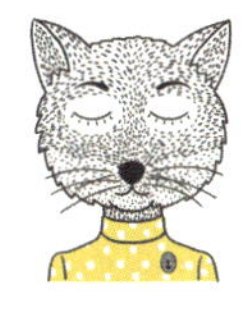
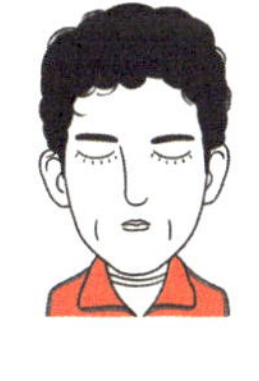
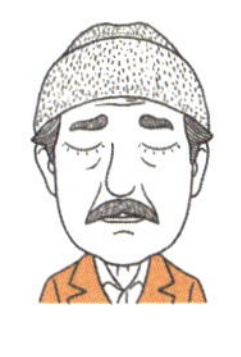
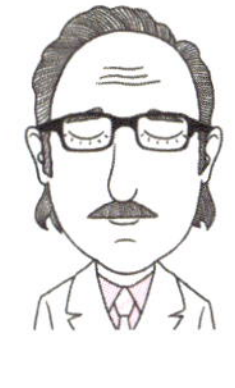

WES ANDERSON TRIBUTE

Editor, concept, and project director
Anna Minguet

Project's selection, design and layout
Eva Minguet (Monsa Publications)
Cover design
Eva Minguet (Monsa Publications)
Introduction and text edition
Monsa Publications
Translation by SomosTraductores

Cover image by Ben Biondo
Back cover by Patrick Concepción

INSTITUTO MONSA DE EDICIONES
Gravina 43 (08930)
Sant Adrià de Besòs
Barcelona (Spain)
Tlf. +34 93 381 00 50
www.monsa.com
monsa@monsa.com

Visit our official online store!
www.monsashop.com

Follow us!
Facebook: @monsashop
Instagram: @monsapublications

Second edition: 2019 January
ISBN: 978-84-16500-57-4
D.L. B 17399-2017
Printed by Cachimán Gráfic

by Eva Minguet

WES ANDERSON

TRIBUTE

monsa

INTRO

Who would not want to live in a Wes Anderson movie? His films are full of pastel colours (underscoring a vintage style), unusual characters depicting children as adults and adults as children, visual excesses and a storyline as crazy as it is fast-paced, not to mention his soundtracks overflowing with good taste.
Wes Anderson films have something that makes them unique, no doubt. All you need is a few minutes to see that you are enjoying one of his cinematic wonders. Think of how he abuses ancient and precious objects from an era in when all artefacts and machines worked analogically. For example: Where did the ubiquitous record players and LPs in *Moonrise Kingdom* end up? Or Margot's typewriter in *The Royal Tenenbaums*?
The filmmaker has attracted loyal collaborators—including Bill Murray, Jason Schwartzman, Owen Wilson, Anjelica Huston, Kumar Pallna—who breathe life into characters with a unique essence.

This is a tribute book to Wes Anderson and the universe he has created. It highlights his most prominent characters such as Margot, Mr Fox, Sam & Suzy, Zero, Steve Zissou... his vintage trend, his nostalgic but not sad touch, his meticulously arranged sets and his obsession with symmetry.

Twenty-two international artists unveil their most personal perspectives through one or several illustrations, expressing in a sentence what this wonderful, timeless and sympathetic filmmaker means to them.

¿A quién no le gustaría vivir dentro del cine de Wes Anderson? Sus películas llenas de colores pastel para enfatizar ese estilo vintage, personajes insólitos en los que presenta a los niños como adultos y los adultos como niños, excesos visuales y una narrativa tan alocada como trepidante, sin mencionar sus bandas sonoras rebosantes de buen gusto.
Se ha demostrado que las películas de Wes Anderson tienen algo que las hace únicas, con tan sólo ver unos pocos minutos ya sabes cuando estás en presencia de alguna de sus maravillas. El abuso de objetos antiguos y preciosos de una época en la que todo artefacto o máquina funcionaba de forma analógica. Por ejemplo: ¿Dónde quedaron esos tocadiscos y vinilos tan presentes en *Moonrise Kingdom*? o ¿La máquina de escribir de Margot en *The Royal Tenenbaums*?
El cineasta también cuenta con fieles colaboradores entre los que siempre encontramos a Bill Murray, Jason Schwartzman, Owen Wilson, Anjelica Huston, Kumar Pallna, dando vida a personajes con una esencia única.

Este es un libro tributo a Wes Anderson y a todo el universo que ha creado. Desde sus personajes más destacados como son Margot, Mr Fox, Sam & Suzy, Zero, Steve Zissou... a su tendencia por lo vintage, su toque nostálgico pero no triste, sus decorados cuidados hasta el último detalle, y su obsesión por la simetría.

Veintidos artistas internacionales nos muestran su visión más personal por medio de una o varias ilustraciones, expresando en una frase lo que significa para ellos este maravilloso, atemporal y simpático cineasta.

Image by Alejandro Giraldo (right page)

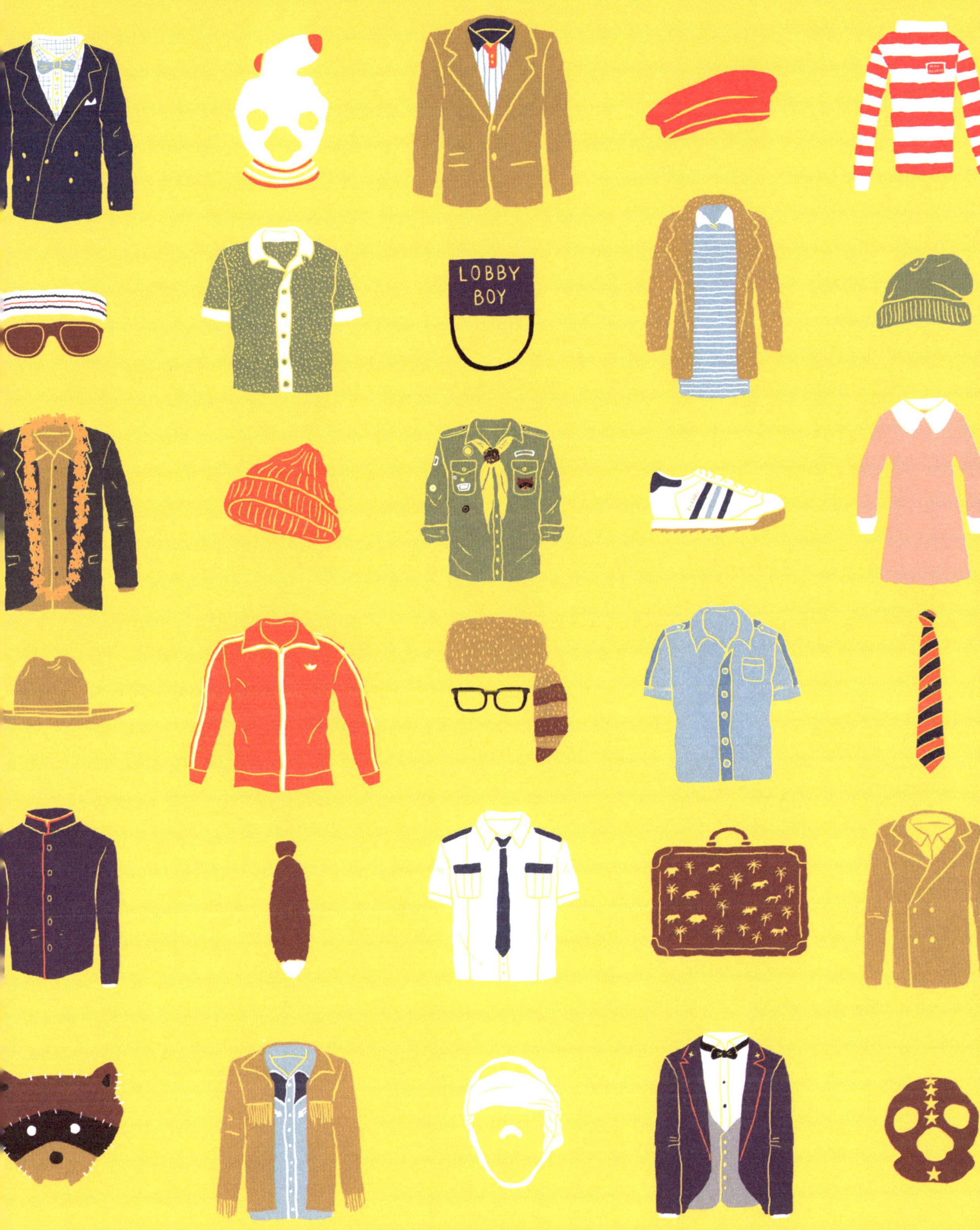
LOBBY
BOY

INDEX

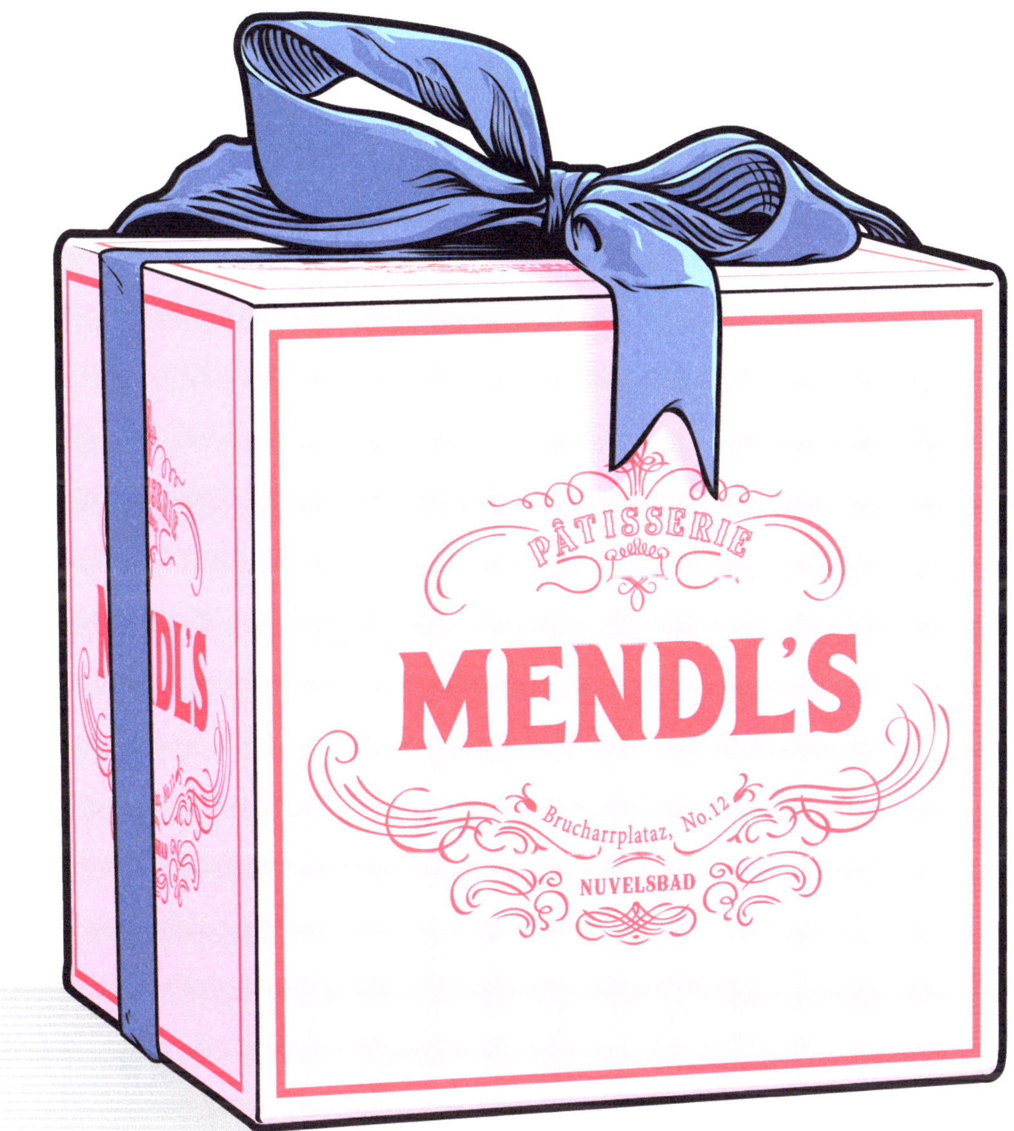

Image by Joshua Budich

GUILLAUME MORELLEC

www.guillaumemorellec.com
Instagram: @guillaumemorellec
Twitter: @gmorellec
Facebook: @Guillaume-Morellec

"I LOVE THE SWEET MADNESS THAT EMANATES FROM THE CHARACTERS OF WES ANDERSON, AND WHICH CONFERS TO HIS WORKS A TRUE POETRY"

Born in 1983, Guillaume Morellec is a french designer and illustrator living in Paris. After working several years in creating logos, brochures and websites in Paris and Montreal, he decided to take a new career orientation and now works as a graphic designer and freelance illustrator working for press, edition, fashion... His passions for Cinema and Video Game influences his work which is now regularly exhibited internationally in galleries such as Spoke Art Gallery, Hero Complex Gallery, Bottleneck Gallery...

Nacido en 1983, Guillaume Morellec es un diseñador e ilustrador francés que vive en París. Después de trabajar varios años en la creación de logos, folletos y sitios web en París y Montreal, decidió tomar una nueva orientación profesional y ahora trabaja como diseñador gráfico e ilustrador freelance para prensa, edición, moda ... Su pasión por el cine y los videojuegos ha influenciado su obra, la cual se expone con regularidad internacionalmente en galerías como la Spoke Art, Hero Complex, Bottleneck...

The Grand Budapest Hotel (right page)

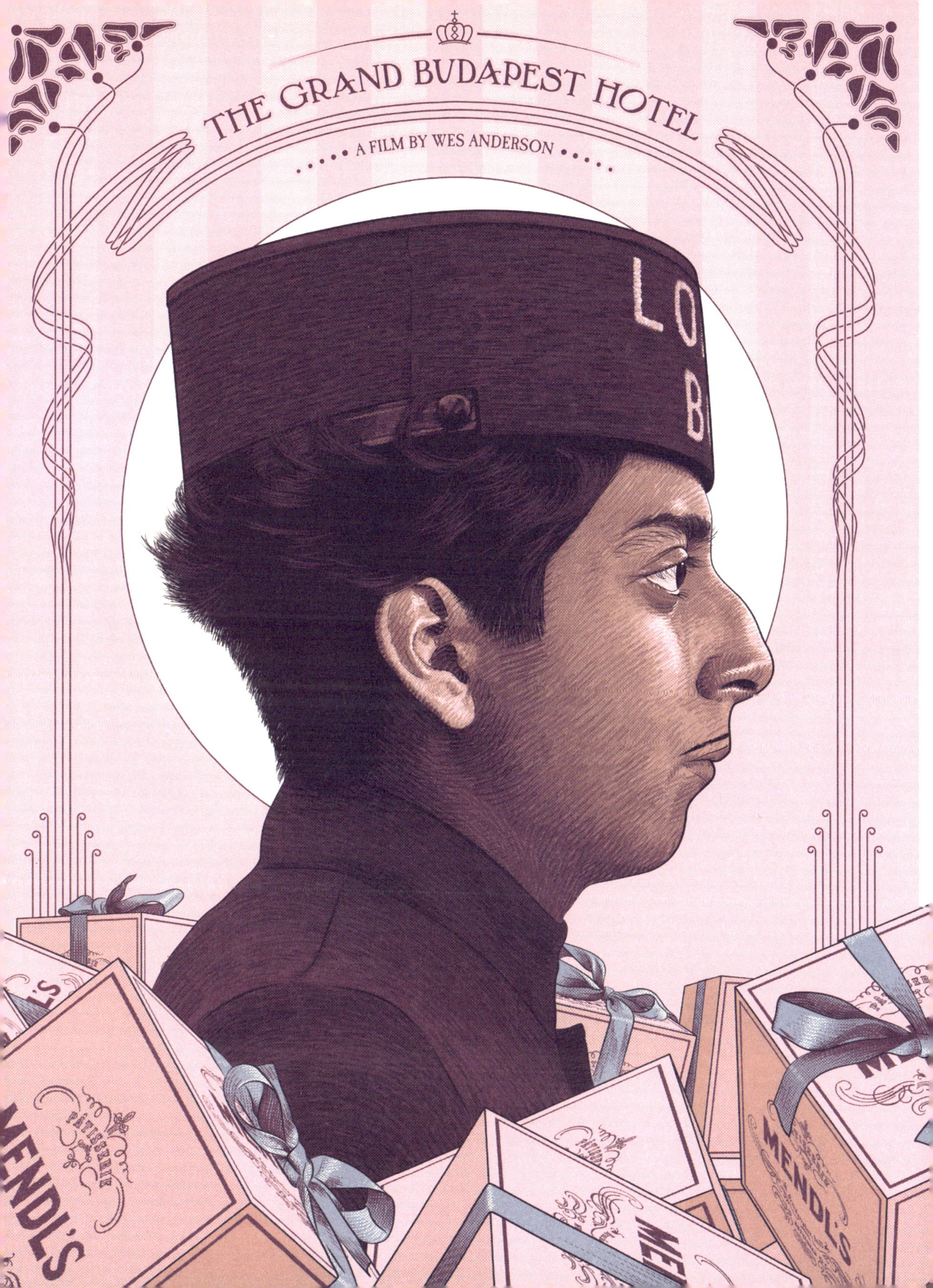
THE GRAND BUDAPEST HOTEL
A FILM BY WES ANDERSON
MENDL'S
PÂTISSERIE
MENDL'S

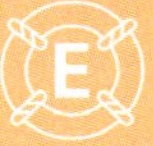

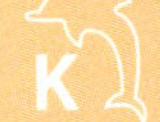

The deeper you go, the weirder life gets.

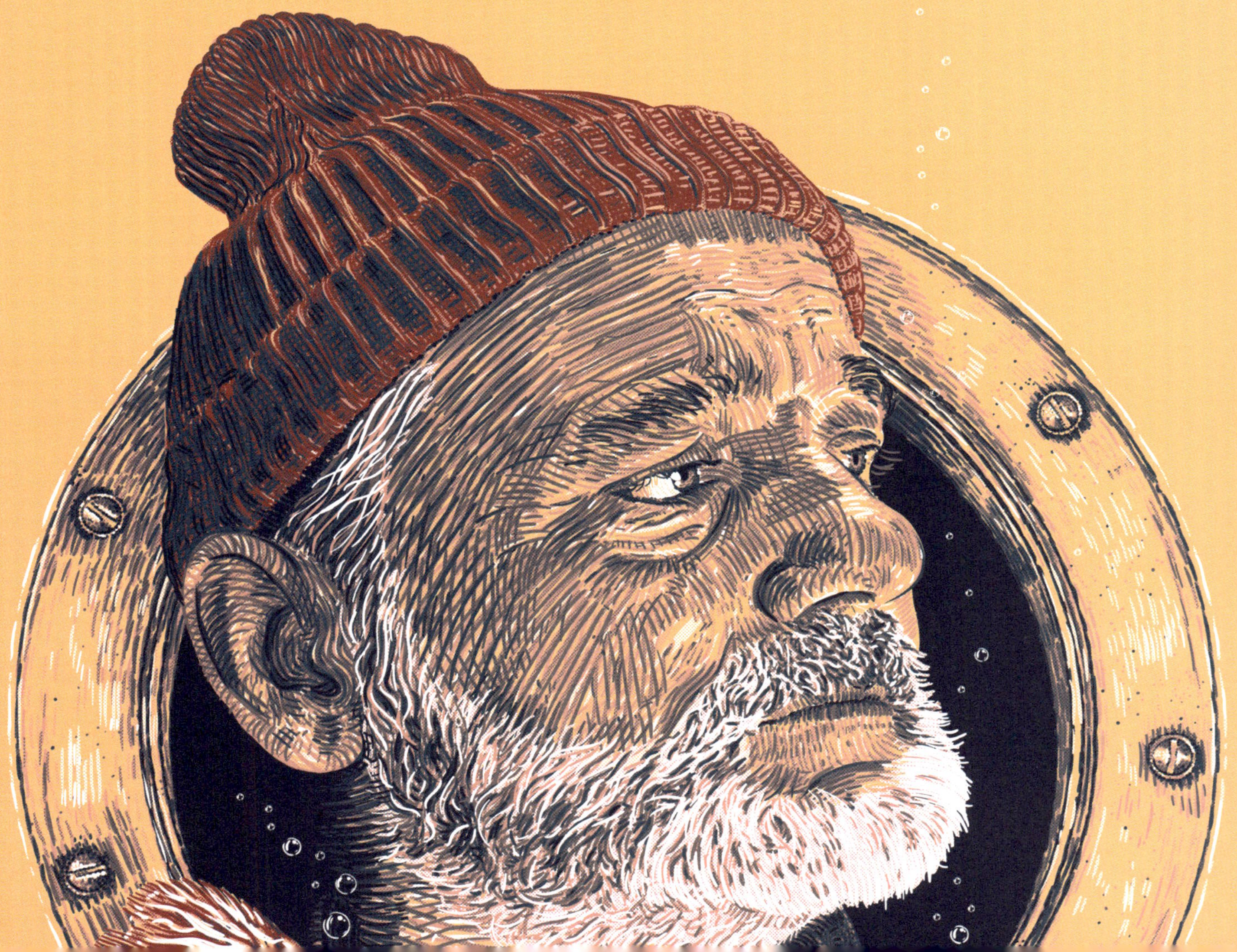

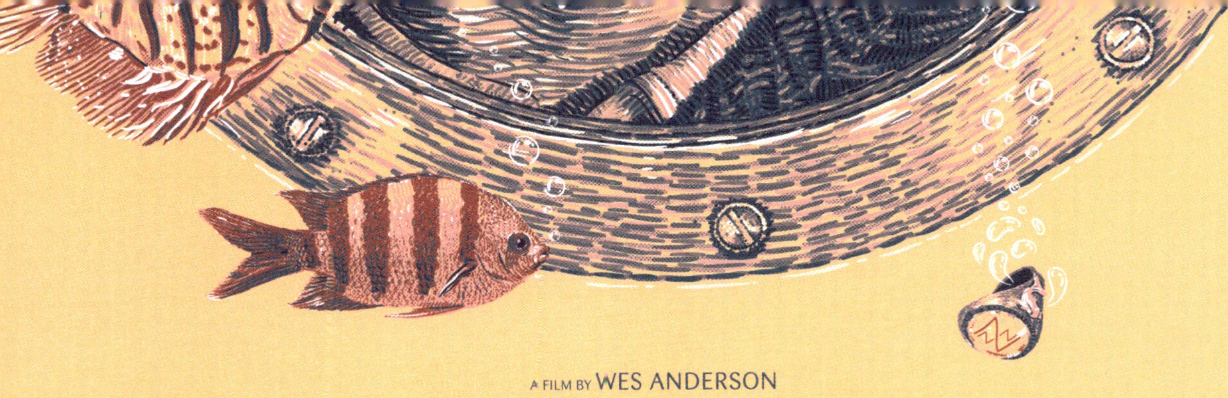

A FILM BY WES ANDERSON

THE LIFE AQUATIC
- WITH STEVE ZISSOU -

Bill **MURRAY** Owen **WILSON** Cate **BLANCHETT** Anjelica **HUSTON** Willem **DAFOE** Jeff **GOLDBLUM** Michael **GAMBON** Bud **CORT**

TOUCHSTONE PICTURES presents an AMERICAN EMPIRICAL PICTURE "THE LIFE AQUATIC WITH STEVE ZISSOU"
BILL MURRAY OWEN WILSON CATE BLANCHETT ANJELICA HUSTON WILLEM DAFOE JEFF GOLDBLUM MICHAEL GAMBON BUD CORT
casting by DOUGLAS AIBEL music supervisor RANDALL POSTER music by MARK MOTHERSBAUGH costume designer MILENA CANONERO
edited by DAVID MORITZ production designer MARK FRIEDBERG director of photography ROBERT YEOMAN, ASC executive producer RUDD SIMMONS
produced by WES ANDERSON BARRY MENDEL SCOTT RUDIN written by WES ANDERSON NOAH BAUMBACH

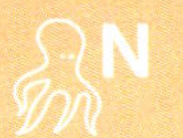

R RESTRICTED
SOME LANGUAGE AND NUDITY

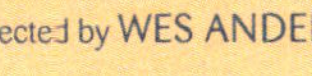

directed by WES ANDERSON

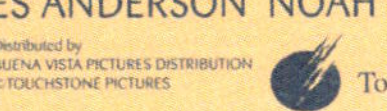

Distributed by
BUENA VISTA PICTURES DISTRIBUTION
©TOUCHSTONE PICTURES

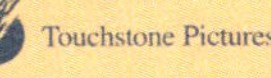

Touchstone Pictures

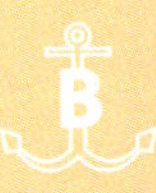

The Life Acquatic with Steve Zissou

IVONNA BUENROSTRO

www.ivonnabuenrostro.tumblr.com
Instagram: @heartbeatsclub
Facebook: @heartbeatsclub
Tumblr: heartbeatsclub.tumblr.com

"DRAWING WES CHARACTERS WAS THE BEGINNING OF MY OBSESSION FOR DRAWING MOVIES"

Ivonna Buenrostro is an illustrator originally from Mexico.

Her project Heartbeats Club is an attempt to belong together with the films, series, books and music she relates to, feels or admires.

With this personal project, she has managed to create a piece of art that had been sent to more than 15 countries.

Ivonna Buenrostro es una ilustradora de origen mexicano.

Su proyecto Heartbeats club es un intento de pertenecer a las películas, series, libros o música con los que se relaciona, siente o admira.

Mediante este proyecto personal, ha logrado crear arte que ha sido enviado a más de 15 países.

Sam Shakusky (right page)

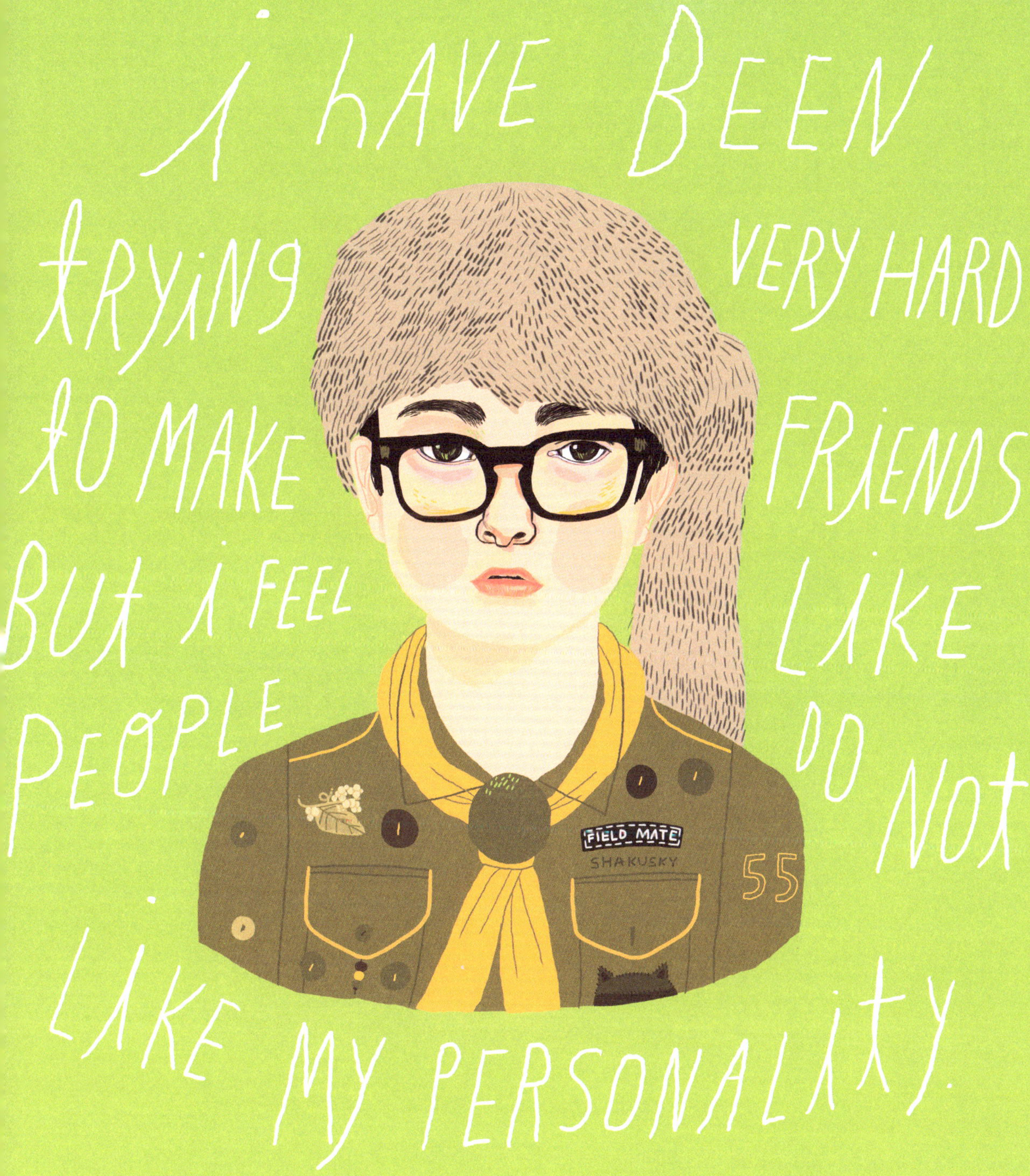

i HAVE BEEN
trying VERY HARD
to MAKE FRIENDS
But i FEEL LiKE
PEOPLE DO NOT
LiKE MY PERSONALity.

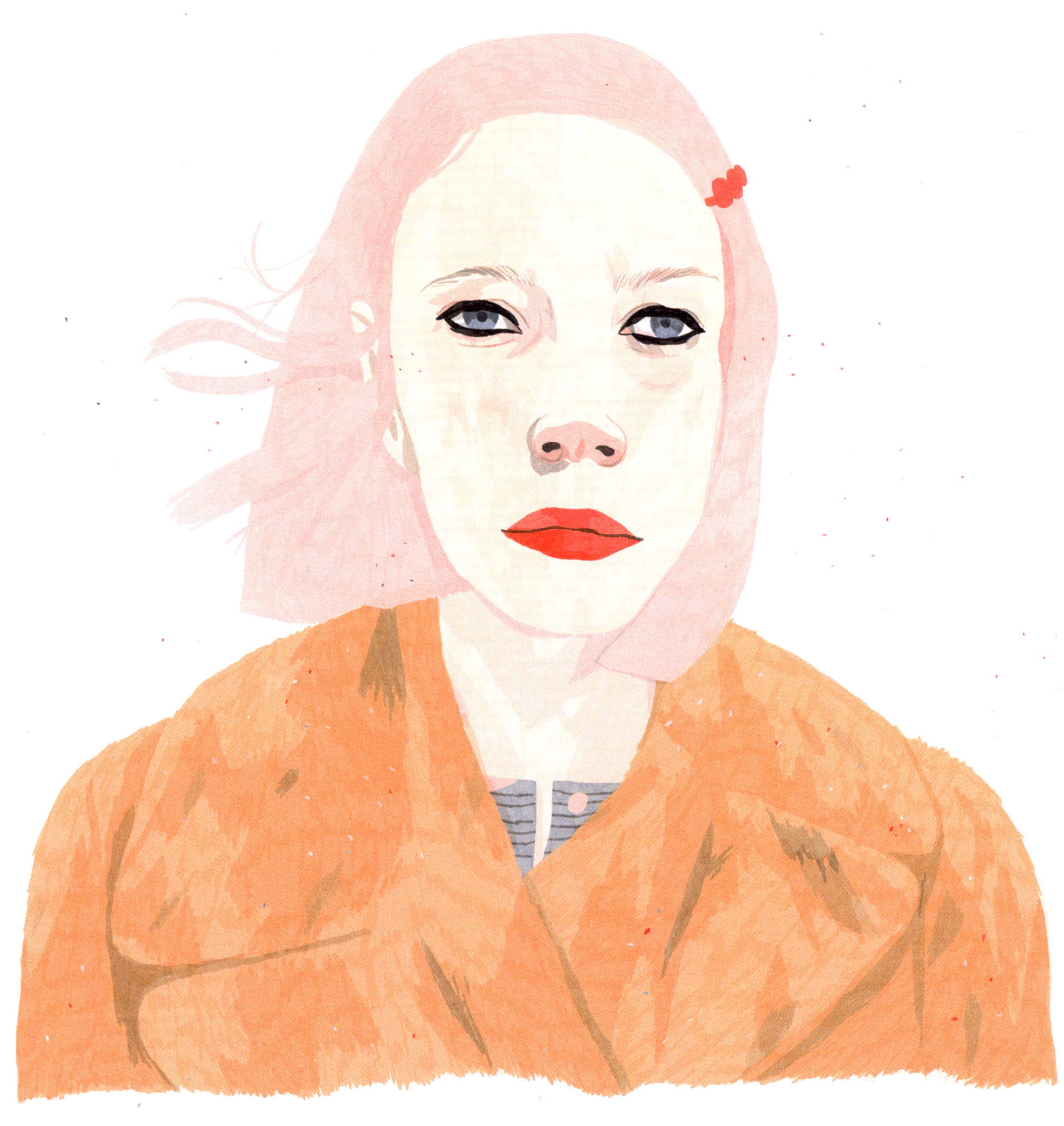

I DON'T DO TOO MUCH TALKING THESE DAYS

These Days (The Royal Tenenbaums)

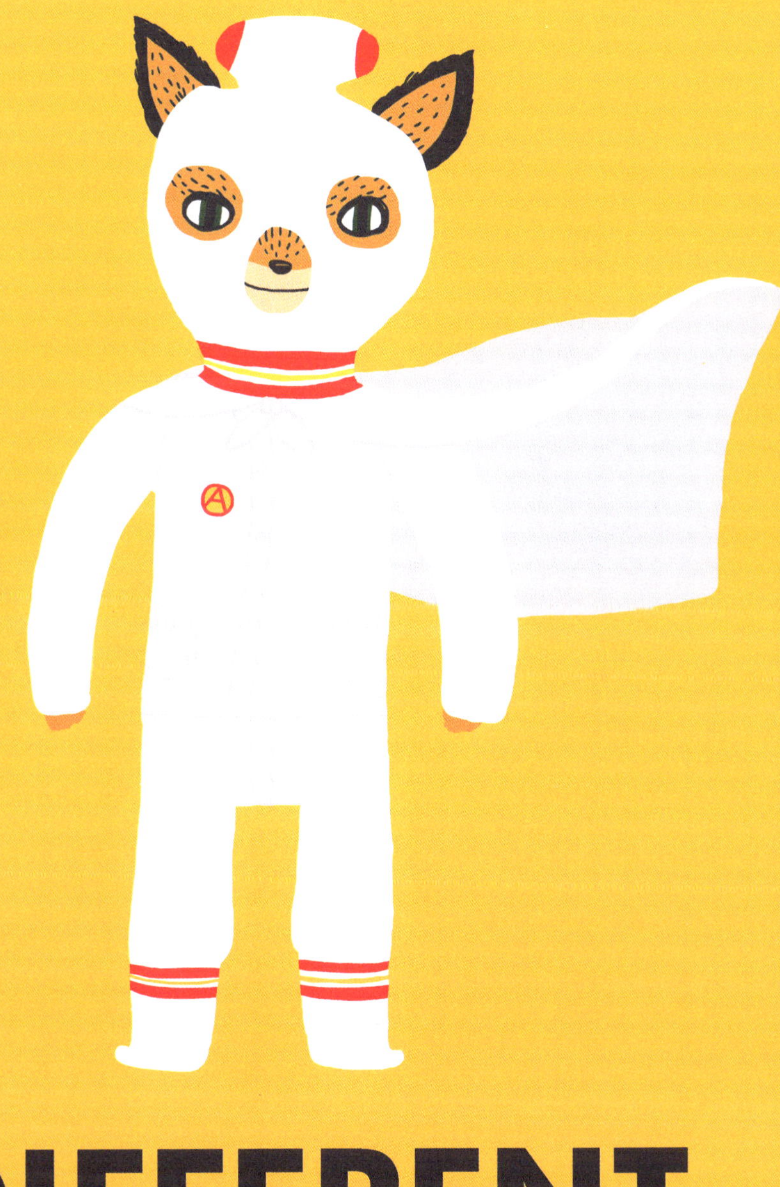

DIFFERENT

Different (Fantastic Mr. Fox)

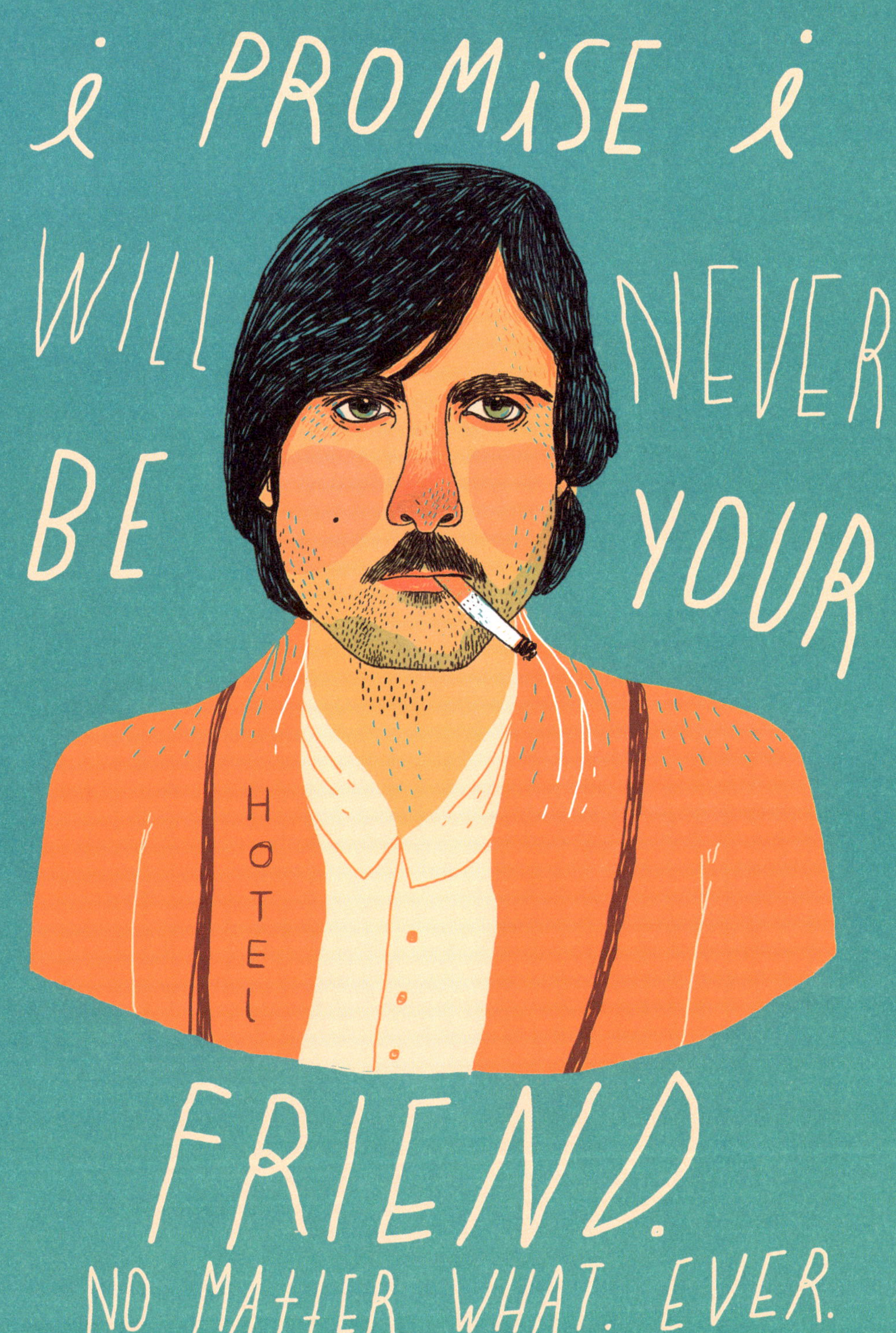

Hotel Chevalier (The Darjeeling Limited)

IS HE FLIRTING WITH YOU?

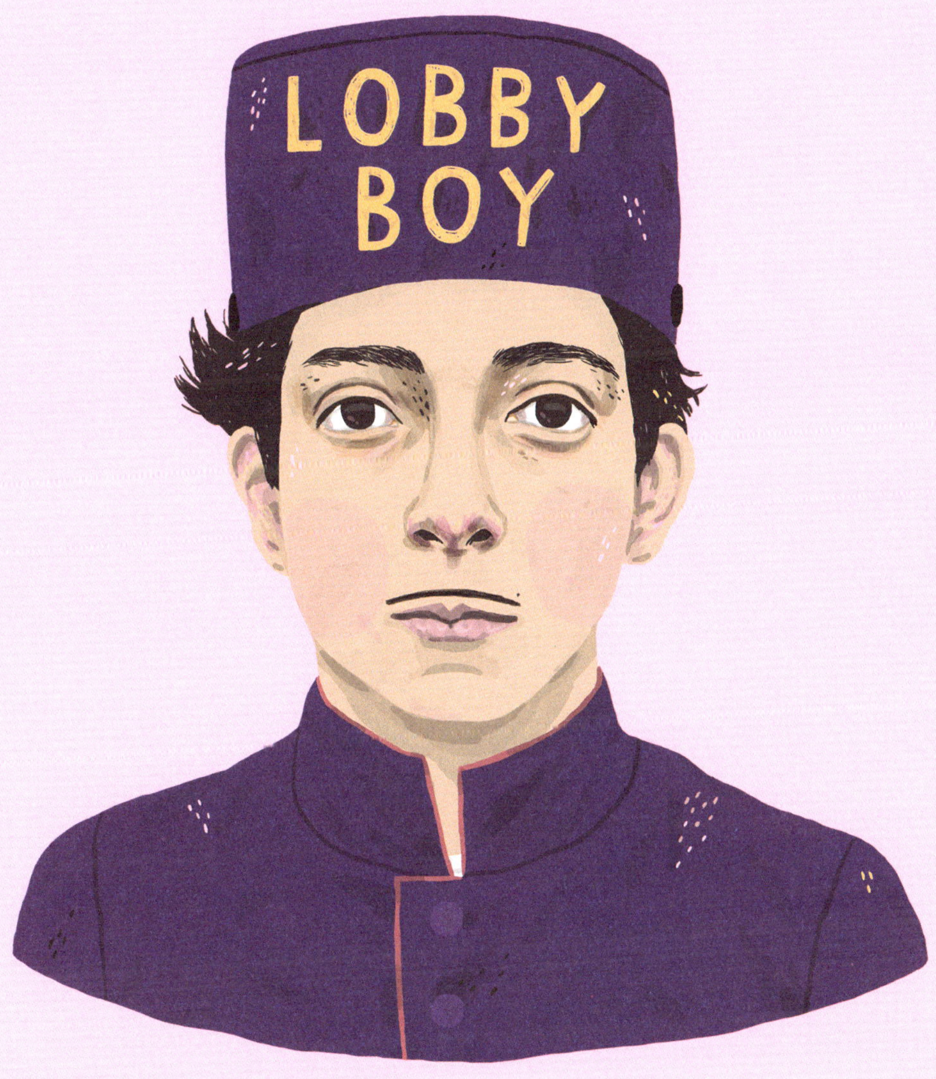

Lobby Boy (Grand Budapest Hotel)

IBRAHEEM YOUSSEF

www.ibraheemyoussef.com
Twitter: @ibraheemyoussef
Facebook: @The-Artwork-of-Ibraheem-Youssef

"THERE IS A SUBTLE YET RICH BEAUTY TO WES ANDERSON'S FILMS. IN MY ARTWORK, I AIM TO CONVEY THAT SUBTLETY THROUGH MINIMALISM AND SYMBOLISM"

Ibraheem Youssef is an Canadian/Egyptian Designer that is currently based in Hong Kong.

His work has been featured by The Guardian, The Independent, Der Speigel, El País, Digital Artist, SlashFilm, Universal/NBC, Wired Magazine, Empire Magazine and recognized by Cannes, Clios, Graphis & How Magazine and exhibited in cities such as San Francisco, Los Angeles, New York, Miami, Toronto, Breda, Cairo and Paris to mention a few.

He also only wears an all white outfit during the day, and the same outfit in all black at night.

Ibraheem Youssef es un diseñador canadiense/egipcio que vive actualmente en Hong Kong.

Su obra ha sido presentada por The Guardian, The Independent, Der Spiegel, El País, Digital Artist, SlashFilm, Universal/NBC, Wired Magazine, Empire Magazine y reconocida por Cannes, Clios, la revista Graphis & How y expuesta en ciudades como San Francisco, Los Ángeles, Nueva York, Miami, Toronto, Breda, El Cairo y Paris, entre otras.

Ibraheem lleva durante el día un traje blanco y durante la noche el mismo traje pero en color negro.

The Life Acquatic with Steve Zissou (right page)

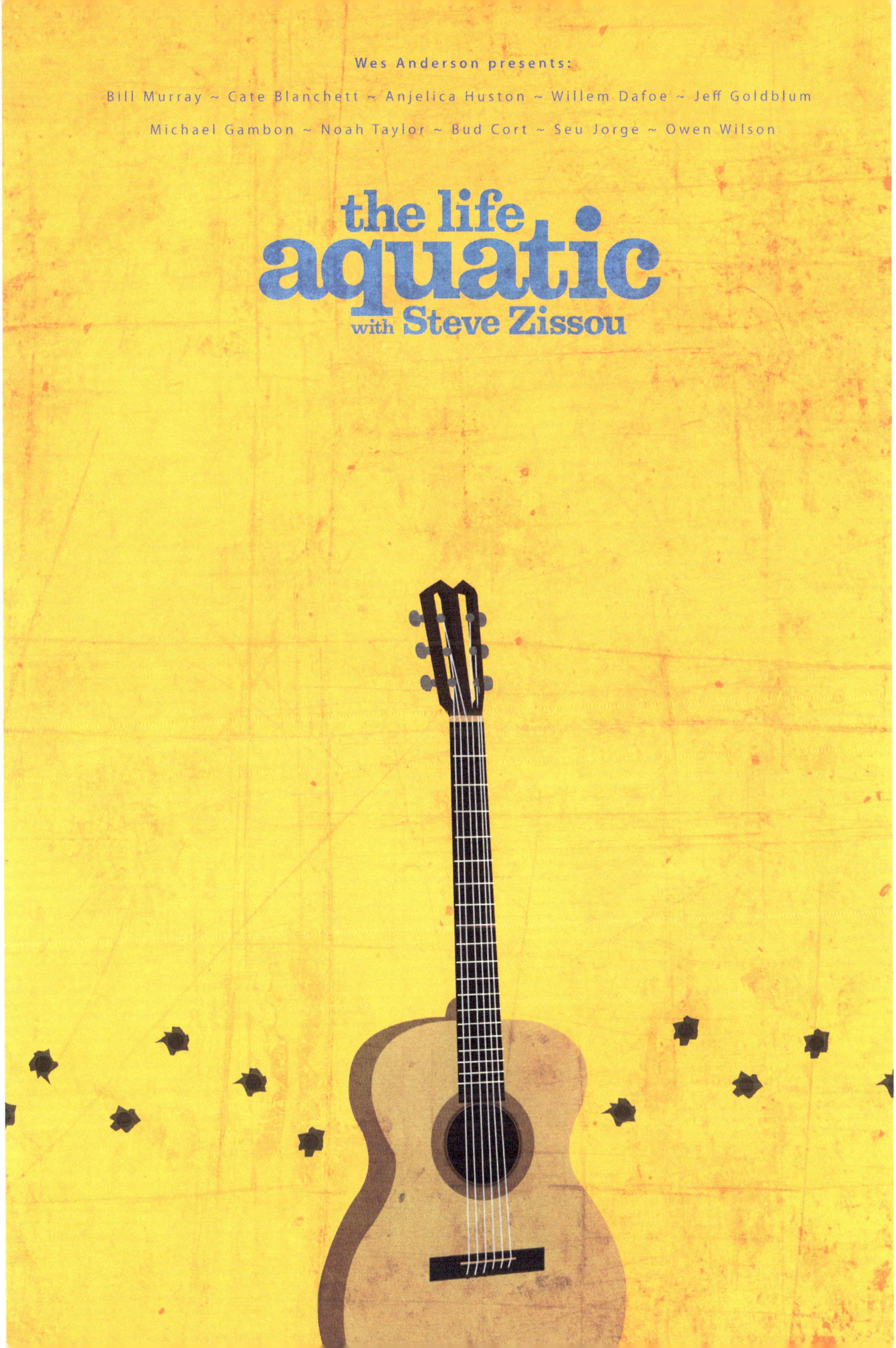

Wes Anderson presents:

Bill Murray ~ Cate Blanchett ~ Anjelica Huston ~ Willem Dafoe ~ Jeff Goldblum

Michael Gambon ~ Noah Taylor ~ Bud Cort ~ Seu Jorge ~ Owen Wilson

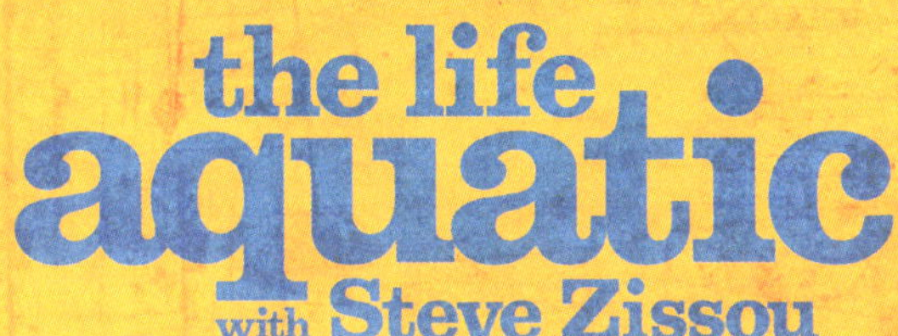

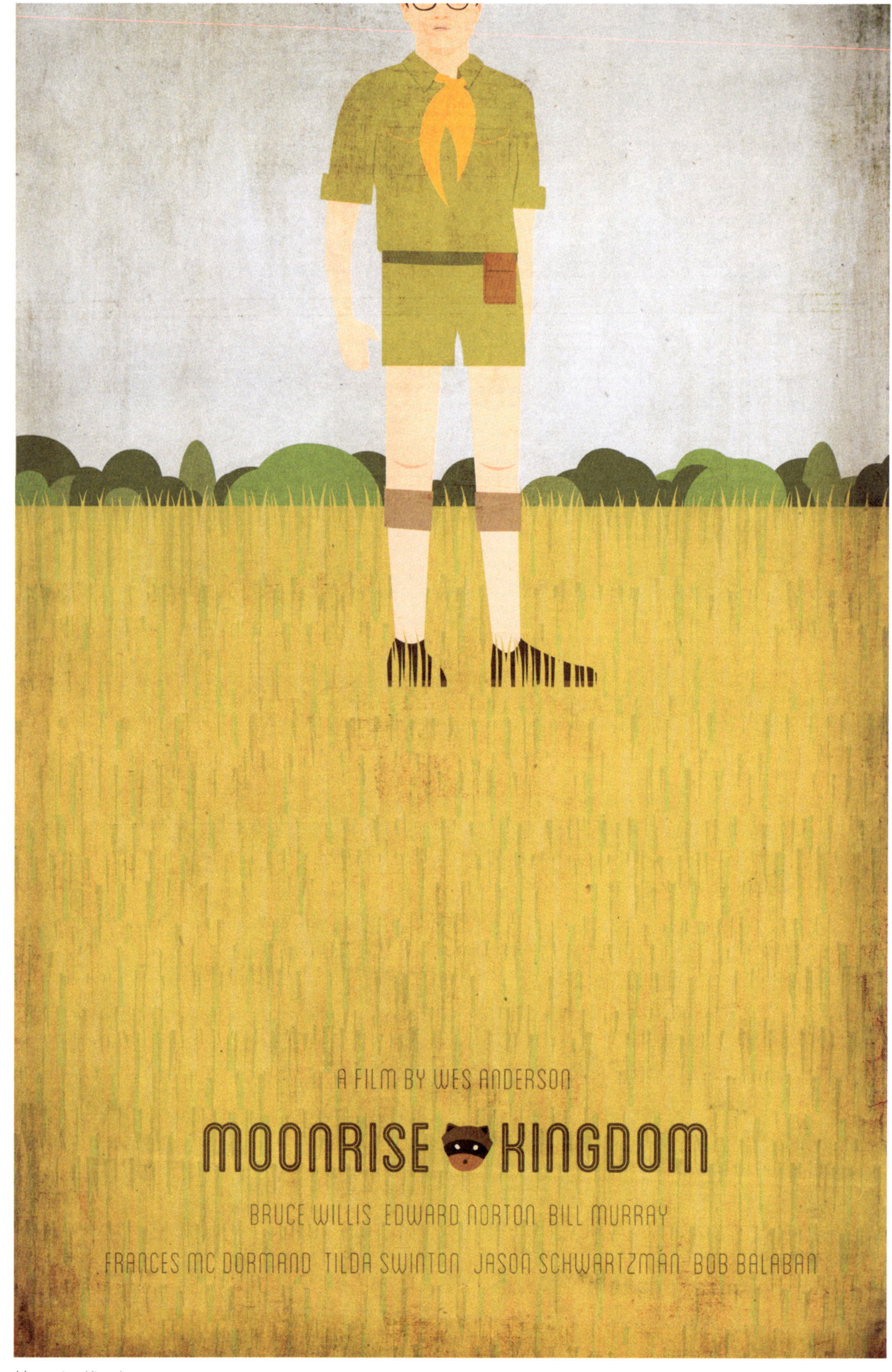

Moonrise Kingdom

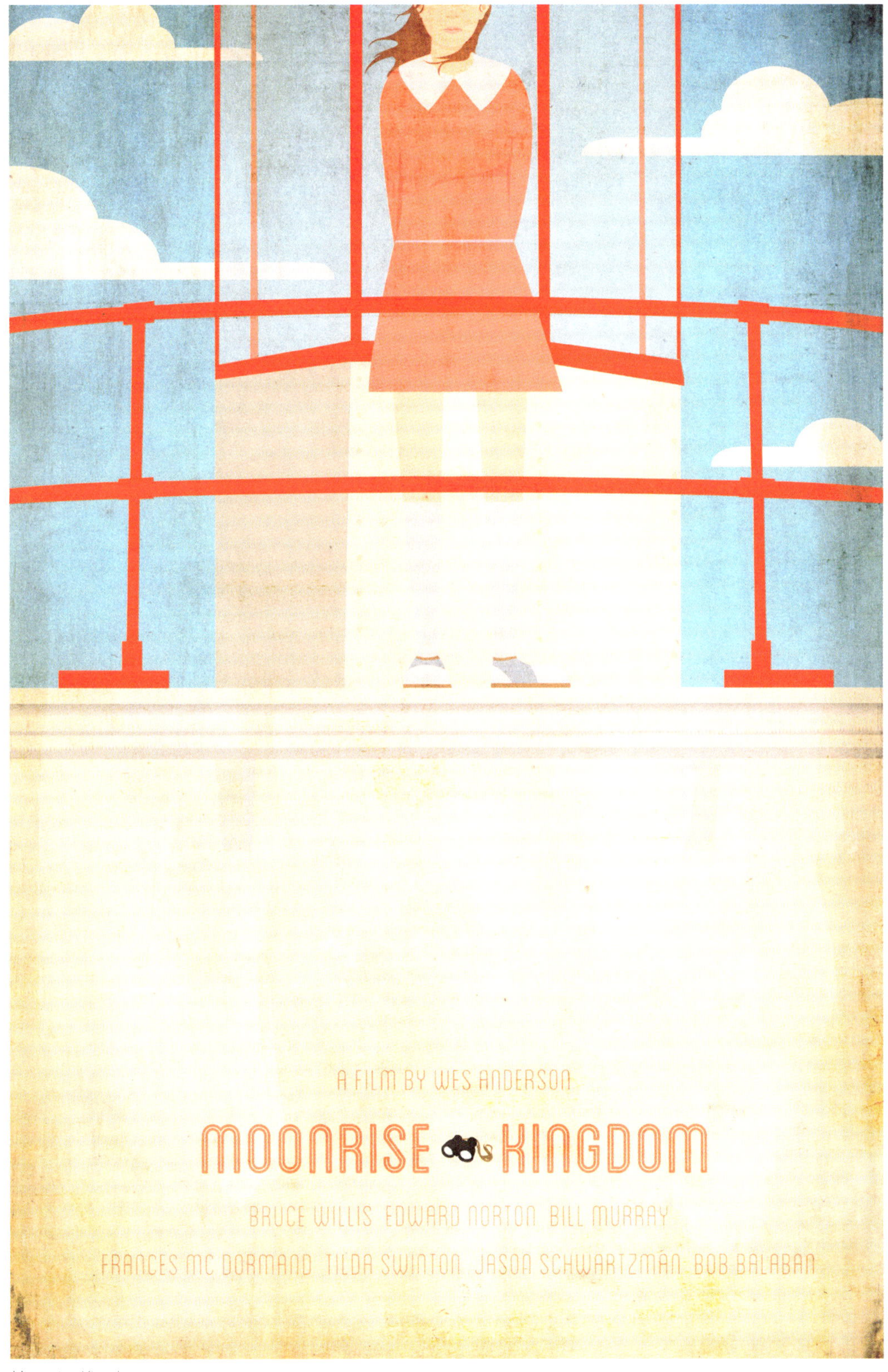

Moonrise Kingdom

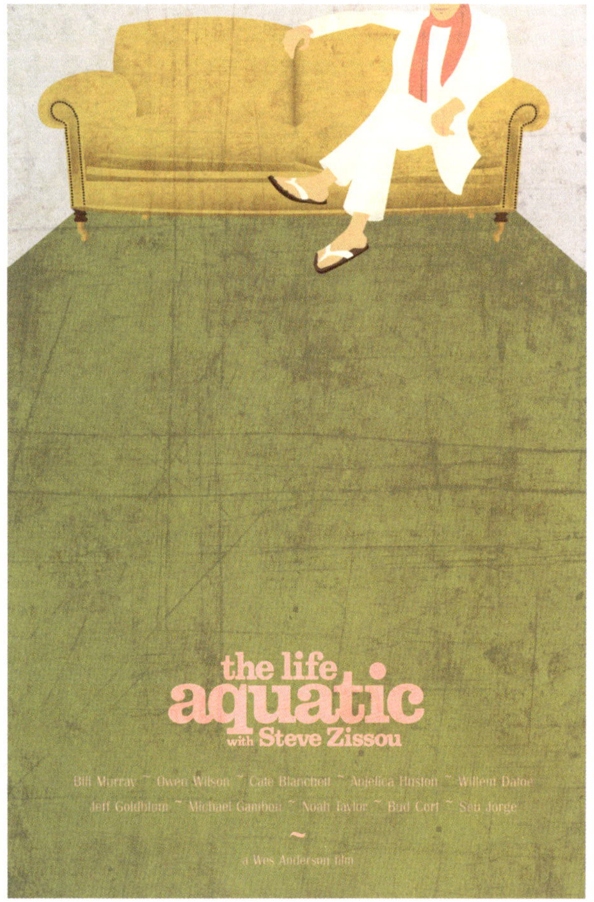

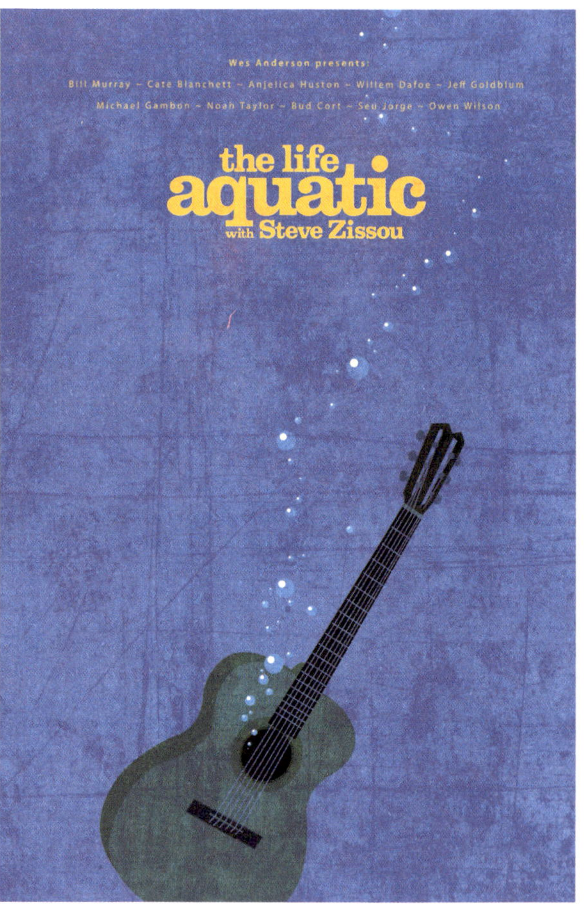

The Life Acquatic with Steve Zissou (both pages)

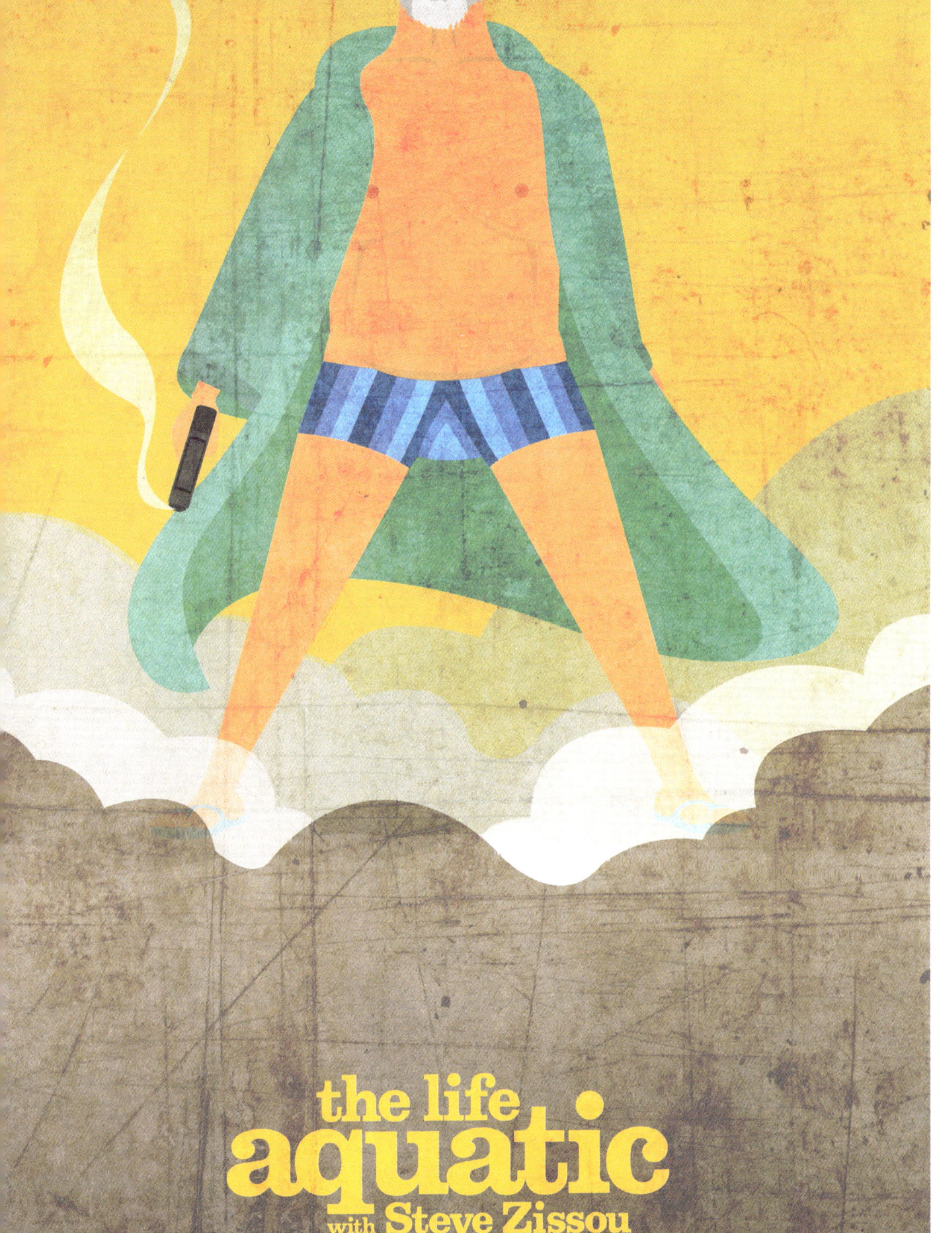
the life
aquatic
with Steve Zissou
Bill Murray ~ Owen Wilson ~ Cate Blanchett ~ Anjelica Huston ~ Willem Dafoe
Jeff Goldblum ~ Michael Gambon ~ Noah Taylor ~ Bud Cort ~ Seu Jorge
~
a Wes Anderson film

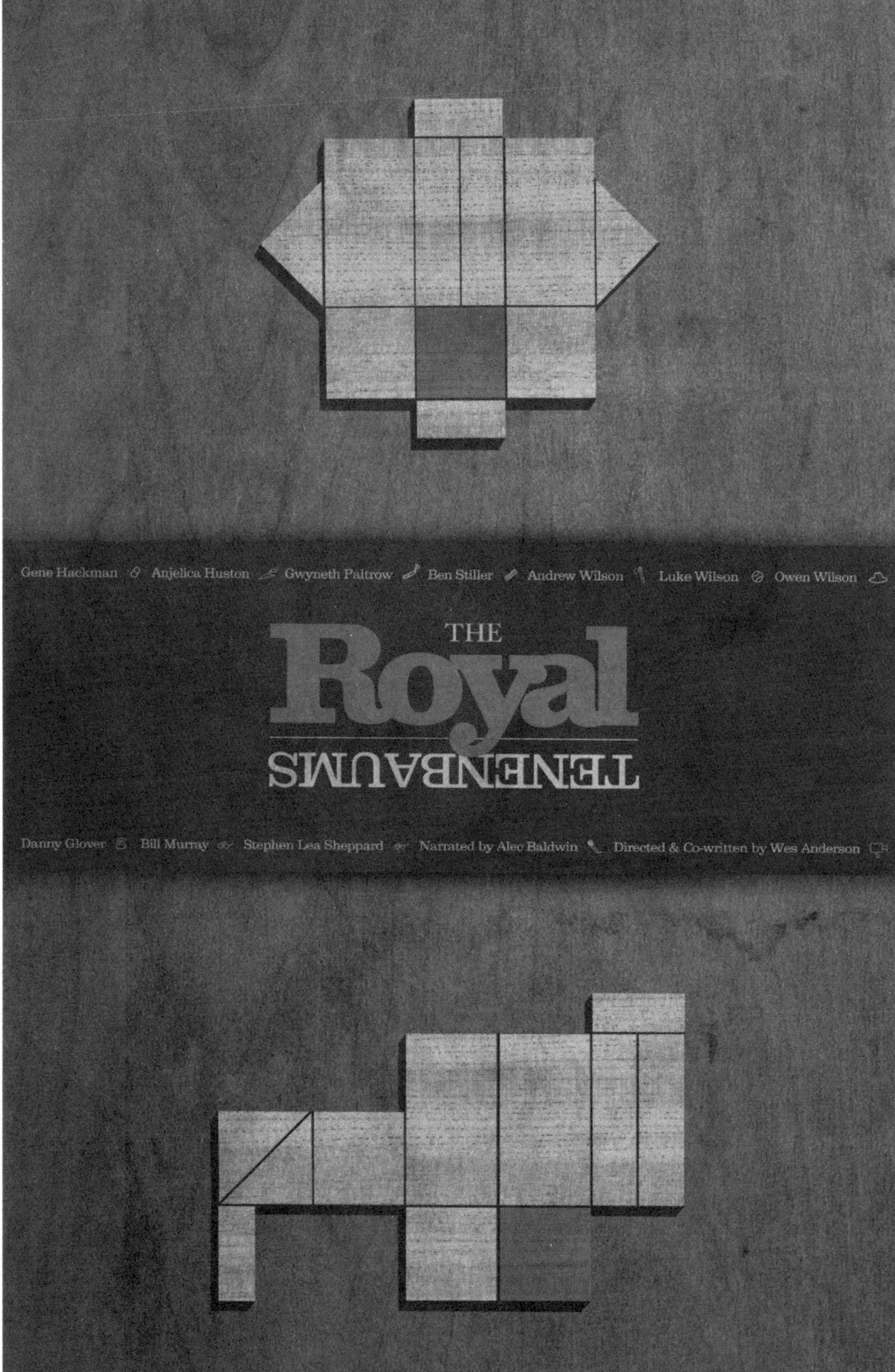

The Royal Tenenbaums

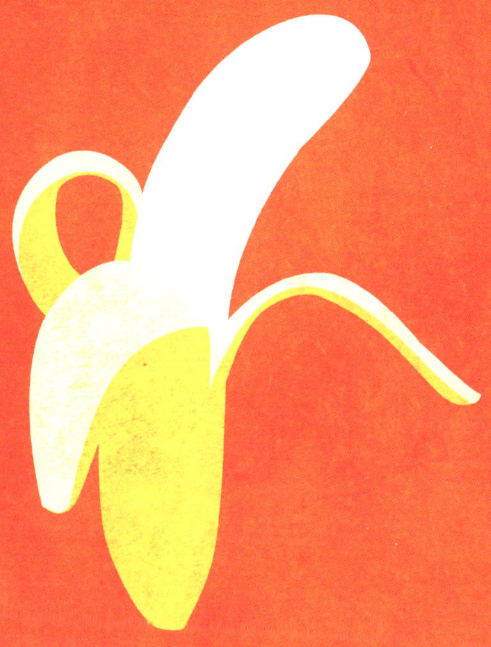

BOTTLE

Luke Wilson Owen Wilson James Caan Robert Musgrave Lumi Cavazos

ROCKET

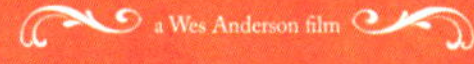

Bottle Rocket

SARA FRATINI

www.sarafratini.com
Instagram: @sara_fratini
Twitter: @sarafratini
www.facebook.com/sarafra
www.sarafratini.tumblr.com

"I THINK WE'RE JUST GONNA TO HAVE TO BE SECRETLY IN LOVE WITH EACH OTHER AND LEAVE IT AT THAT, RICHIE"

-Margot Tenenbaums-

Sara Fratini, Venezuela, 1985. At age three she tried to draw with her feet but seeing the results she decided to switch to her hands. Since then, she carries a pencil and a notebook everywhere she goes. In the early years, her notebook and case caused some falls, but today they are an excuse to get away and draw at any time. She studied Fine Arts at the Universidad Complutense de Madrid and illustration in Nancy, France. Since 2012 she is responsible for the Guarimba International Film Festival for which she organizes an annual exhibition of posters by artists from around the world. She has painted murals in different European cities

Sara Fratini, Venezuela, 1985. A los tres años ya intentaba dibujar con los pies pero al ver que no resultaba decidió cambiar los pies por las manos y desde entonces lleva un lápiz y un cuaderno a todas partes. Los primeros años, cuaderno y estuche fueron motivo de algunas caídas, hoy son una excusa para escapar y dibujar en cualquier momento. Cursó la licenciatura de Bellas Artes en la Universidad Complutense de Madrid y estudios de ilustración en Nancy, Francia. Desde 2012 se hace cargo de La Guarimba International Film Festival en el que organiza una exposición anual de carteles de artistas de todo el mundo. Ha realizado murales en diferentes ciudades Europeas.

Grand Budapest Hotel (right page)

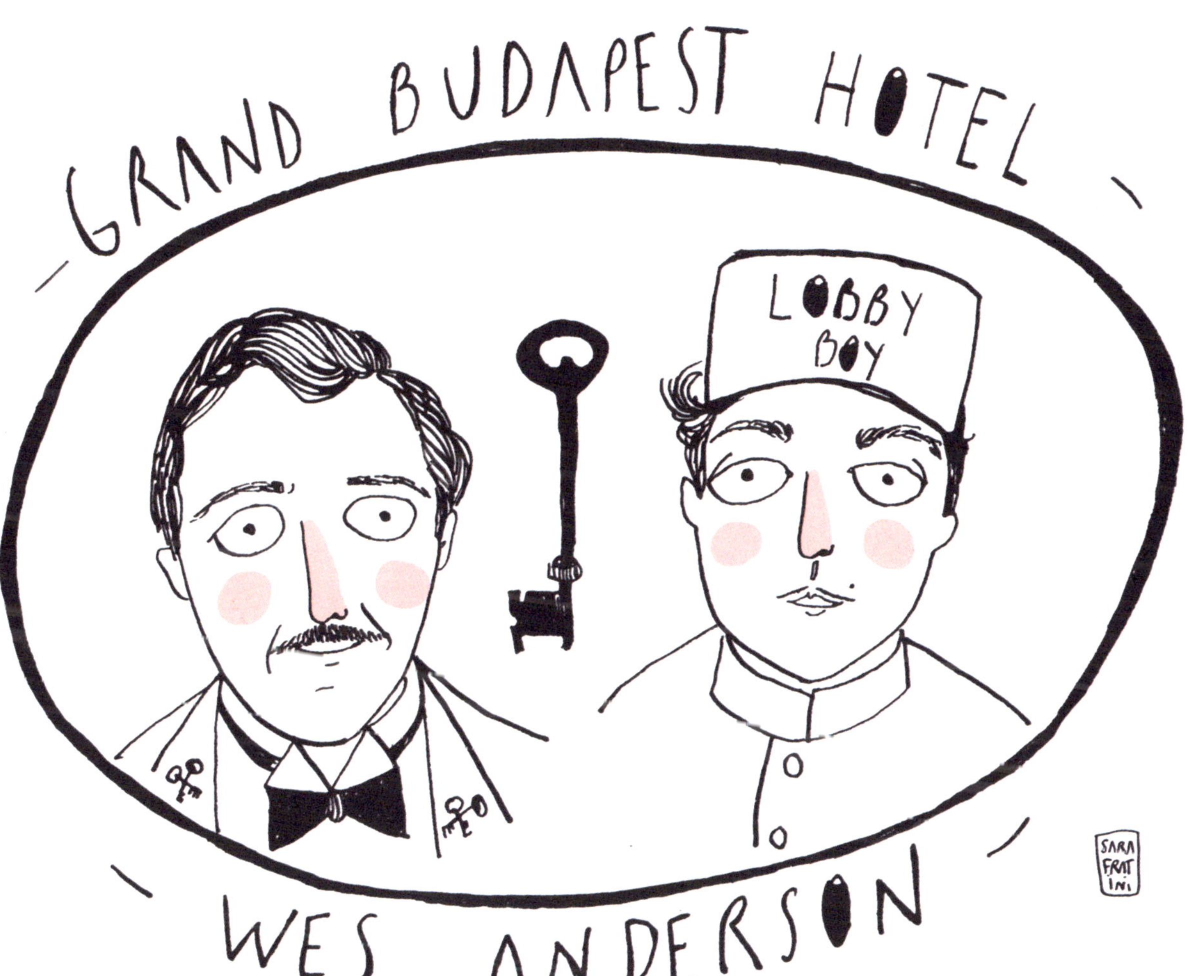
GRAND BUDAPEST HOTEL
LOBBY BOY
WES ANDERSON
SARA FRATINI

www.gokceinan.com
www.behance.net/inangokce

"BRAND NEW NOSTALGIA"

Born in 1987 in Mersin, Turkey. Studied and mastered in illustration and fine arts. Sold her soul by working as senior art director in several advertising agencies. Enjoy painting, trying to focus on watercolor and acrylic. Crazy about symmetry and colors as Wes. Loves Wes. Living in Istanbul, trying to cross boundaries.

Nacida en 1987 en Mersin, Turquía. Estudió y se especializó en ilustración y bellas artes. Se dejó el alma trabajando como directora principal de arte en varias agencias de publicidad. Disfruta de la pintura, intentando centrarse en la acuarela y el acrílico. Le vuelve loca la simetría y los colores, igual que a Wes. Ama a Wes. Vive en Estambul, tratando de traspasar fronteras.

Rushmore - Max Fischer (right page)
Gökçe İnan, 2013

RUSHMORE

A FILM BY WES ANDERSON

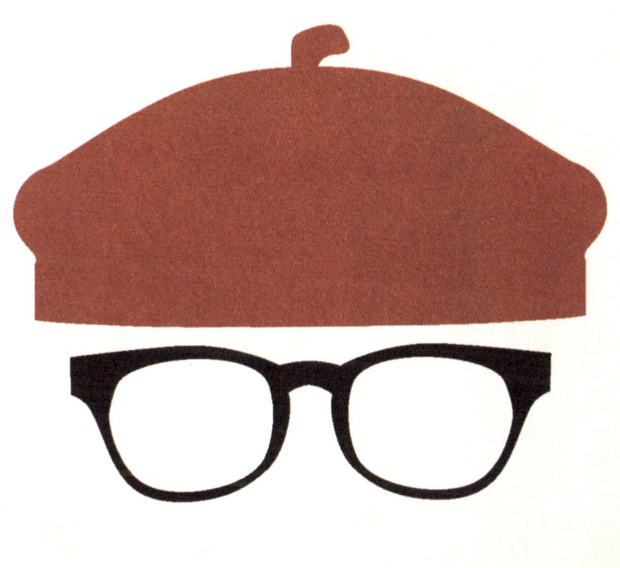

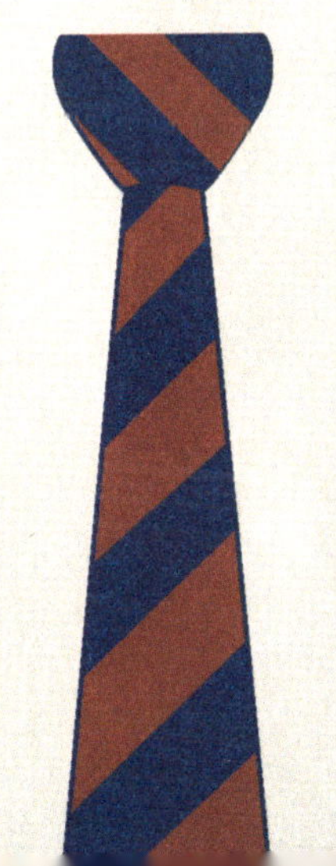

MOONRISE KINGDOM

A FILM BY WES ANDERSON

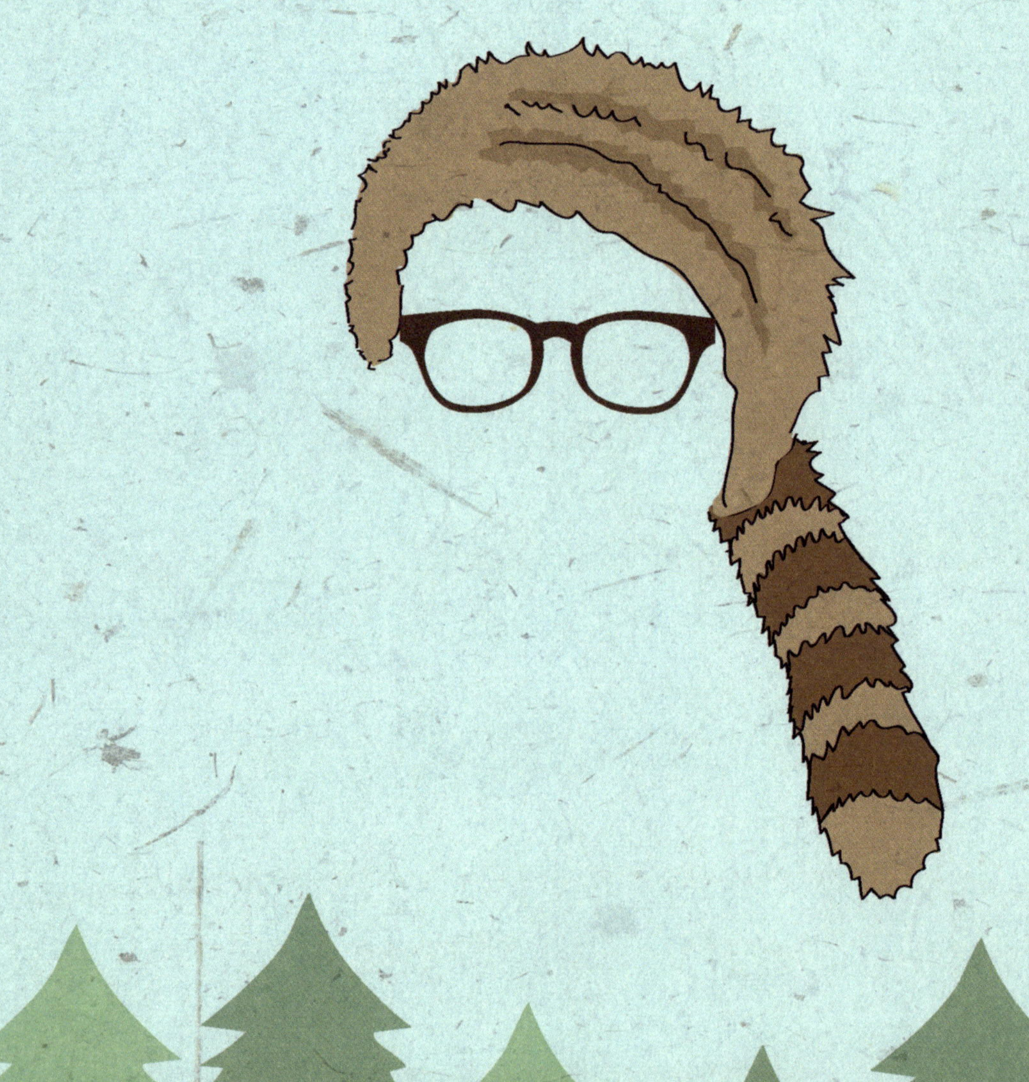

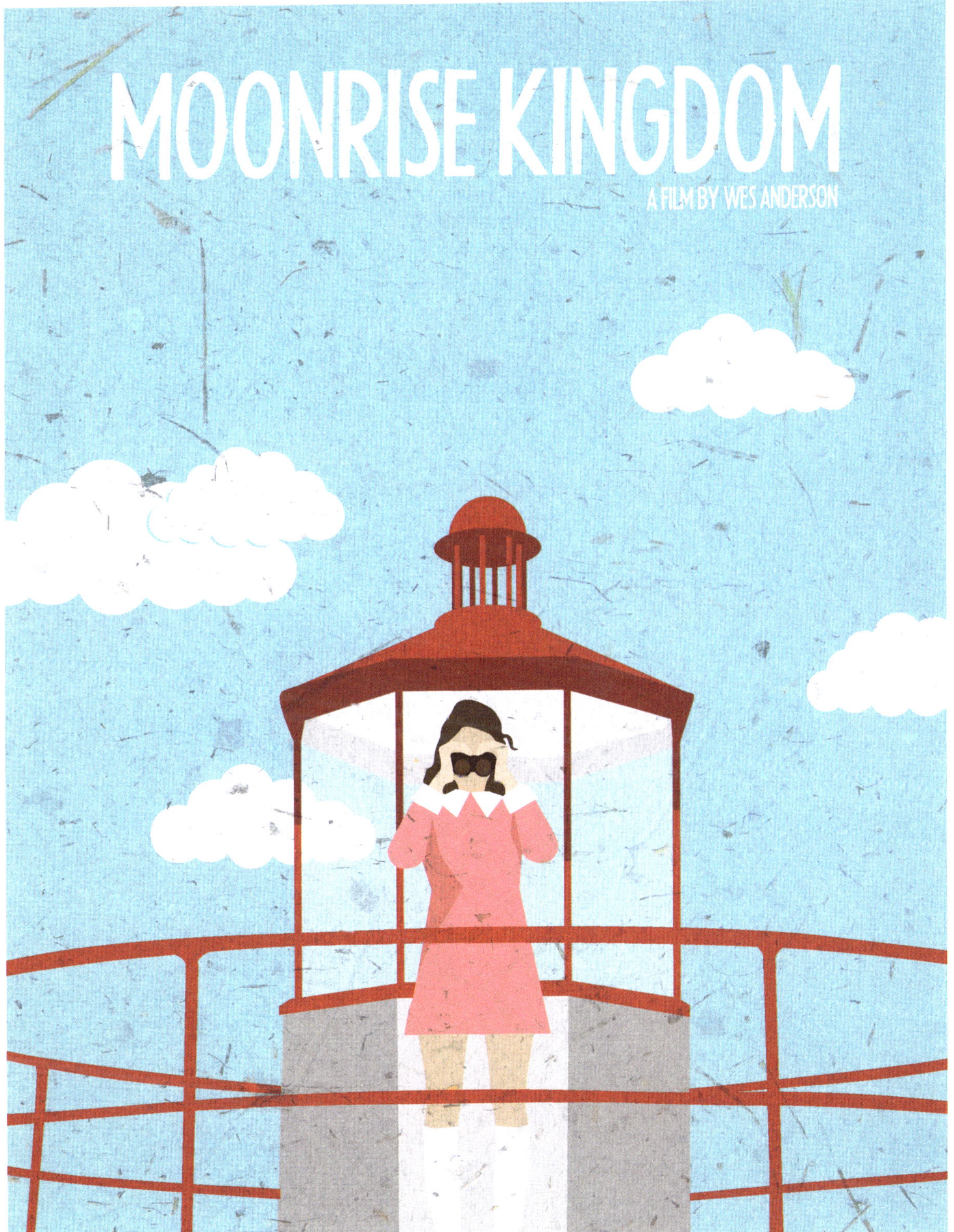

Moonrise Kingdom - Suzy / Gokçe Inan, 2013
Moonrise Kingdom - Sam (left page) / Gokçe Inan, 2013

THE ROYAL TENENBAUMS

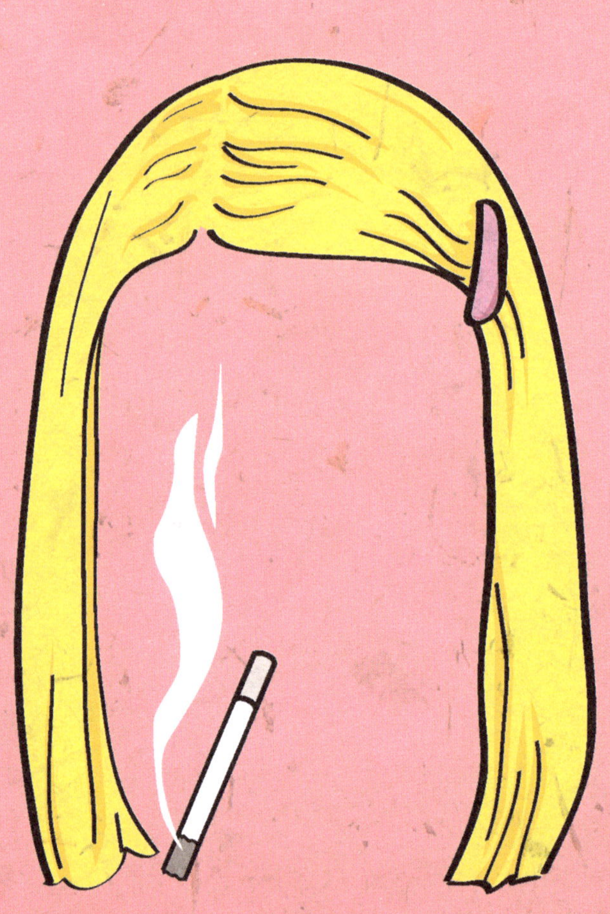

The Royal Tenenbaums - Margot&Richie
Gökçe Inan, 2013

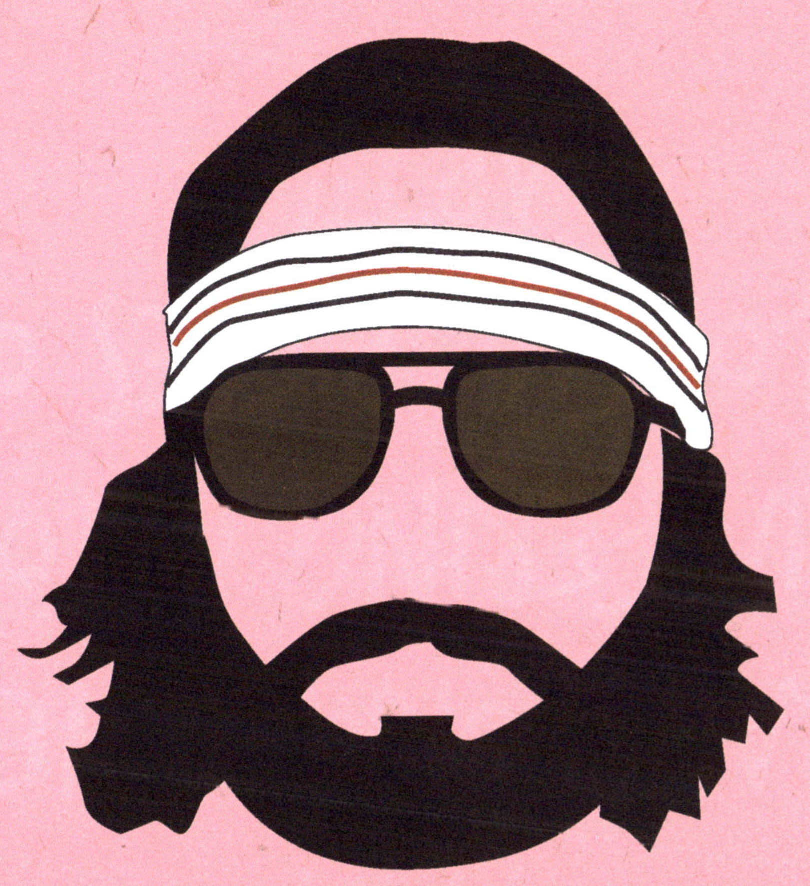

A FILM BY WES ANDERSON

NATALIA DE FRUTOS

www.nataliadefrutos.com
www.instagram.com/nataliadefrutos
www.behance.net/nataliadefrutos

"I LOVE HIS CHARACTERS, THE COLOUR PALETTE, THE SOUNDTRACKS... HIS FILMS ARE A PRESENT FOR SENSES!"

Natalia de Frutos is a Spanish graphic illustrator and graphic designer with a degree in Graphic Design for Advertising from the School of Art in Oviedo, the city where she grew up.

Her work stands out for its fresh and colourful style, highlighting pastel tones, geometric shapes and a purely digital image treatment.

She finds her inspiration in cinema, travel, music... or anything brimming with an artistic component.
She still remembers the first time she saw a Wes Anderson movie—it was like love at first sight. His treatment of the image as well as the use of colour and symmetrical compositions have guided her own work.

Natalia de Frutos es una ilustradora y diseñadora gráfica española titulada en Gráfica Publicitaria por la Escuela de Arte de Oviedo, ciudad en la que se crió.

Su trabajo se caracteriza por un estilo fresco y colorido, destacando los tonos pastel, las formas geométricas y un tratamiento puramente digital de la imagen.

Encuentra su inspiración en el cine, los viajes, la música... o cualquier cosa cargada de un componente artístico.
Aún recuerda la primera vez que vio una película de Wes Anderson, fue como un flechazo a primera vista. El tratamiento de la imagen así como el uso del color y las composiciones simétricas, le han sido de guía para el desarrollo de su trabajo.

Margot (right page)

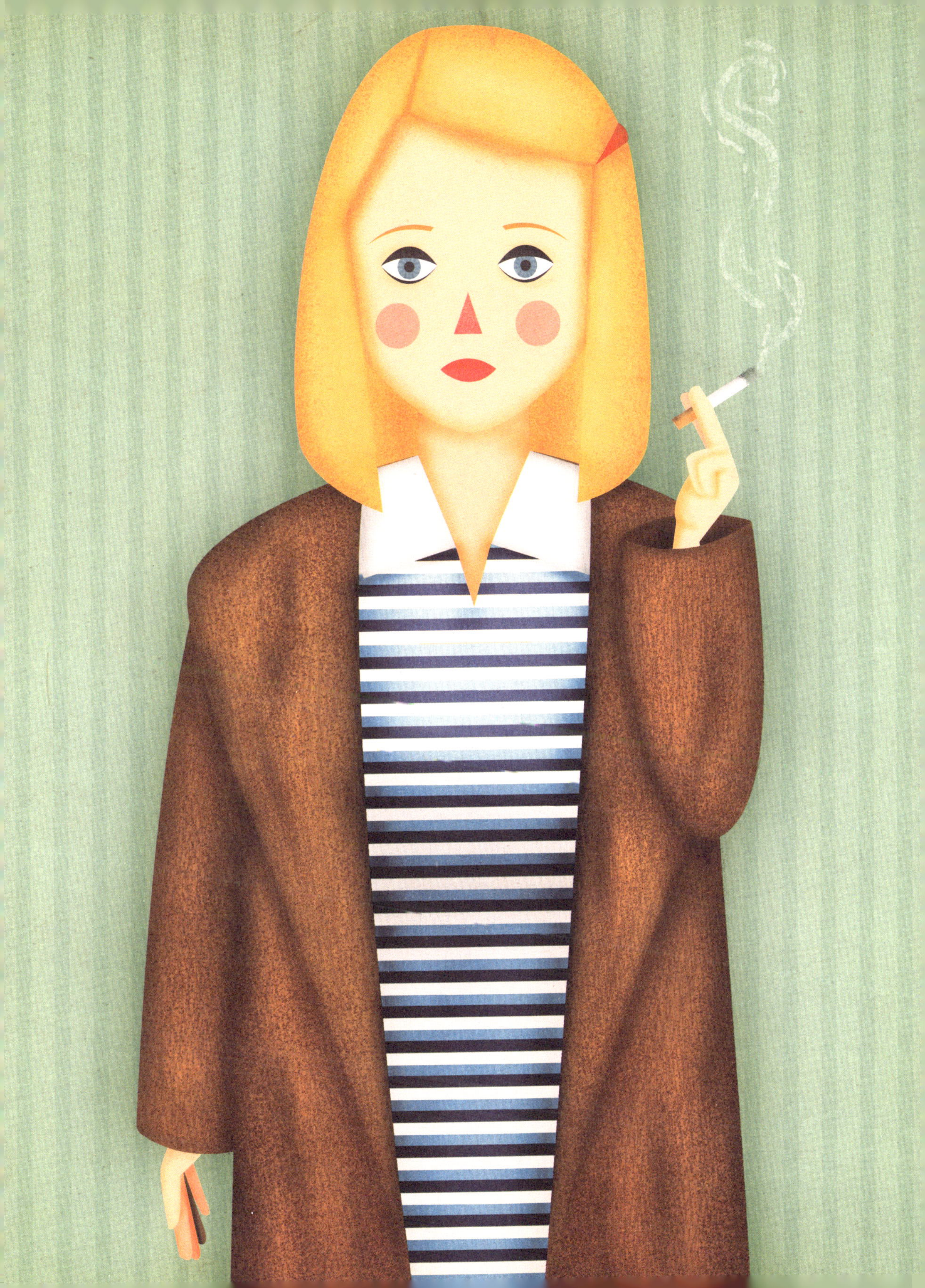

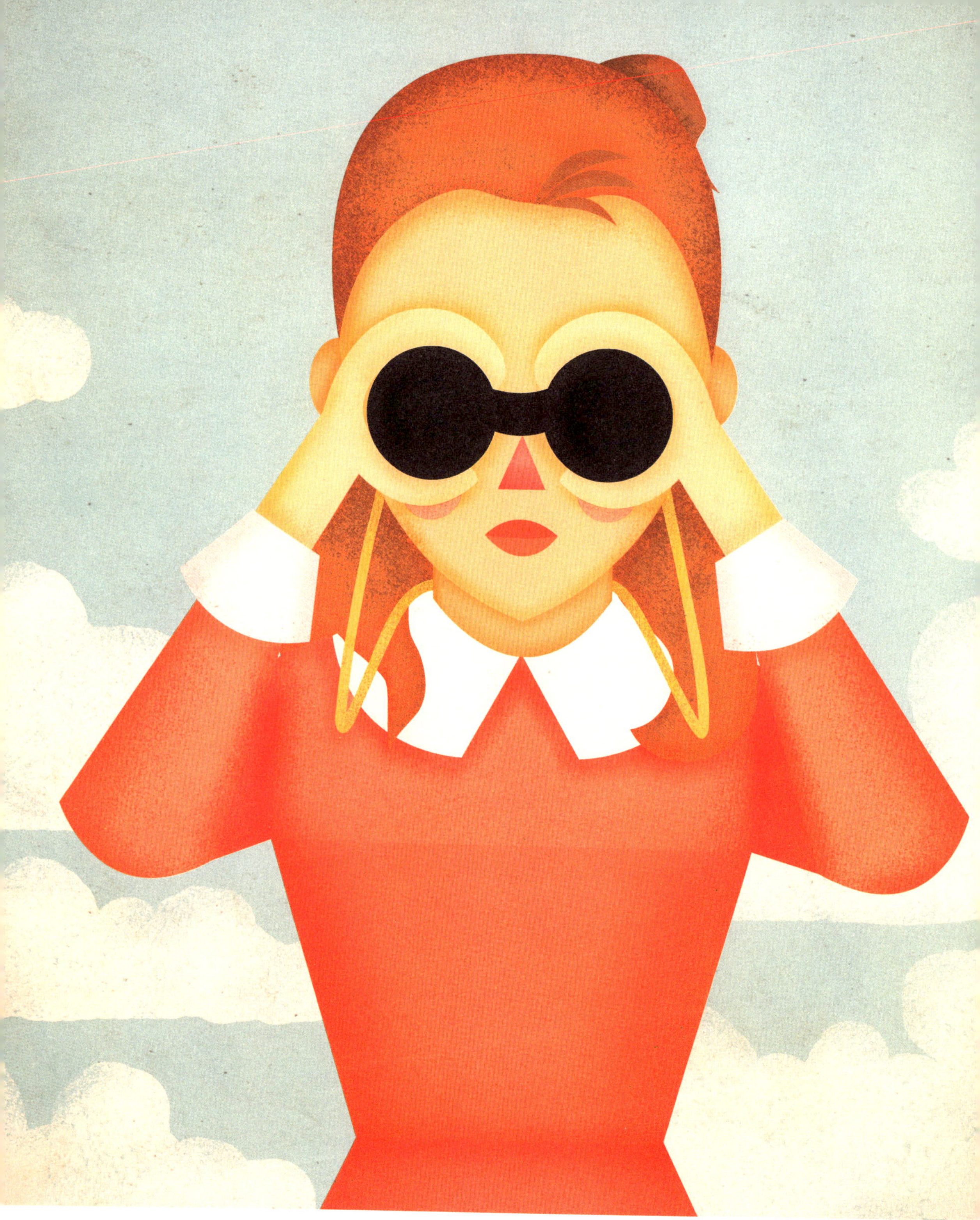

Suzy

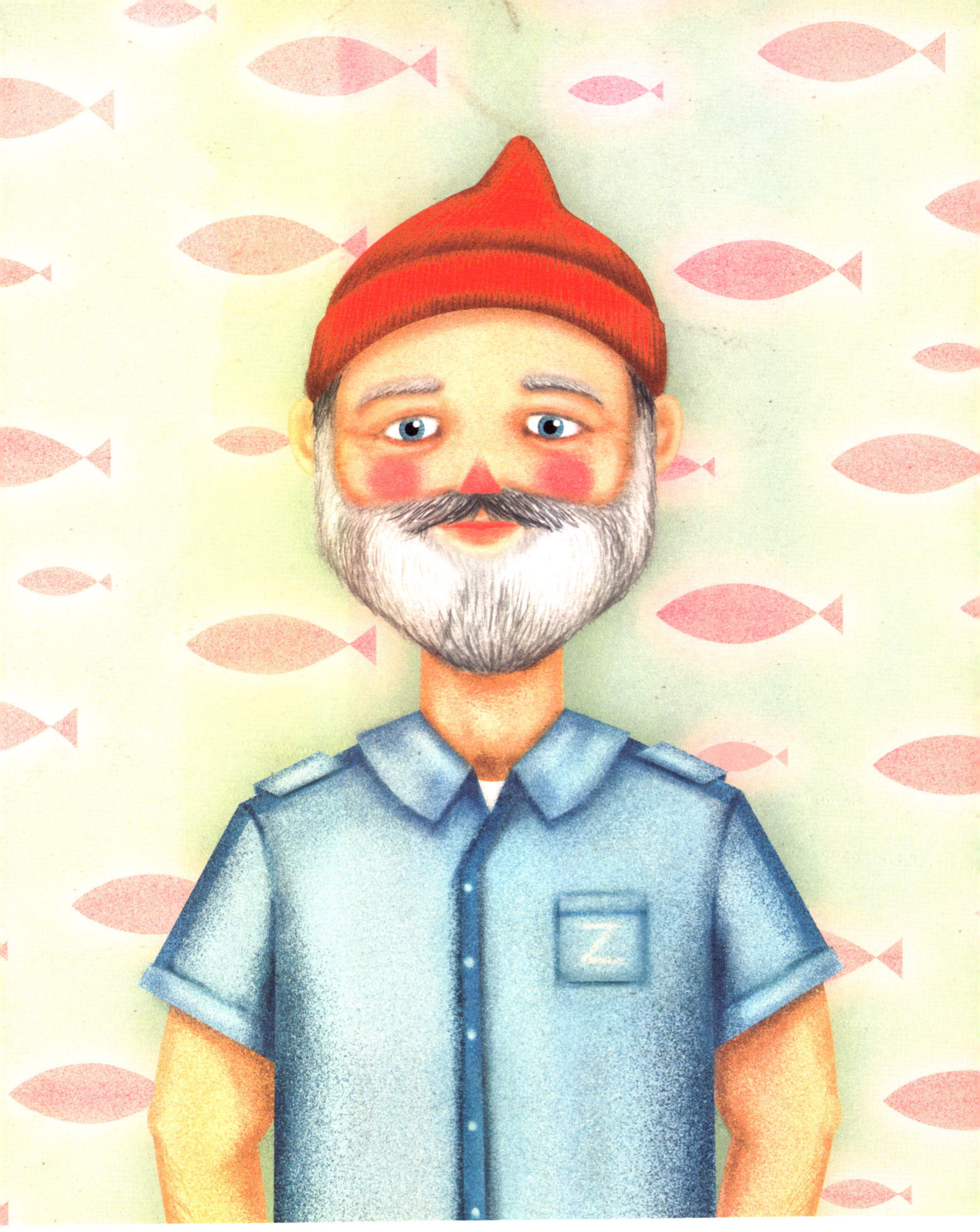

Zissou

JAMES OCONNELL

www.james-oconnell.com
www.behance.net/james-oconnell
Instagram: @jamesp0p
Twitter: @jamesp0p

"WES LEAVES NOTHING TO CHANCE"

James Oconnell is a Manchester based creative who has a passion for mixing colour and lines. He applies his minimalistic style to a variety of themes and has created work for the likes of Wired Magazine, Youtube, T3 Magazine, BBC and The Atlantic to name a few. He is hugely inspired by contemporary pop culture in all its forms - from motion pictures, music to advertising and sport. Simplicity is the key to his work allowing the expression of the idea to reign supreme.

James Oconnell es un creador que vive en Manchester, quien siente pasión por la mezcla de colores y líneas. Aplica su estilo minimalista a una variedad de temas y ha creado obras a petición de revistas como la Wired, el canal Youtube, la revista T3, la BBC y The Atlantic, entre otros. Está muy inspirado por la cultura pop contemporánea en todas sus formas: desde el cine y la música hasta la publicidad y el deporte. La sencillez es la clave de su obra, permitiendo que la expresión de la idea reine de manera suprema.

The Royal Tenenbaums (right page)

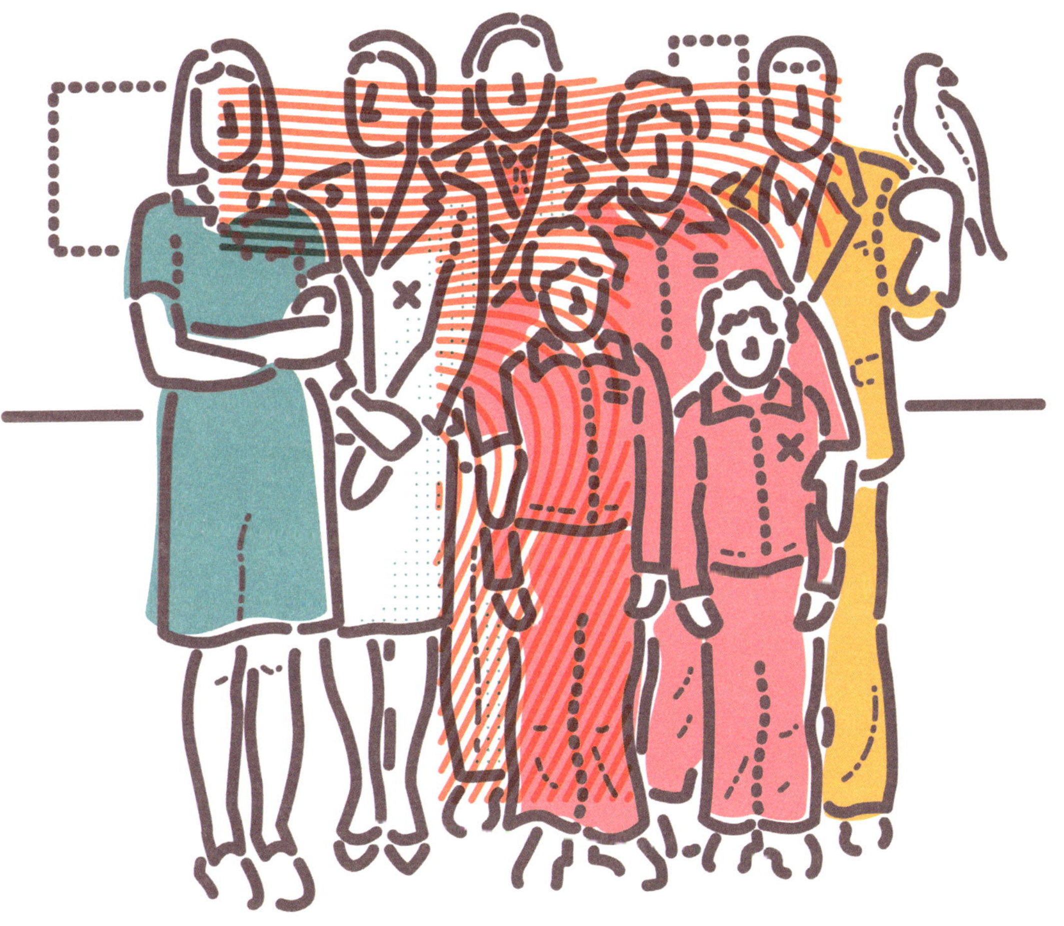

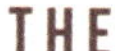
THE

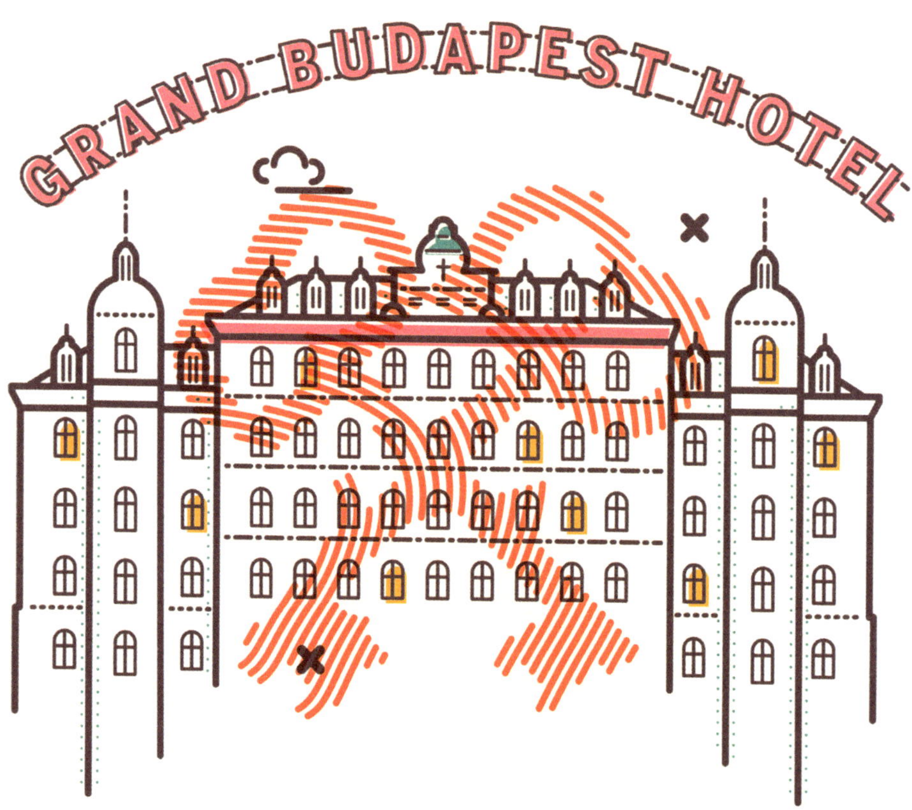
GRAND BUDAPEST HOTEL

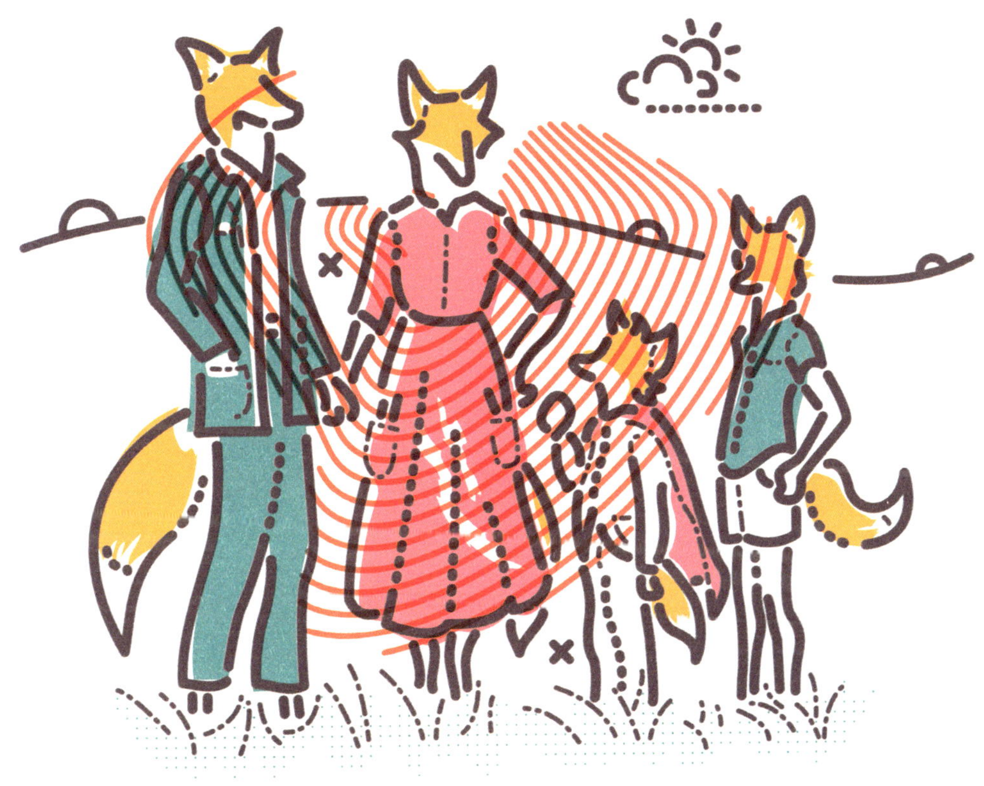

Fantastic Mr. Fox
Grand Budapest Hotel (left page)

SAM GILBEY

www.samgilbeyillustrates.com
Instagram: @samgilbey
Twitter: @samgilbey
Facebook: @samgilbeyillustrates

"WES' METICULOUS FILMS TRANSPORT ME TO A SUMPTUOUS YET MELANCHOLY PARALLEL UNIVERSE THAT I ALWAYS LOVE TO VISIT"

Sam has been drawing the pop culture he loves for as long as he can remember, and illustrating professionally since 2004. His distinctive painterly illustrations have been featured in books, magazines, comics and exhibitions worldwide.

Over the years he's worked for a wide range of clients including Edgar Wright, Paramount Pictures, Picturehouse Cinemas, Sony Pictures and Working Title.

He's produced officially licensed pop culture artwork for properties including Marvel's Avengers, Call of Duty, Teenage Mutant Ninja Turtles, The Karate Kid, Flash Gordon and Shepperton Studios, and taken part in more than forty group pop culture exhibitions in the UK and US over the last five years.

All of his Wes Anderson works to date have been created for Spoke Art's annual Wes Anderson tribute exhibitions in San Francisco and New York.

Sam viene dibujando la cultura pop que tanto ama desde que tiene uso de razón, así como ilustrando de manera profesional desde 2004. Sus ilustraciones pictóricas distintivas han aparecido en libros, revistas, comics y exposiciones de todo el mundo.

Durante años ha trabajado para una amplia gama de clientes, incluyendo Edgar Wright, Paramount Pictures, Picturehouse Cinemas, Sony Pictures y Working Title.

Ha producido obras de cultura pop con licencia oficial incluyendo *Marvel's Avengers*, *Call of Duty*, *Teenage Mutant Ninja Turtles*, *The Karate Kid*, *Flash Gordon* y *Shepperton Studios*, y ha participado en más de cuarenta exposiciones de cultura pop en Reino Unido y Estados Unidos durante los últimos cinco años.

Todas sus obras de Wes Anderson hasta la fecha han sido creadas para exposiciones tributo a Wes Anderson, las cuales se exponen anualmente en la galería Spoke Art, en San Francisco y Nueva York.

Steve Zissou (right page)

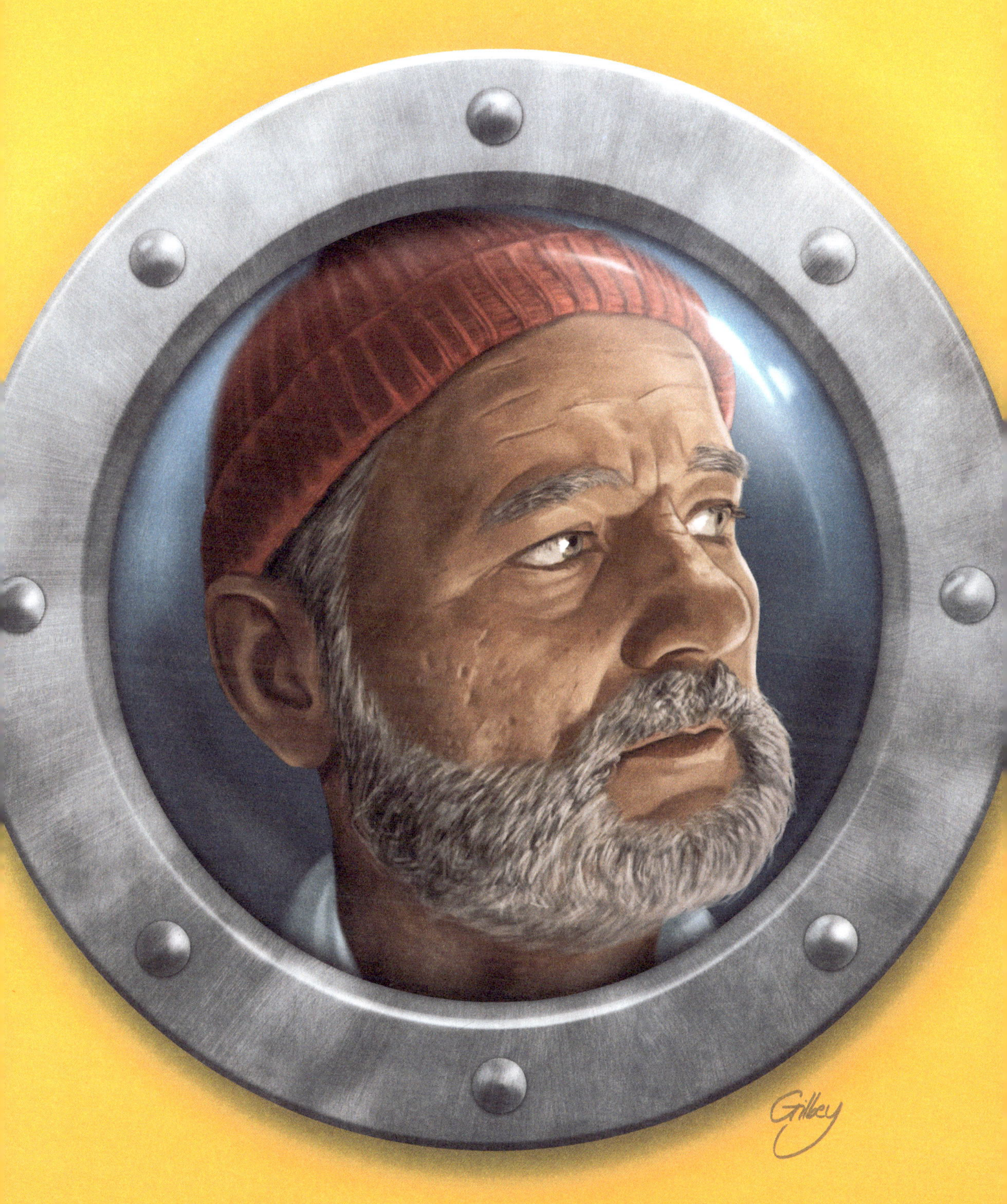
Gilbey

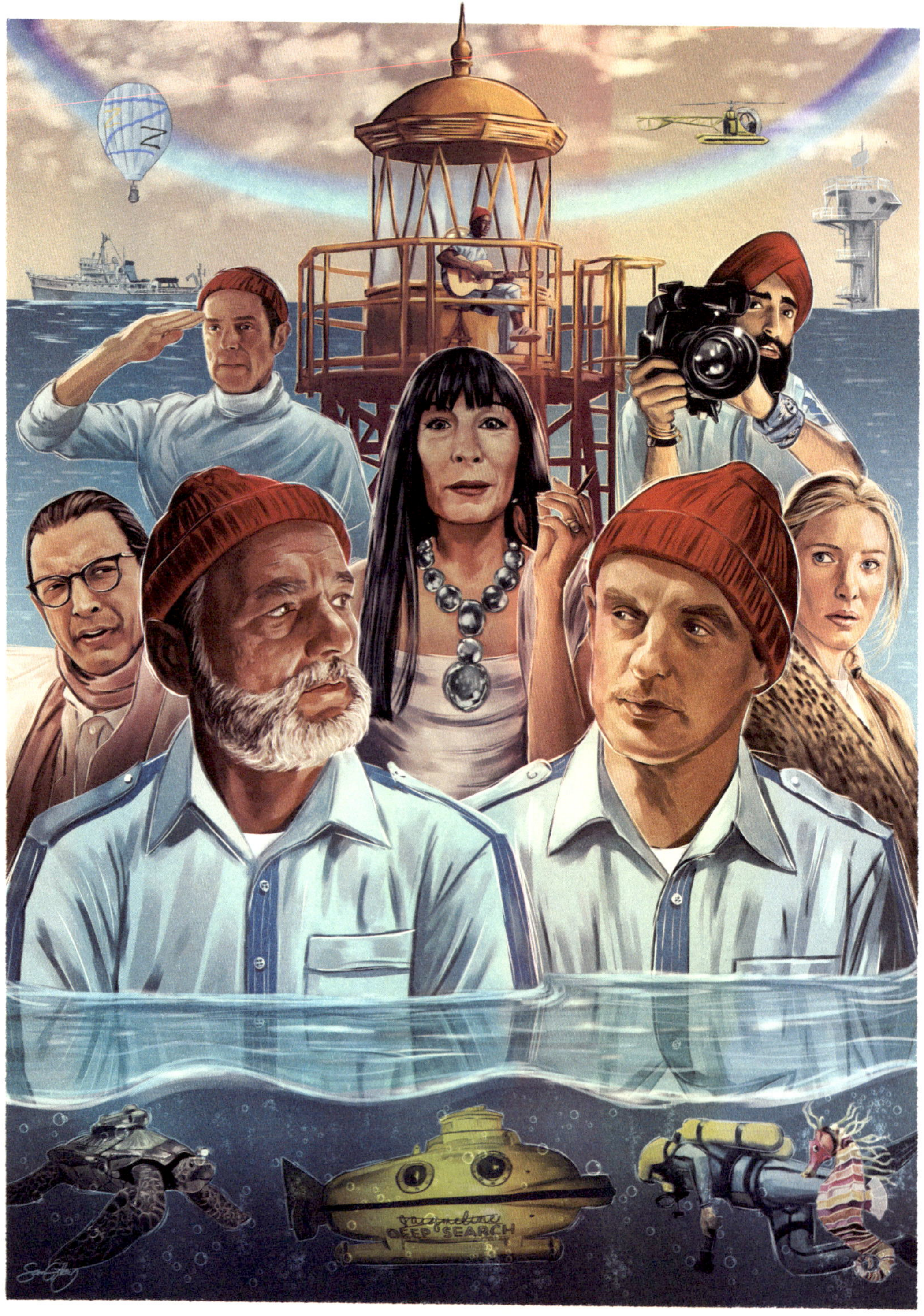

I Hate Fathers, and I Never Wanted to Be One

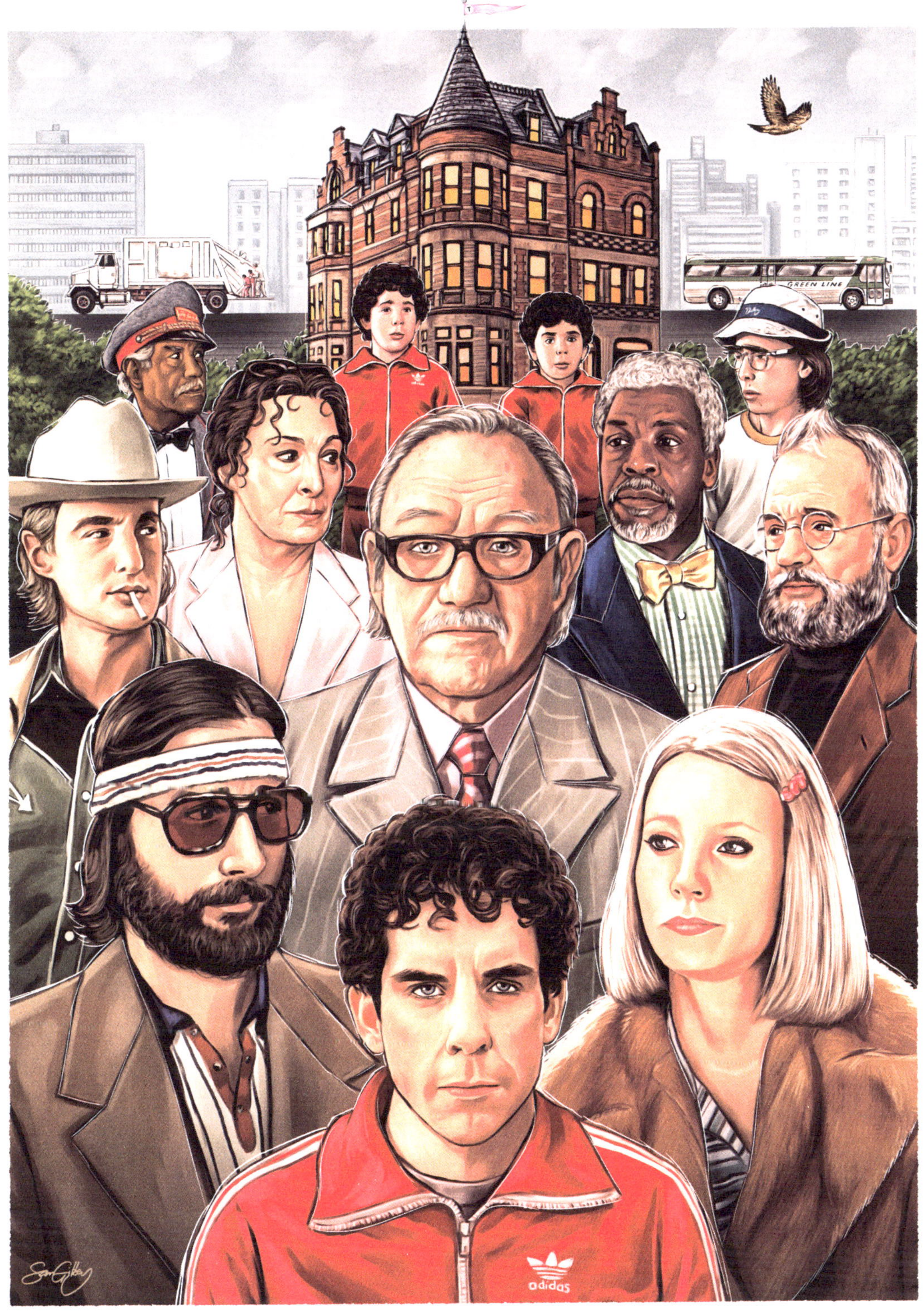

You Still Consider Me Your Father?

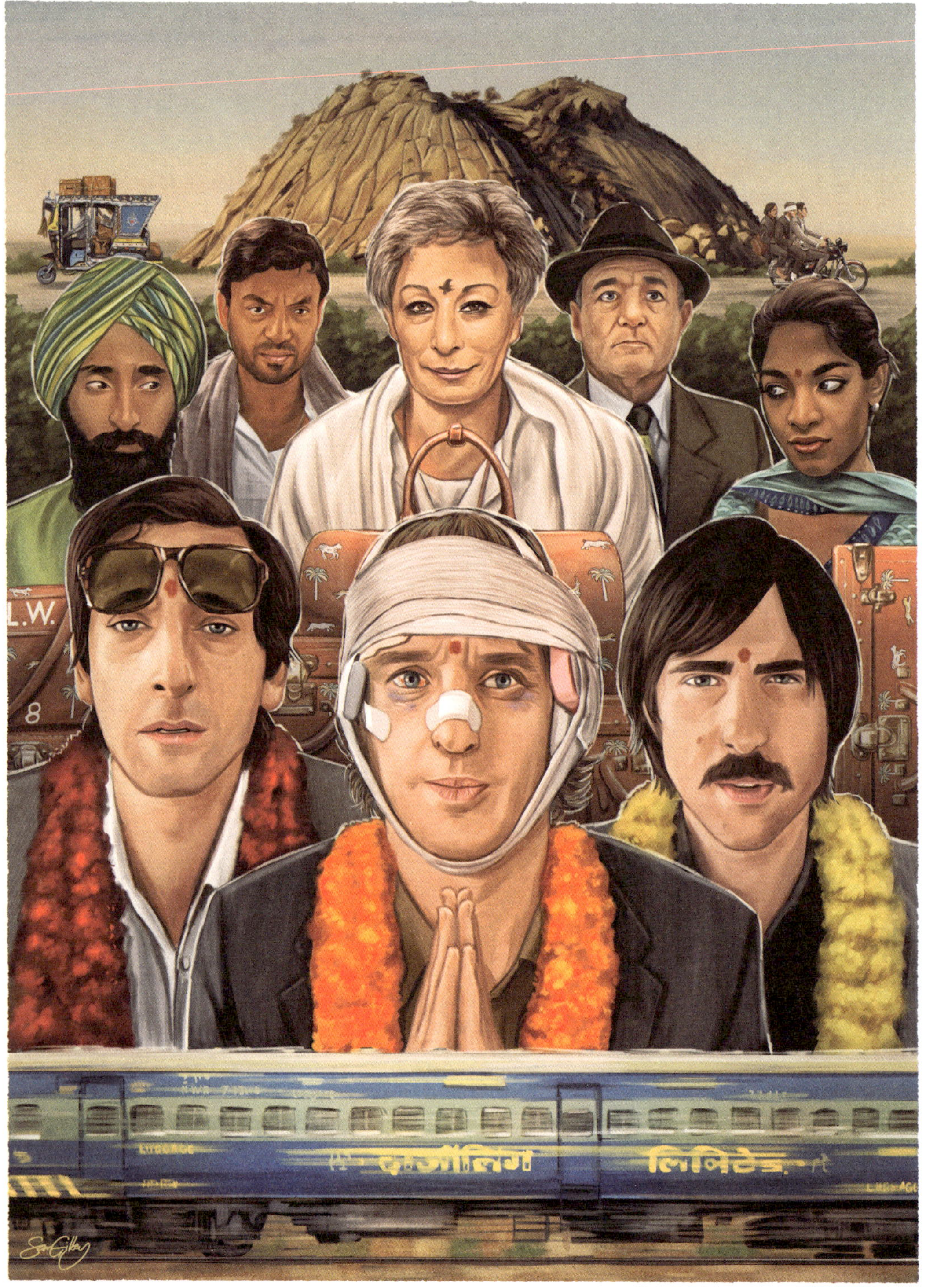

I Wonder if the Three of Us Would've Been Friends in Real Life?

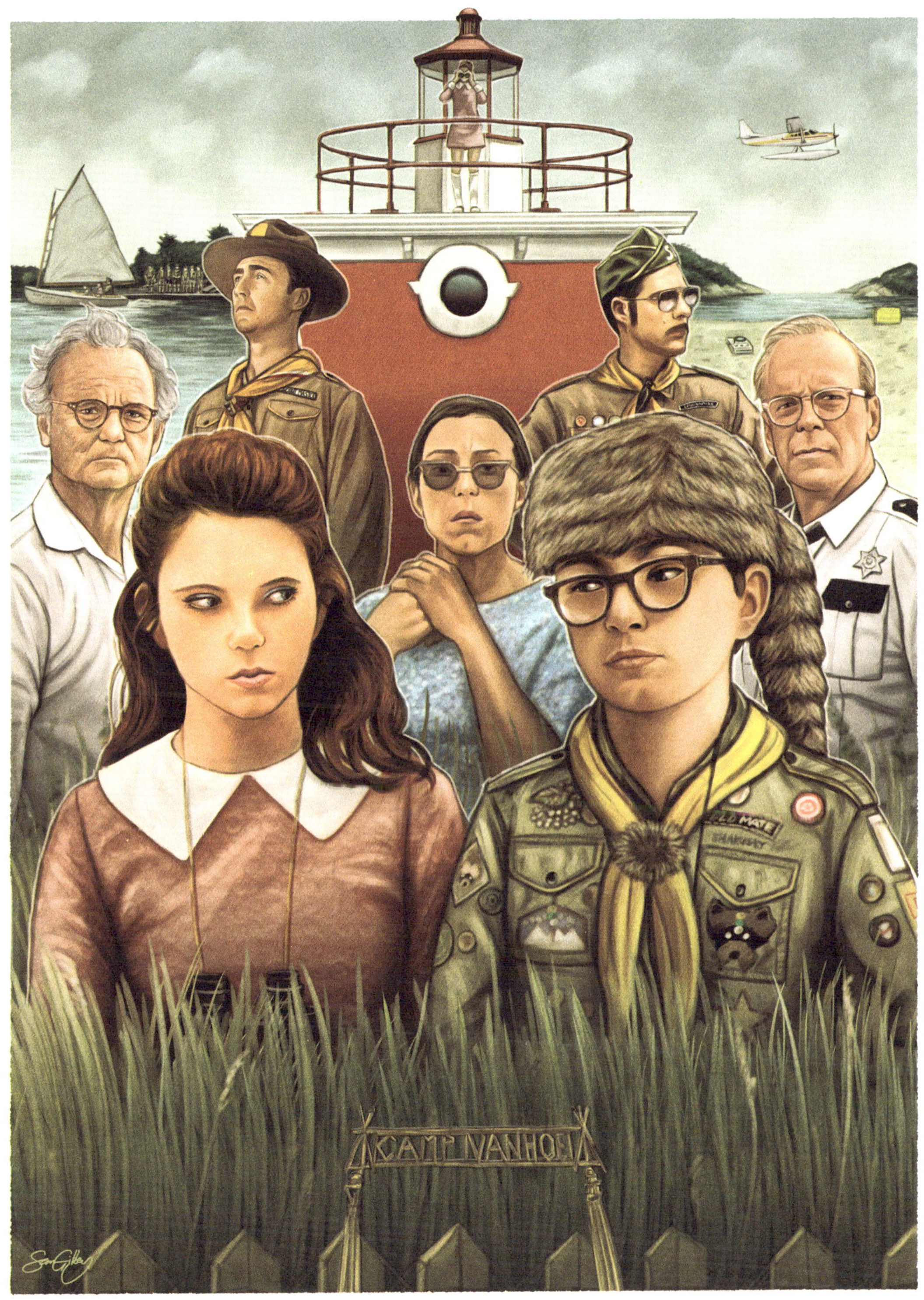

When We First Met Each Other, Something Happened To Us

MARIA HERREROS

www.mariaherreros.com
Instagram: @mariaherreros
www.facebook.com/Maria-Herreros

"THE STORYLINE HAS NEVER BEEN ONE OF MY STRONG POINTS"

"Maria Herreros (Valencia, 1983) is an artist based in Barcelona from where she creates art for the rest of the world. The basic aim of her work is to express the most instinctive components of human beings.

Gathering different illustrations by Maria Herreros might feel like taking a walk through a botanical garden in the middle of a big city. Duality is implicit in everything she does, and flipping through her books is like walking through the beautiful and the ugly, the sweet and the crude, the intimate and the foreign. Perhaps it is her particular colour range, her bizarre originality, her floral ornamentation or her stimulating honesty. Without being able to pin down exactly what the secret is, we feel that Maria manages to break aesthetic clichés and make us fall in love through imperfection. Graphic refinement is off limits in her illustrations but there is something beautiful in each of her characters that captures the eye. At that point personality opens up powerfully and flows out unabashedly from each figure, unveiling the most sincere beauty—impossible to dismiss by the light of a look that blinds us. And that is where we finally find Maria, drawing glances."

Text by Virginia Capellas.

"Maria Herreros (Valencia, 1983), artista con sede en Barcelona desde donde desarrolla su trabajo hacia el resto del mundo. El objetivo base de su obra es expresar lo más instintivo del ser humano.

Reunir distintas ilustraciones de Maria Herreros bien podría parecerse a dar un paseo por un jardín botánico en medio de una gran ciudad. La dualidad está implícita en todo lo que hace, y hojear sus libros es como caminar entre lo bello y lo feo, lo dulce y lo bruto, lo íntimo y lo extraño. Tal vez se encuentre en su particular gama cromática, en su originalidad bizarra, en su ornamentación floral o su estimulante honradez, pero sin saber bien cuál es exactamente el secreto, Maria consigue romper clichés estéticos y enamorar mediante la imperfección. El preciosismo está prohibido en sus ilustraciones pero hay algo bello en cada uno de sus personajes que no te deja escapar. Es entonces cuando la personalidad se abre paso poderosa y brota sin complejos de cada figura, emergiendo la belleza más sincera; imposible de descartar por la luz de una mirada que nos ciega. Y ahí es donde finalmente encontramos a Maria, dibujando miradas."

Texto de Virginia Capellas.

Wes Anderson portrait, from the book "Marilyn had eleven toes" Lunwerg (right page)

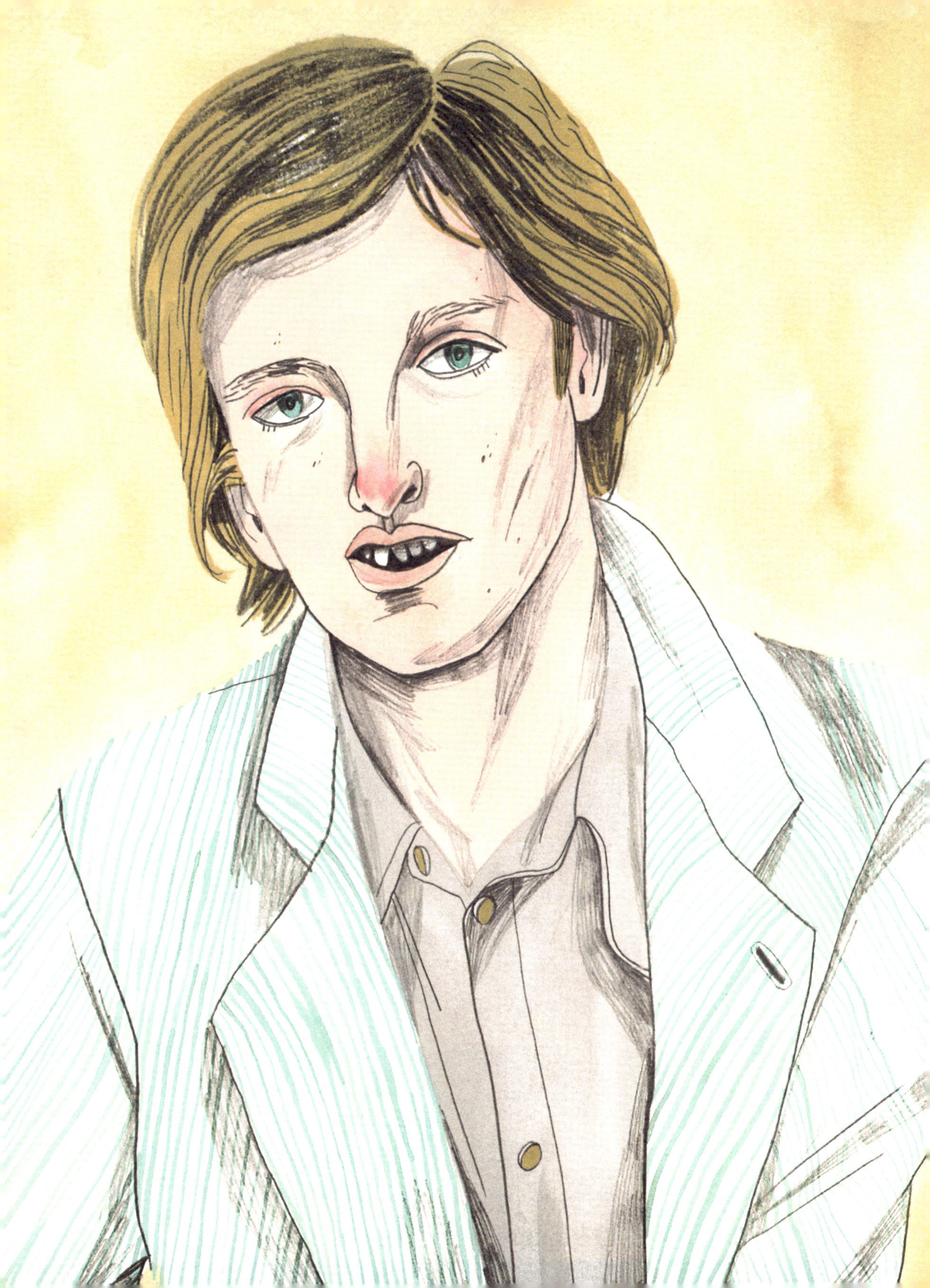

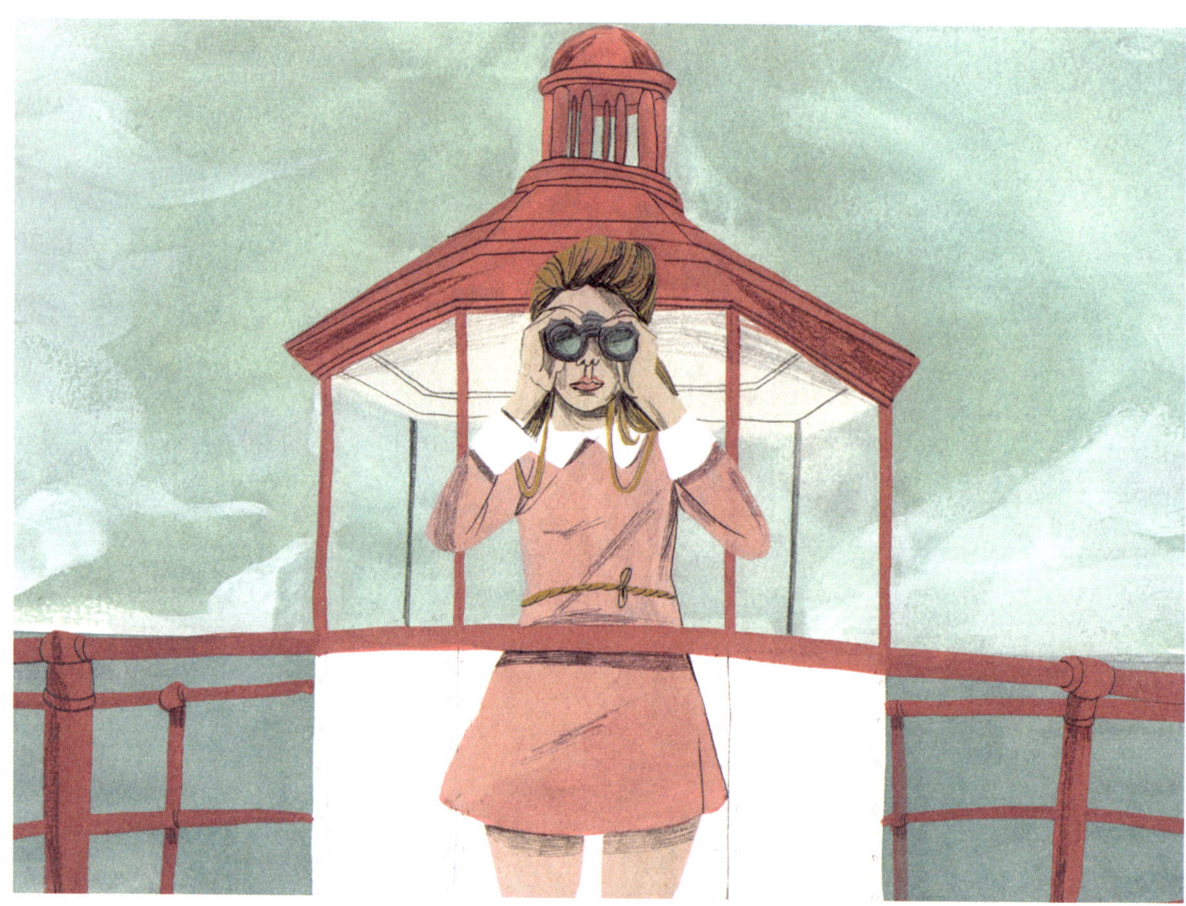

Moonrise Kingdom scene, from the book "Marilyn had eleven toes" Lunwerg

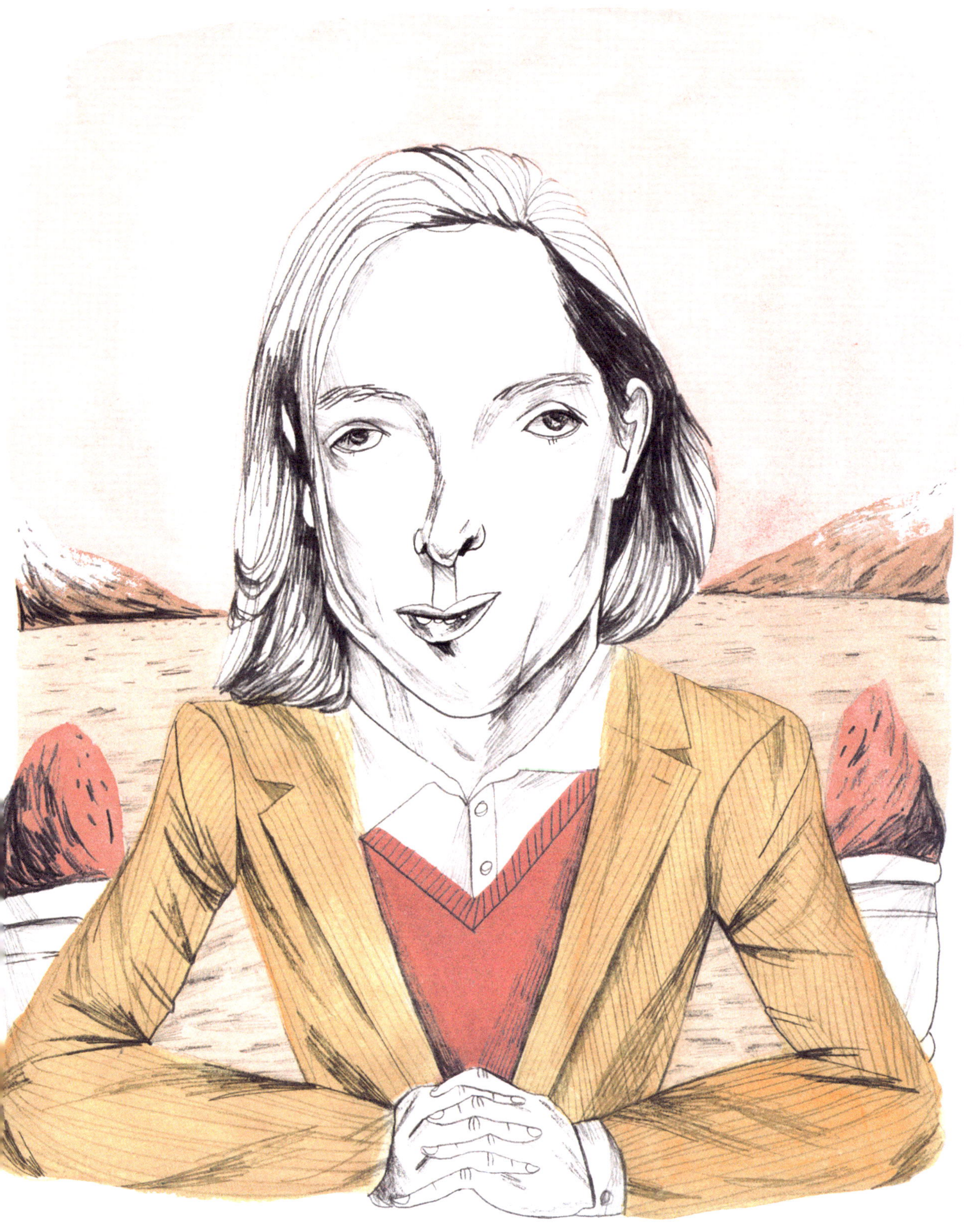

Wes and the symmetry, from the book "Marilyn had eleven toes" Lunwerg

MARIA SUAREZ-INCLAN

www. msinclan.com
Instagram: @m_sinclan
Twitter: @m_sinclan
Facebook: @msinclan

"I LOVE WES'S ATTENTION TO DETAIL AND ART DIRECTION, IT MAKES YOU WANT TO LIVE IN ALL OF HIS MOVIES"

Maria Suarez-Inclan is an illustrator and designer born in 1992 in Madrid. She studied Graphic Design and Psychology at the UCM although at the moment she only works on design and illustration. She lives in London, working as a graphic designer at an advertising agency and at the same time working as a freelance illustrator with clients such as Sony, Heineken, Studiocanal and Disney. What she likes above all is cinema, which is clearly reflected in her works, many of which she sells in specialised galleries in cities like New York, Los Angeles and San Francisco. She is inspired by the advertising of the 1950s, the Franco-Belgian comics, the music of the 60s and in popular culture in general. You can find her walking her dog, holding a cup of coffee or planning different projects.

Maria Suarez-Inclan es una ilustradora y diseñadora nacida en 1992 en Madrid. Estudió Diseño gráfico y Psicología en la UCM aunque actualmente sólo se dedica al diseño y la ilustración. Vive en Londres, trabajando como diseñadora gráfica en una agencia de publicidad y a la vez compagina su trabajo como ilustradora freelance con clientes como Sony, Heineken, Studiocanal o Disney. Lo que más le gusta en el mundo es el cine, cosa que se refleja en sus obras, muchas de las cuales vende en galerías especializadas en ciudades como New York, Los Angeles o San Francisco. Inspirada por la publicidad de los años 50, el cómic franco-belga, la música de los 60 y en general la cultura popular. Puedes encontrarla paseando a su perro, con una taza de café en la mano o planeando diferentes proyectos.

Wes Anderson Family (right page)

WES ANDERSON
FAMILY

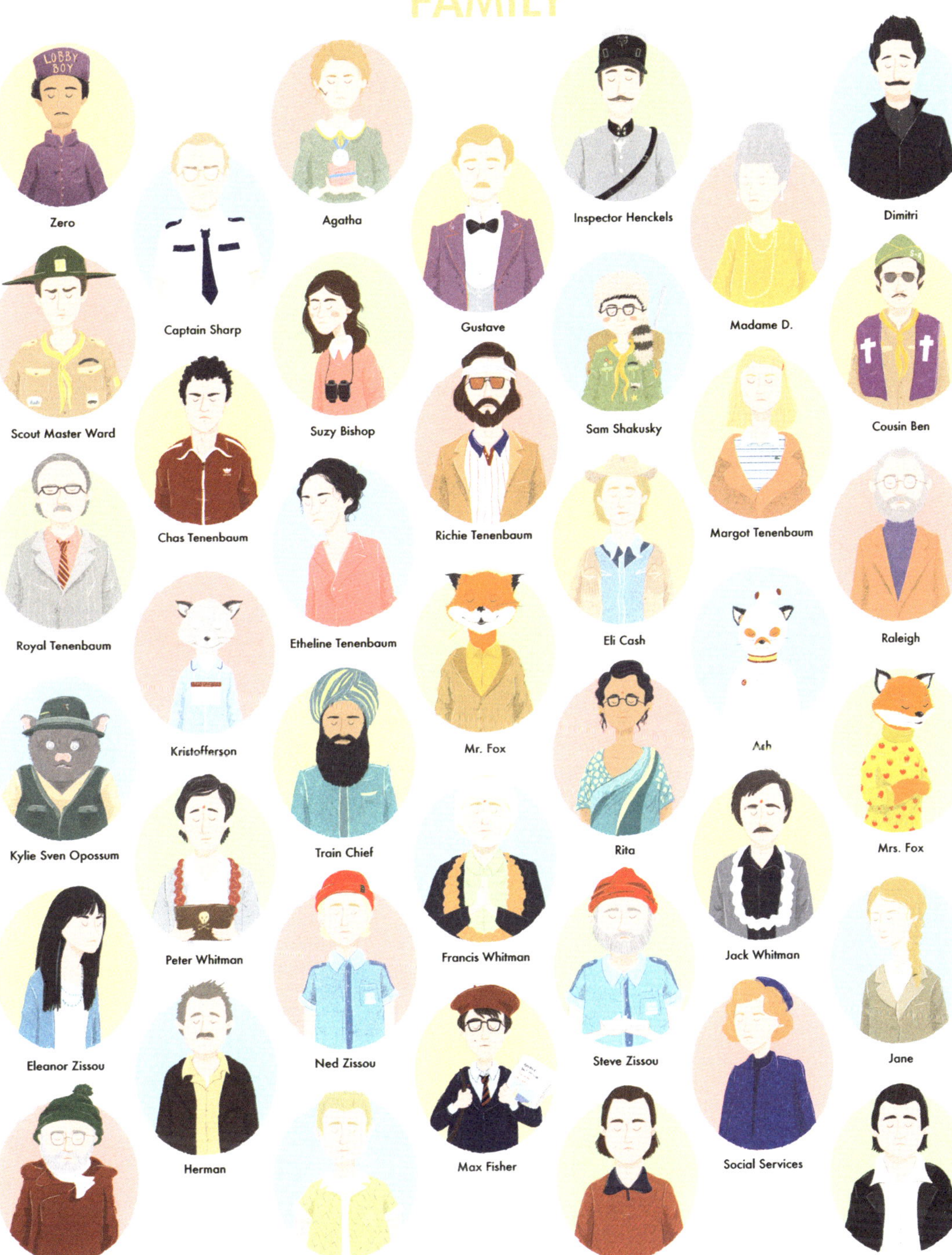

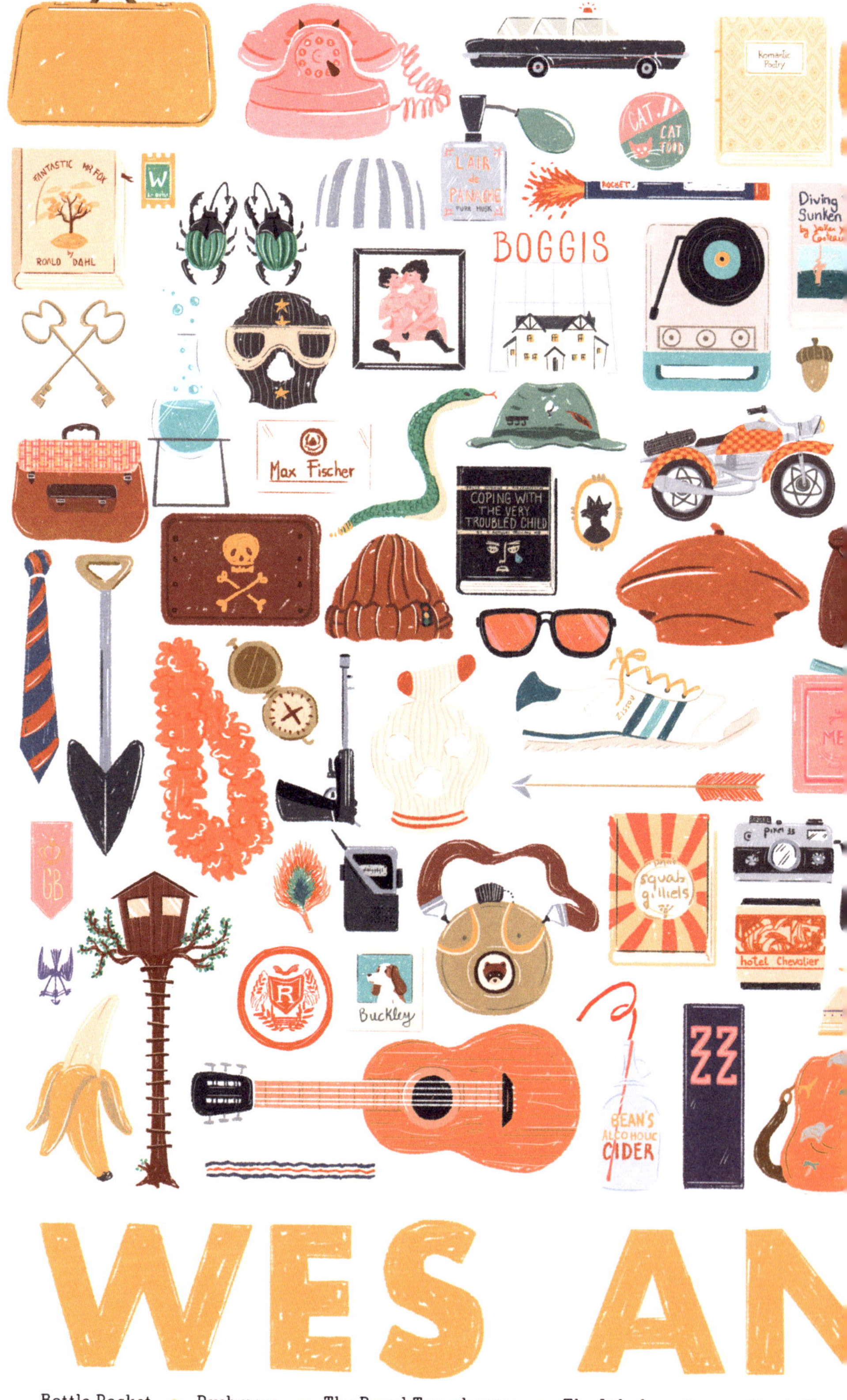

CAT
CAT FOOD
FANTASTIC MR FOX
ROALD DAHL
L'AIR de PANACHE
ROCKET
BOGGIS
Diving Sunken
Max Fischer
COPING WITH THE VERY TROUBLED CHILD
Zissou
Buckley
hotel Chevalier
BEAN'S ALCOHOLIC CIDER
GB
WES AN
Bottle Rocket • Rushmore • The Royal Tenenbaums • The Life Aquatic • Hotel Chev

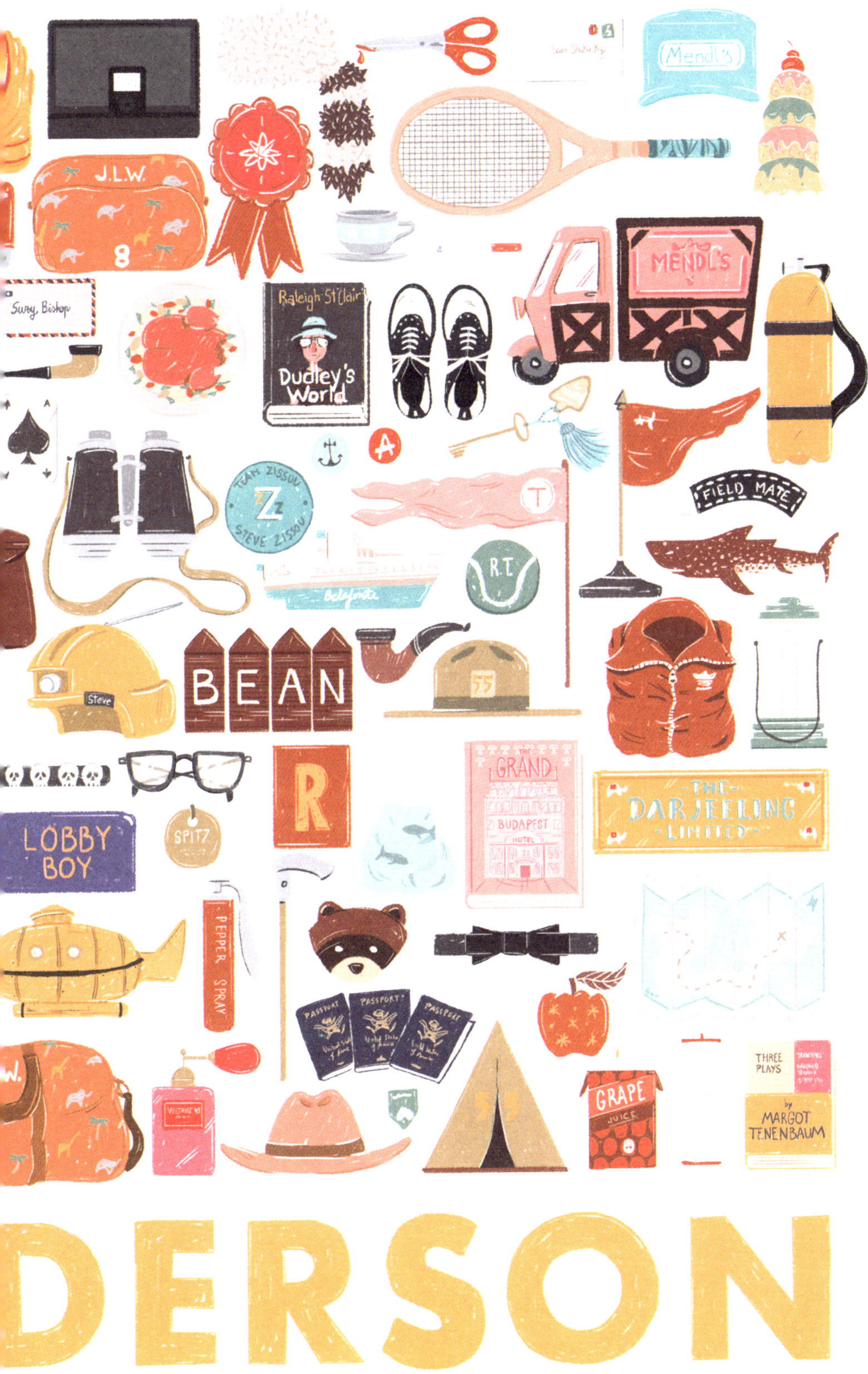

.e Darjeeling Limited • Fantastic Mr. Fox • Moonrise Kingdom • The Grand Budapest Hotel

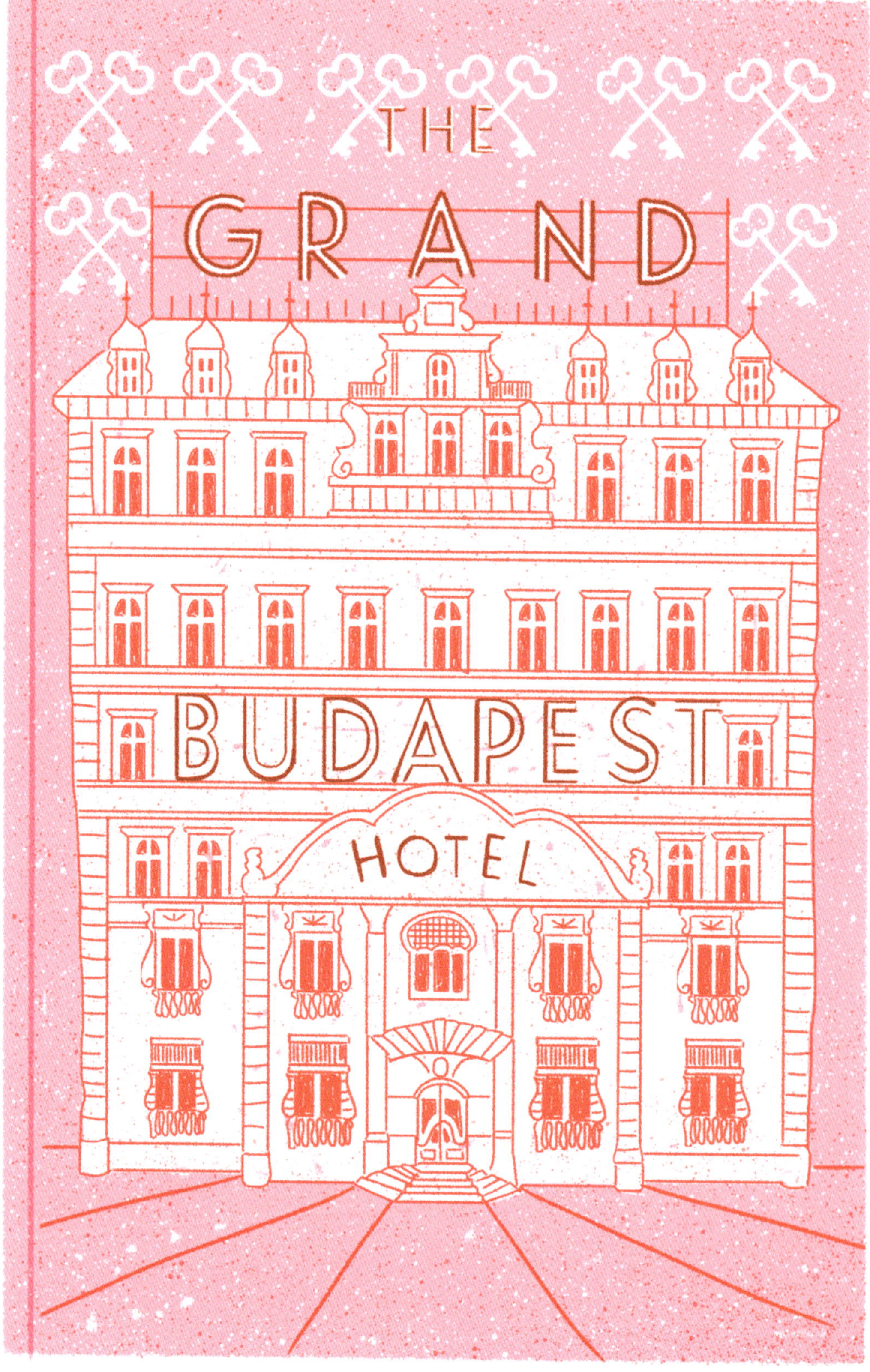
THE
GRAND
BUDAPEST
HOTEL

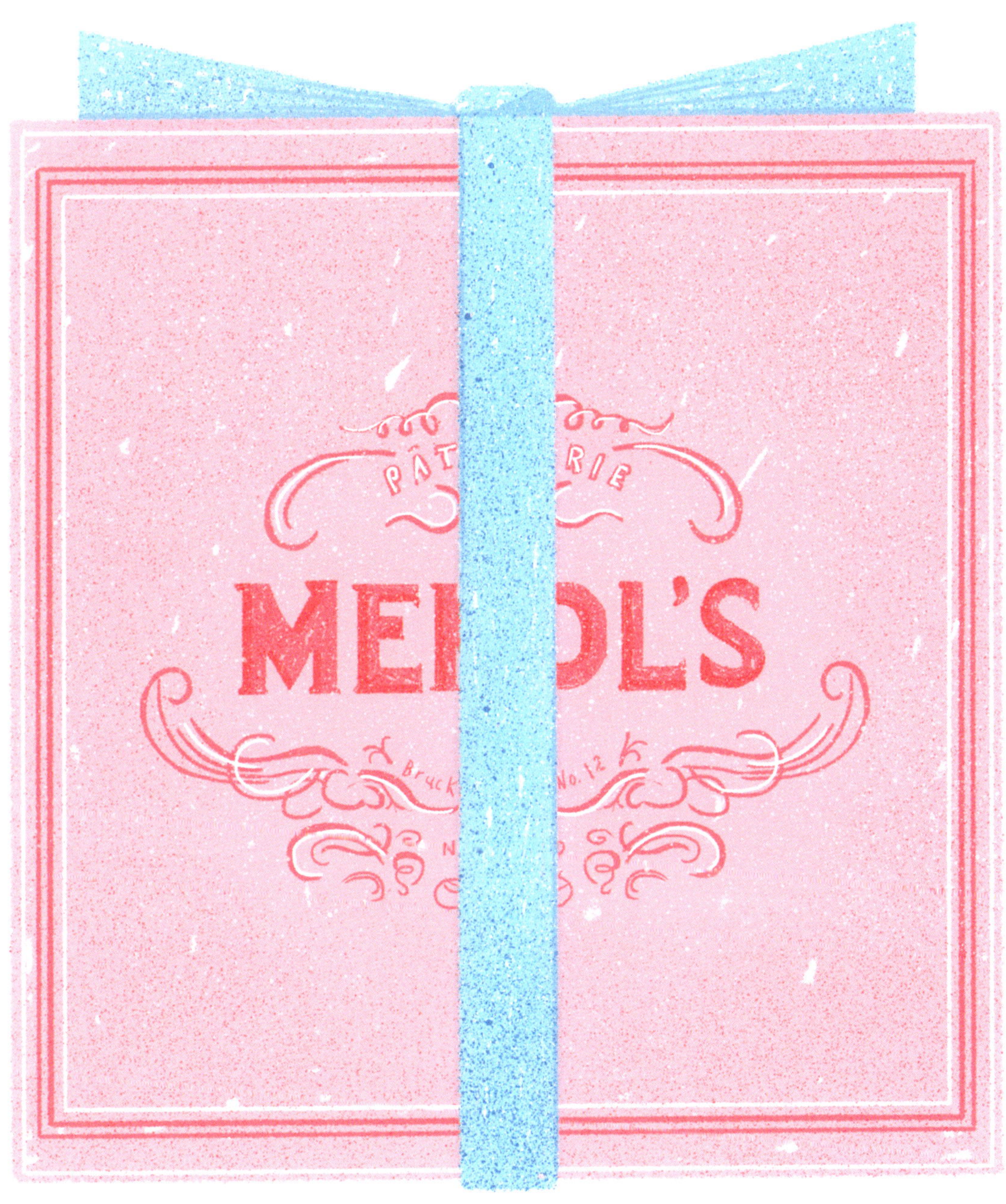

Nothing better than Mendls
Beautiful Reading (left page)

PAULA MORALES

Instagram: @moralespaula
Facebook: @moralespaula
Ello: @paulamorales

"I LOVE YOU BUT YOU DON'T KNOW WHAT YOU'RE TALKING ABOUT"

- Moonrise Kingdom -

Paula Morales (Guatemala 1983) is a transdisciplinary artist who constructs spaces as immersive experiences. She works with video, painting, sculpture and installation. She is interested in the decontextualisation of discarded objects/ technology as tools for altering the ether. Her work usually focuses on colour clusters, glitch, electronic pulses and synthesis, among others. She is interested in creating a sensorial engagement that connects to the aesthetics of the future, plasticity, mortality and repetition as a form of temporal exploration.

Paula Morales (Guatemala 1983) es una artista transdisciplinaria que construye espacios como experiencias inmersivas. Trabaja con video, pintura, escultura e instalación. Interesada en la descontextualización de objetos/tecnología descartados como herramientas de alteración de el éther. Su trabajo suele ser conglomerados de color, glitch, señales electrónicas, y síntesis entre otras. Su interés yace en la creación de compromiso sensorial que referencia la estética del futuro, la plasticidad, mortalidad y la repetición como forma de exploración temporal.

Moonrise Kingdom (right page)

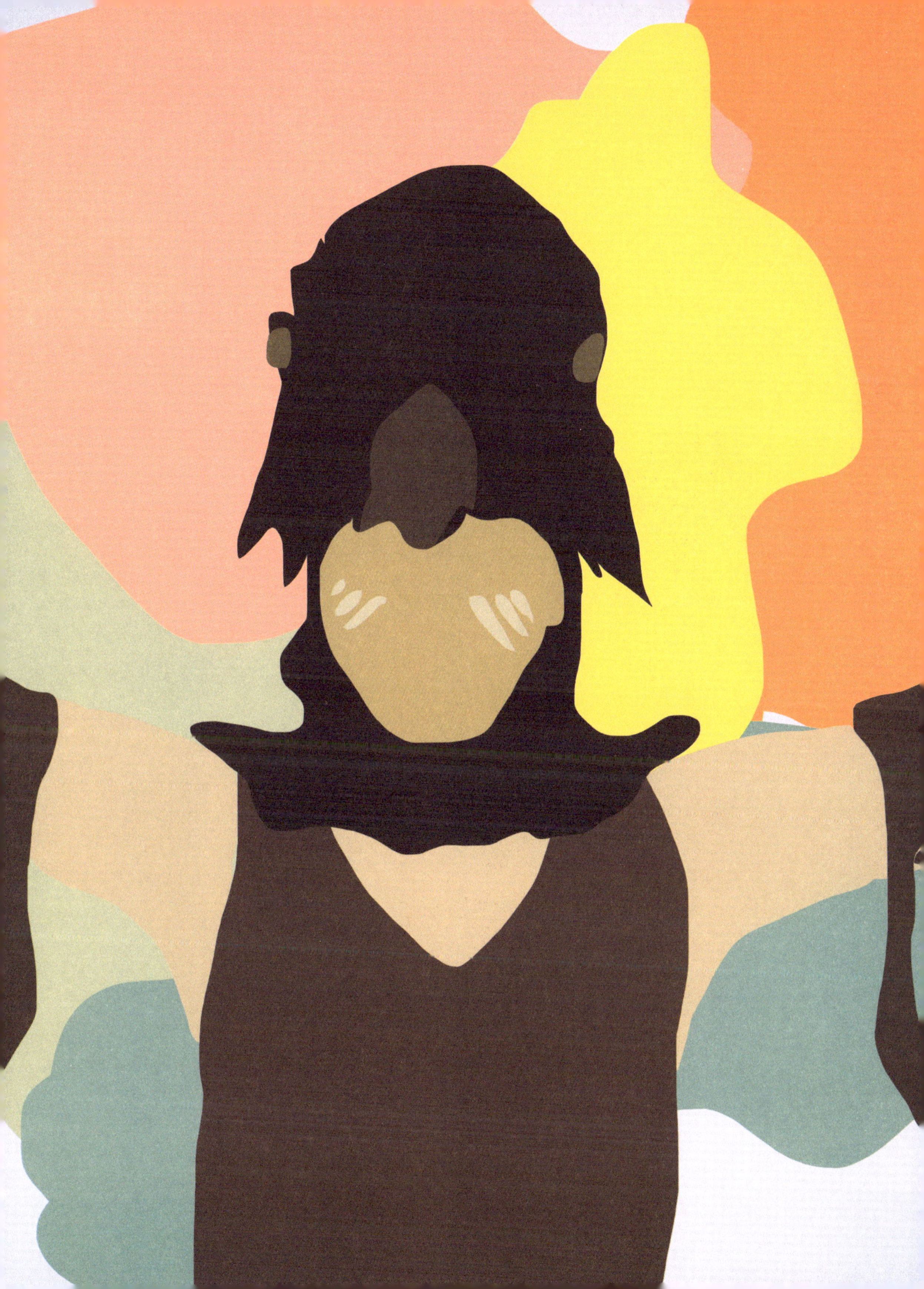

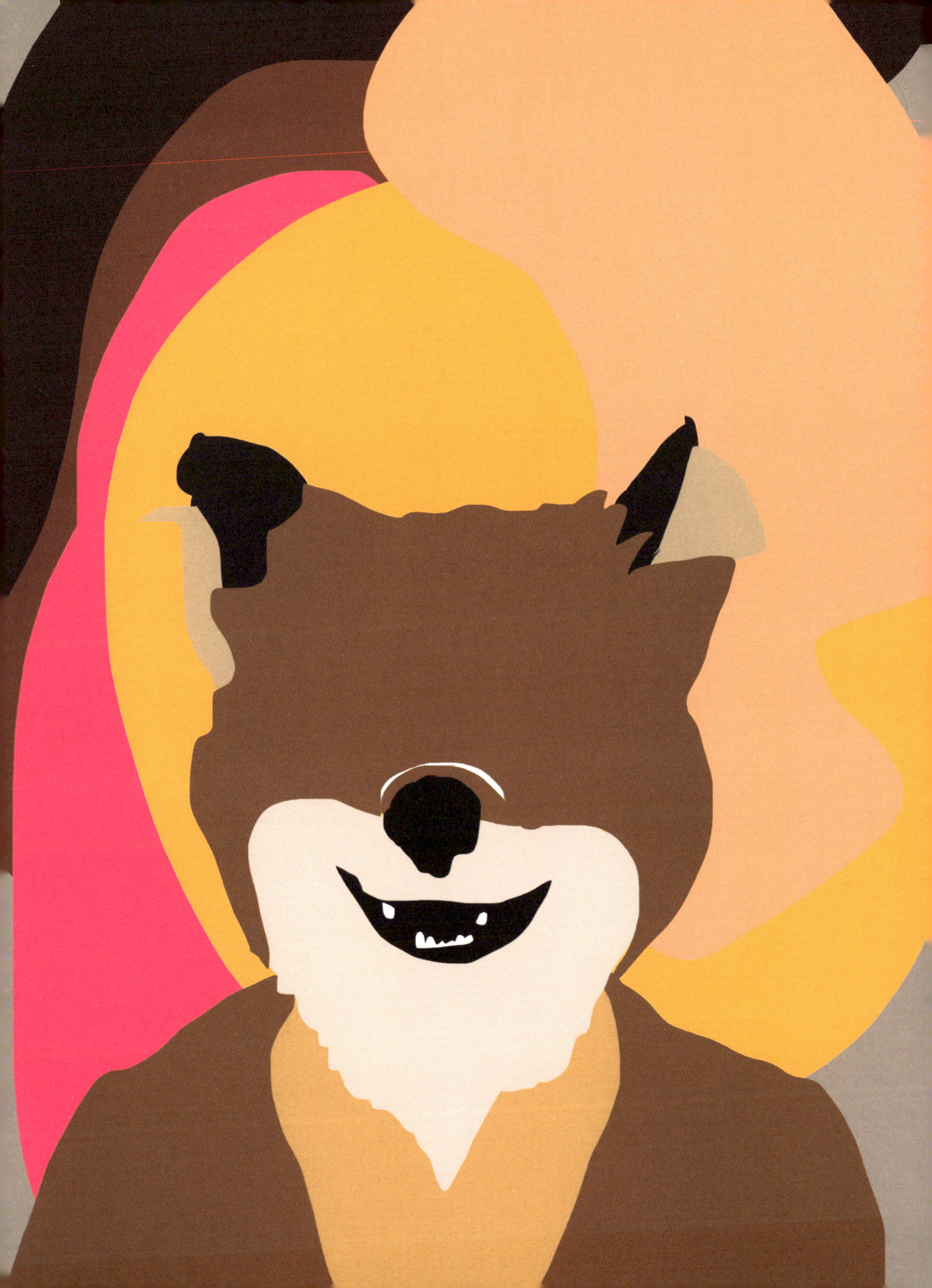

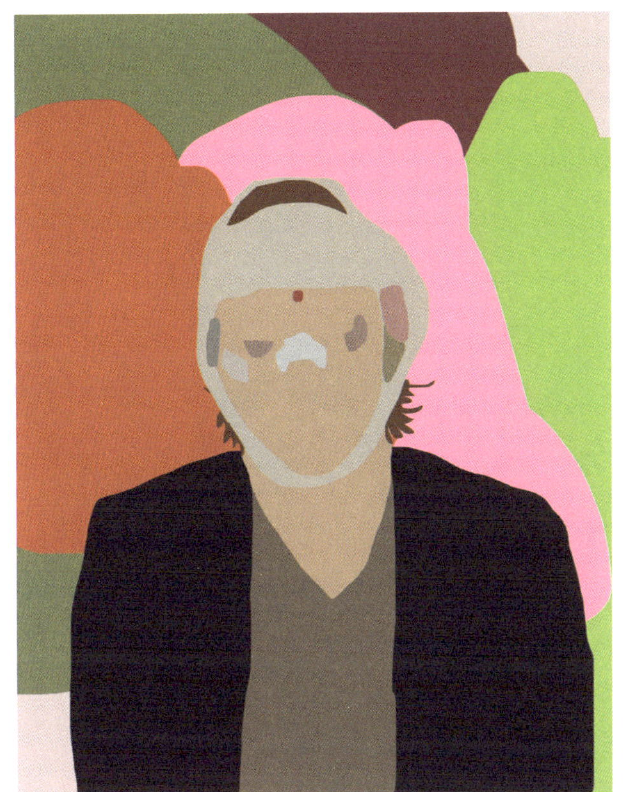

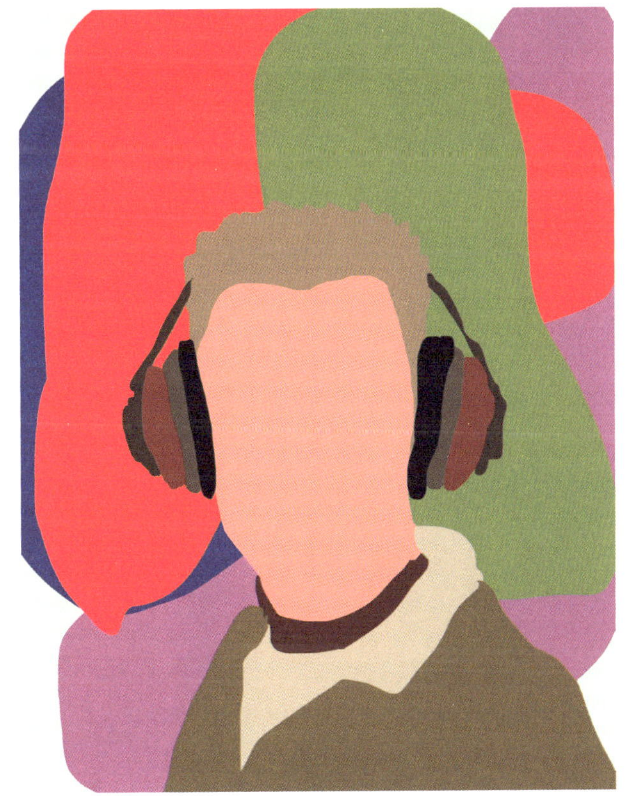

The Darjeeling Limited (top)
Bottle Rocket (bottom)
Fantastic Mr. Fox (left page)

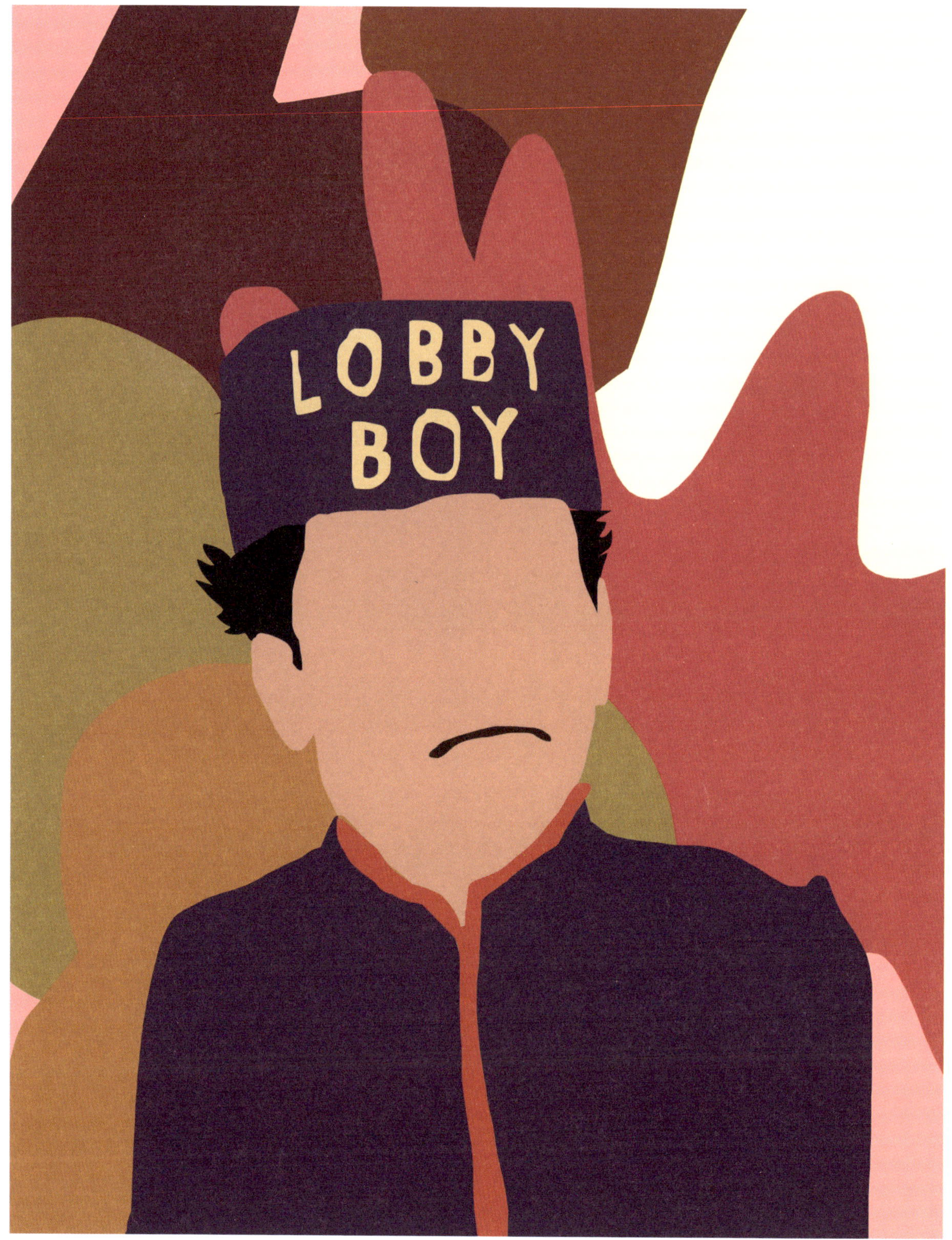

The Grand Budapest Hotel

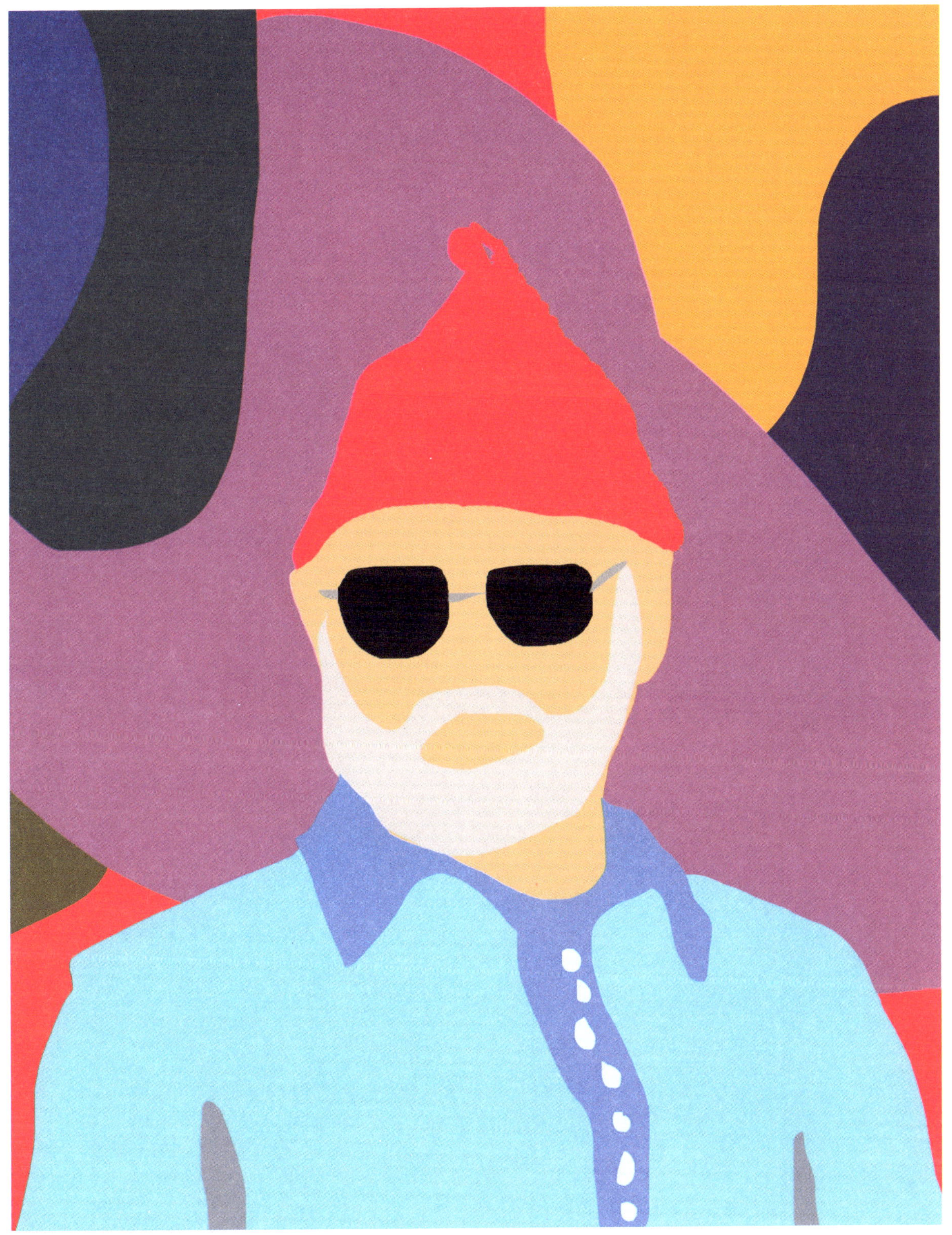

The Life Acquatic with Steve Zissou

TRACIE CHING

www.tracieching.com
Instagram: @tracieching
Twitter: @tracieching
Facebook: @TracieChingDesign

"I AM A MOTH DRAWN TO HIS QUIRKY FLAME"

Tracie Ching is an illustrator and graphic designer living and working in Washington, DC. A self-taught digital artist, Tracie specializes in portraiture featuring complex, graphic line work with a limited palette - a tendency-turned-style after years of working in the medium of silkscreen prints.

While commissioned for a wide range of projects including commercial athletic apparel, editorial illustration, and gallery work, Tracie Ching is best known for her alternative movie posters.

Previous clients include 20th Century Fox, Adidas, AMC, CBS, Google, Lionsgate, Marvel, MGM, Penguin Randomhouse, TIME, Sony Pictures.

Tracie Ching es una ilustradora y diseñadora gráfica que vive y trabaja en Washington D.C. Siendo una artista digital autodidacta, Tracie está especializada en el retrato que destaca una línea de trabajo compleja y gráfica con una paleta limitada: un estilo que se ha convertido en tendencia tras años de trabajo en el medio de la serigrafía.

Si bien se le encomienda una amplia gama de proyectos, incluyendo ropa atlética comercial, ilustración editorial y trabajo en galerías, como más se conoce a Tracie Ching es gracias a sus posters de cine alternativo.

Algunos de sus antiguos clientes son los estudios 20th Century Fox, Adidas, AMC, CBS, Google, Lionsgate, Marvel, MGM, Penguin Randomhouse, TIME o Sony Pictures.

The Royal Tenenbaums (right page)
Collaboration with Spoke Art Gallery in San Francisco for Bad Dads, their annual Wes Anderson tribute art show

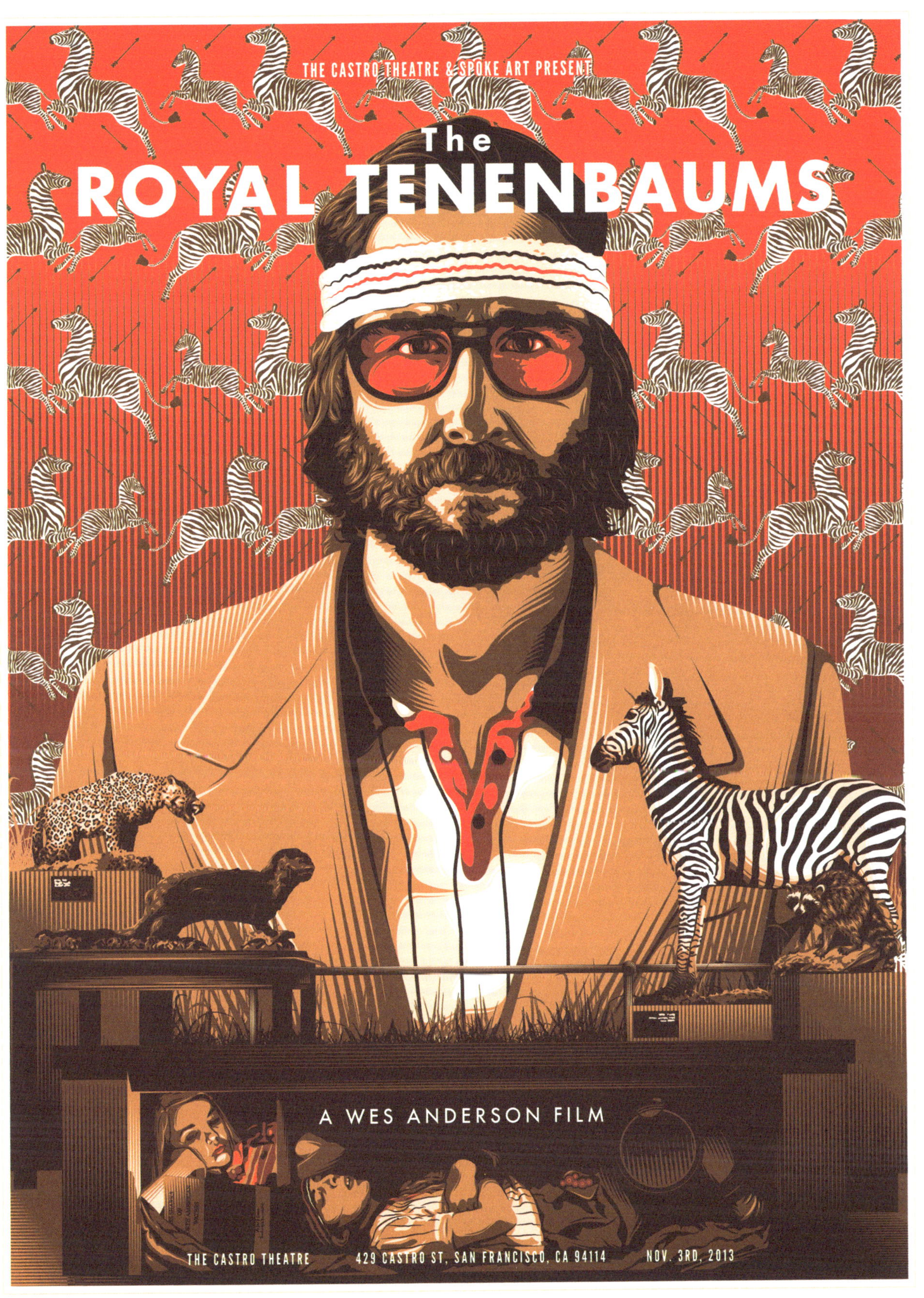
THE CASTRO THEATRE & SPOKE ART PRESENT
The
ROYAL TENENBAUMS
A WES ANDERSON FILM
THE CASTRO THEATRE
429 CASTRO ST, SAN FRANCISCO, CA 94114
NOV. 3RD, 2013

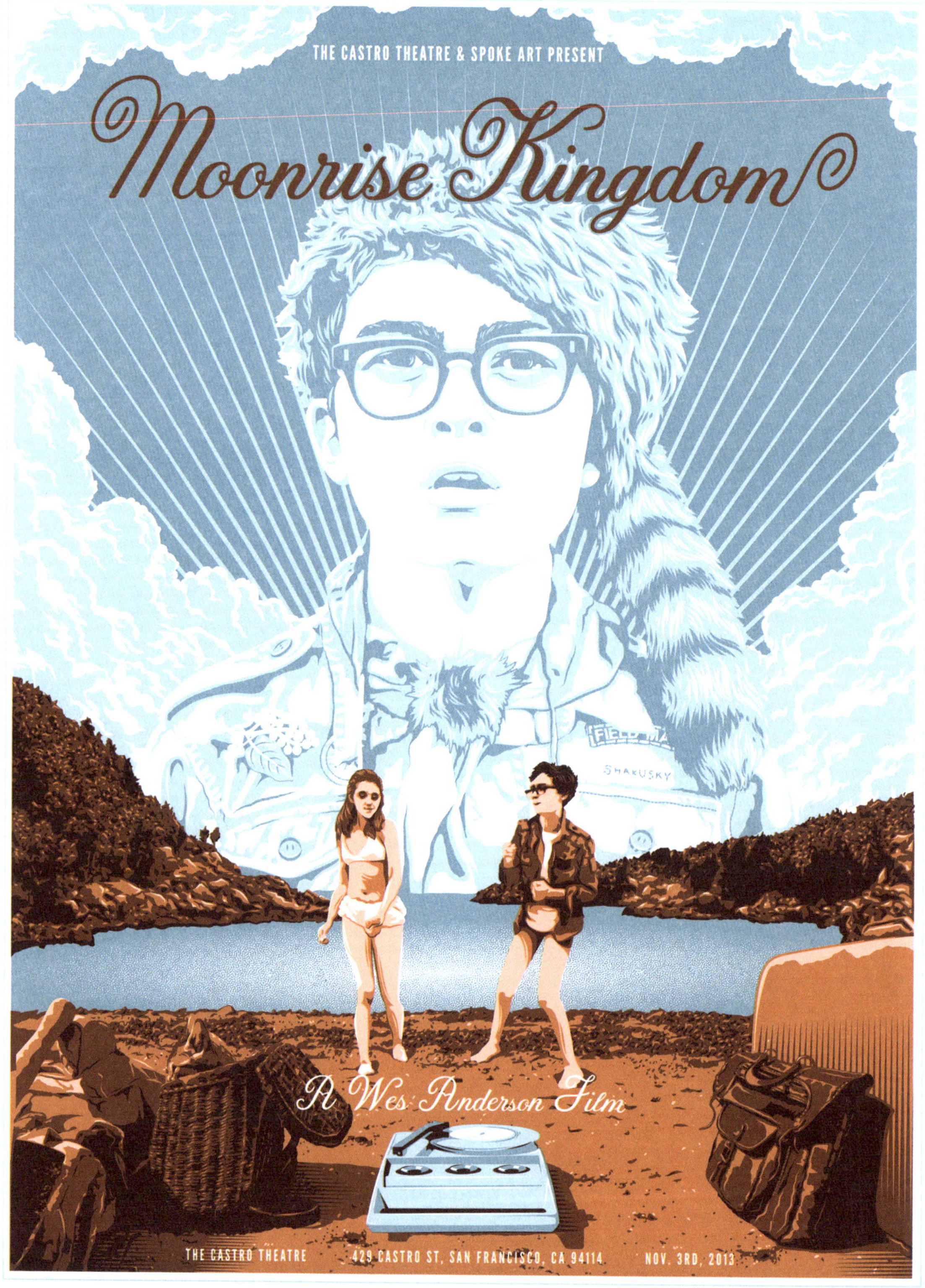

Moonrise Kingdom
Collaboration with Spoke Art Gallery in San Francisco for Bad Dads, their annual Wes Anderson tribute art show

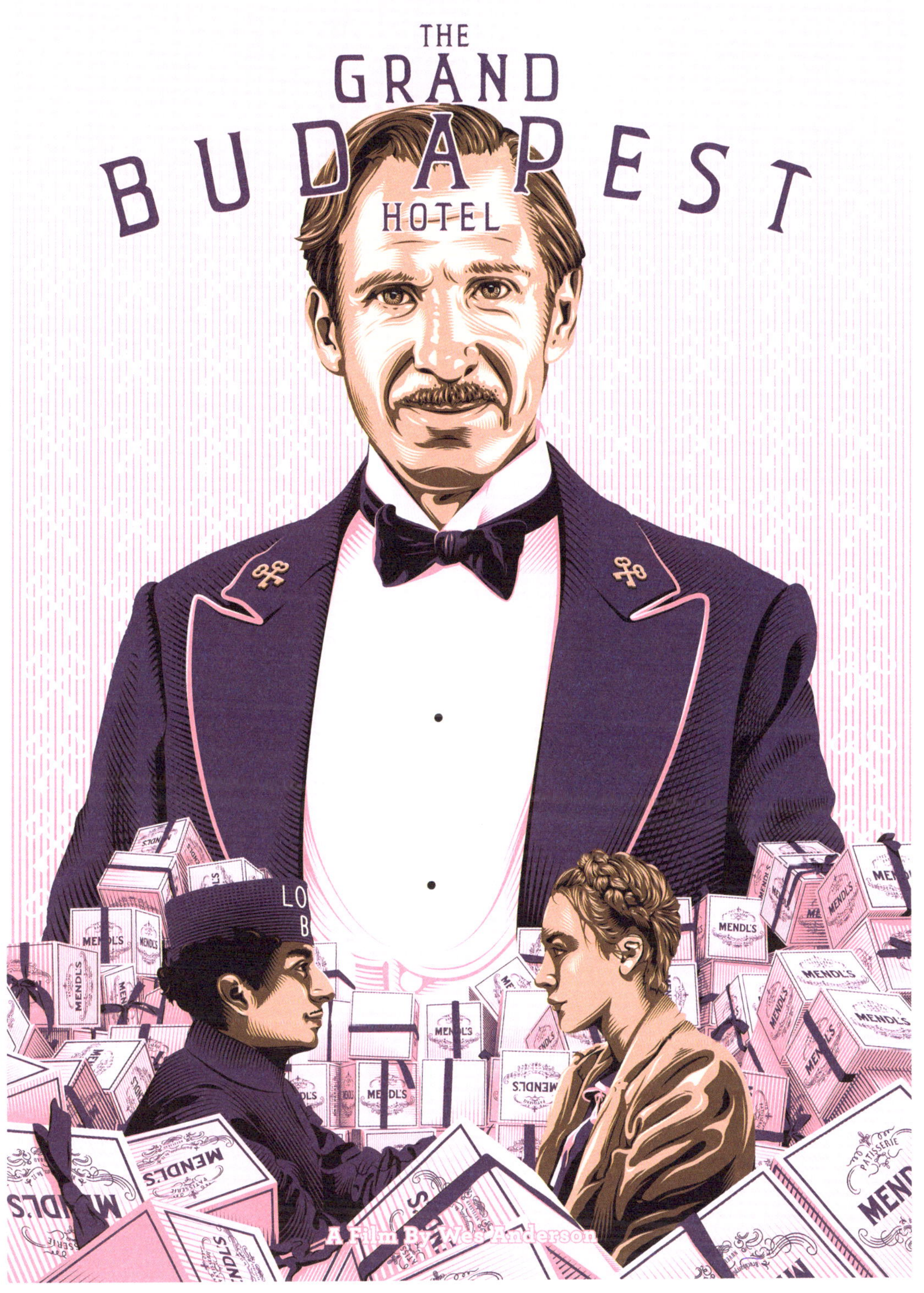

The Grand Budapest Hotel
Collaboration with Spoke Art Gallery in San Francisco for Bad Dads, their annual Wes Anderson tribute art show

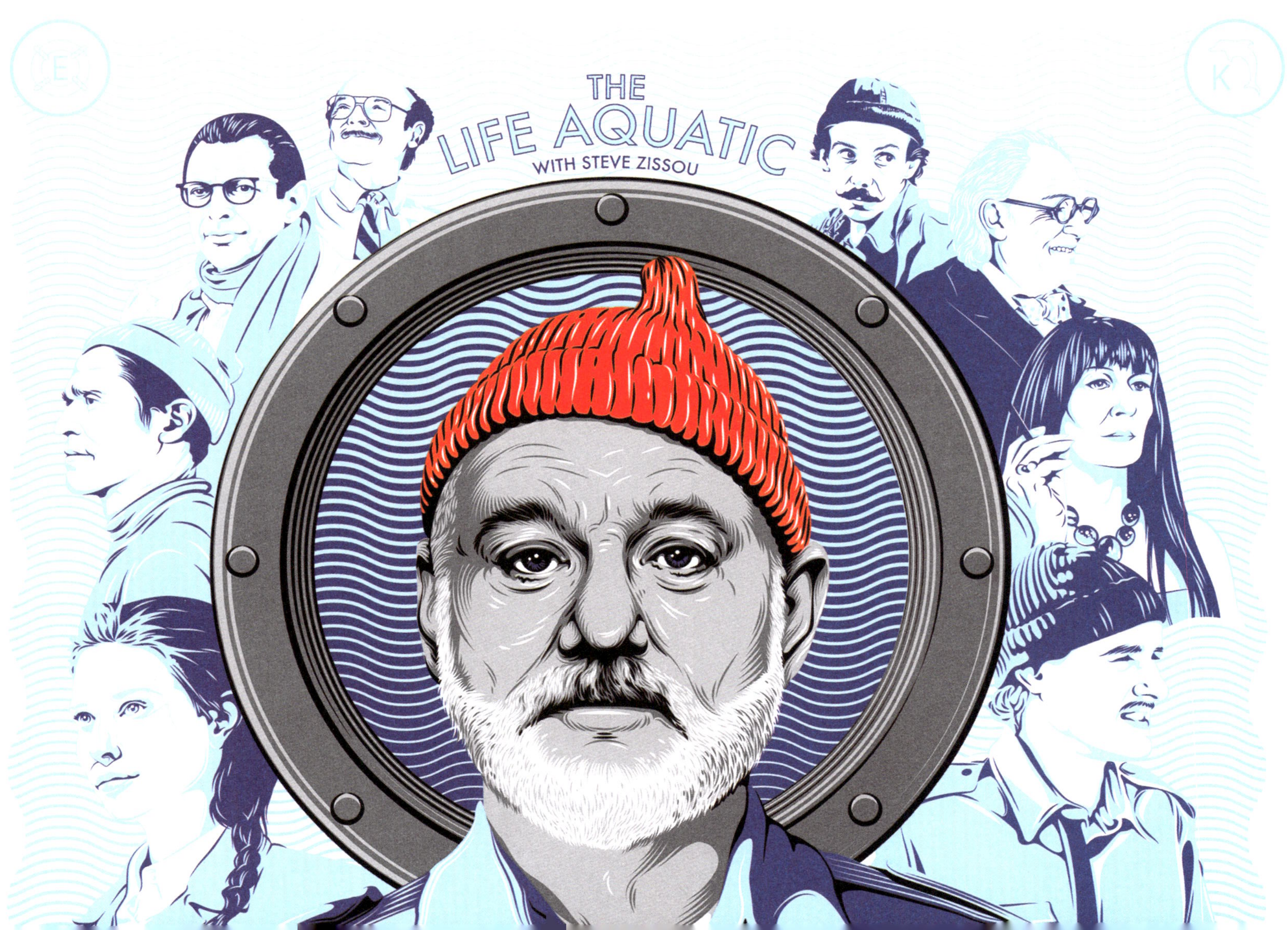
THE
LIFE AQUATIC
WITH STEVE ZISSOU
E
K

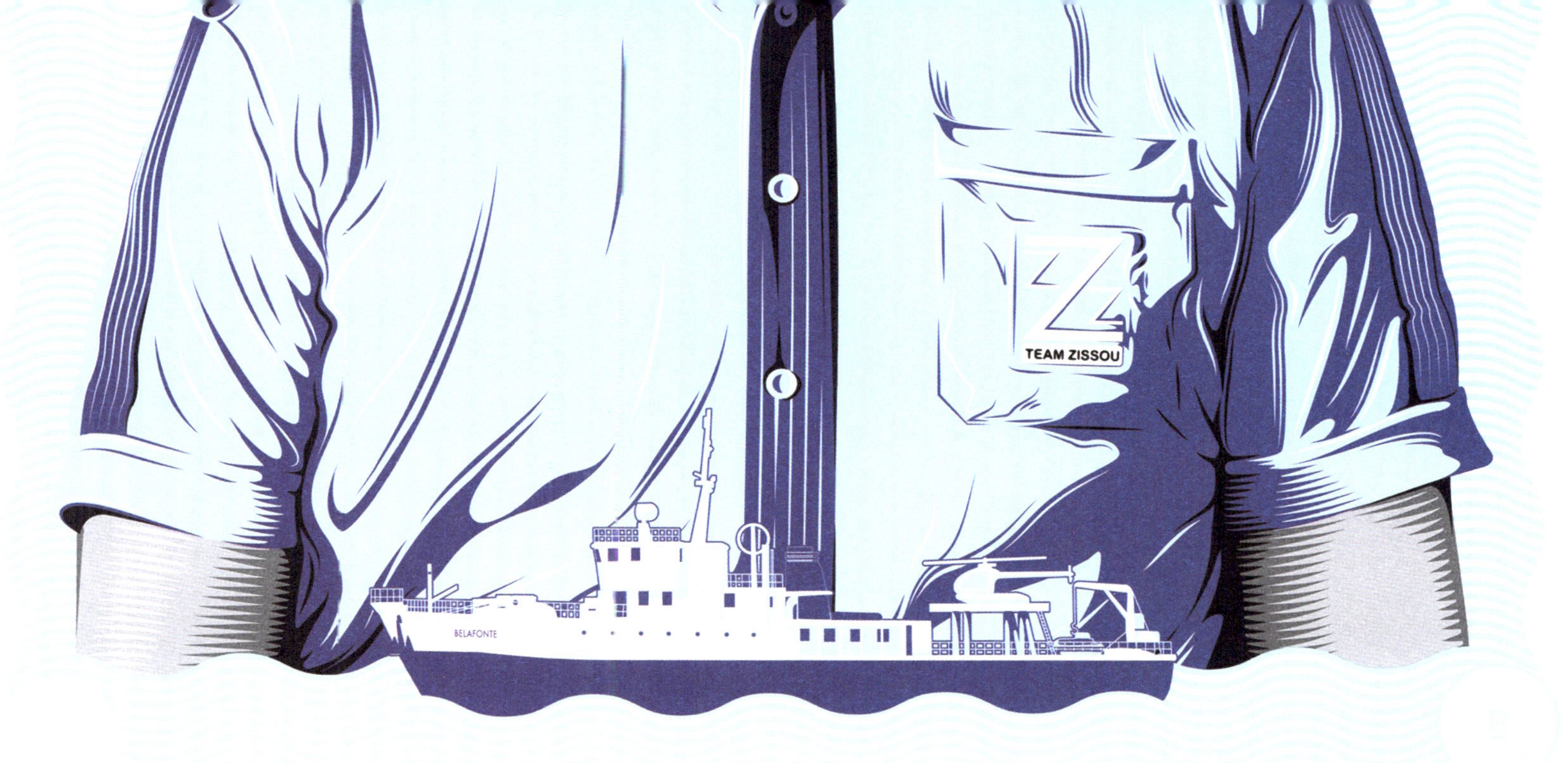

The Life Acquatic with Steve Zissou
Collaboration with Spoke Art Gallery in San Francisco for Bad Dads, their annual Wes Anderson tribute art show

ALEJANDRO GIRALDO

www.alejogiraldo.com
Instagram: @alejogiraldo_
Twitter: @alejogiraldo_

"I WANT TO MAKE PEOPLE FEEL LIKE WES ANDERSON'S MOVIES MAKE ME FEEL"

He is an illustrator from Medellín, Colombia. Currently, he spends his time working on freelance projects for different clients around the world but also takes time to express himself by working on personal projects, which include illustration, lettering and fashion.
When he's not drawing he's probably thinking about what to eat or what to draw next. He loves the ocean and one day he hopes to live in front of the beach.

Ilustrador de Medellín, Colombia. Actualmente, dedica su tiempo a trabajar en proyectos freelance para diferentes clientes en todo el mundo, pero también se dedica tiempo a sí mismo, expresándose mediante el trabajo en proyectos personales, lo cual incluye la ilustración y la moda.
Cuando no está dibujando, probablemente está pensando en qué comer o dibujar próximamente. Le encanta el océano y un día espera vivir frente a la playa.

The characters of Wes Anderson (right page)

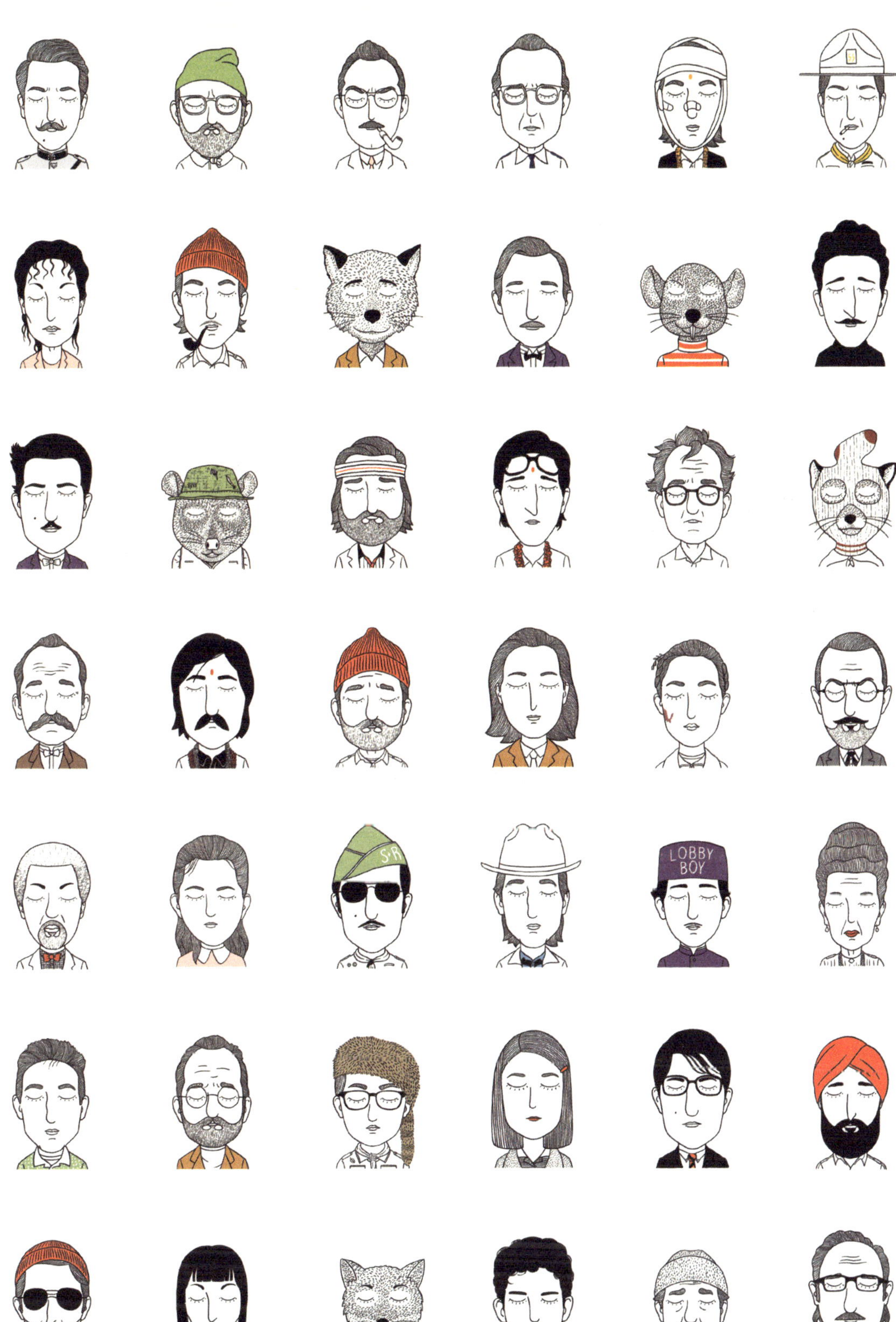
LOBBY
BOY
S·R

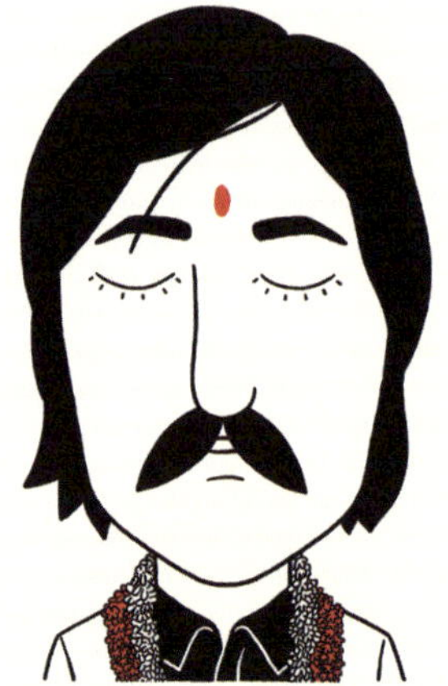
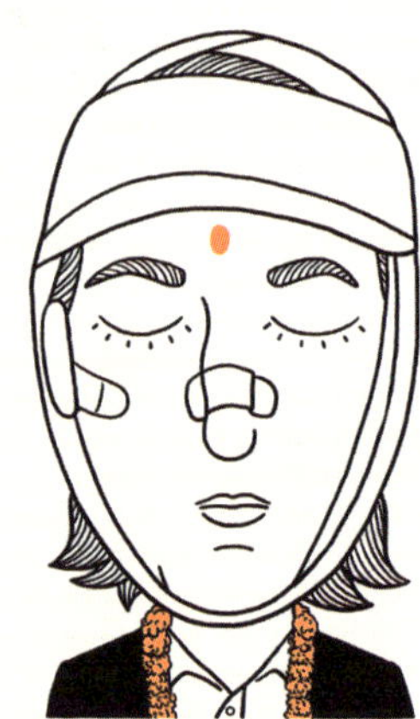
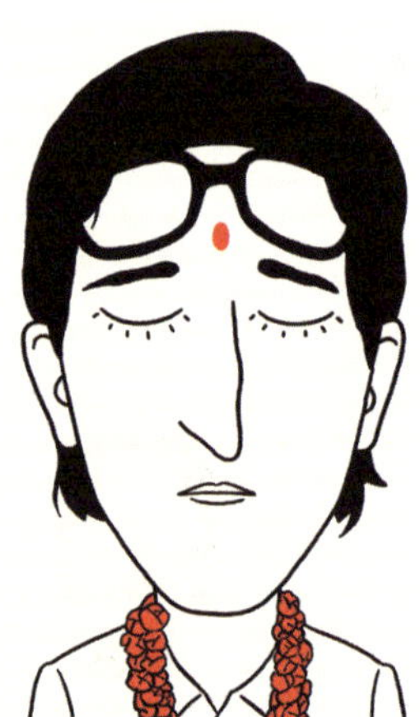

I guess I've still got some more healing to do.

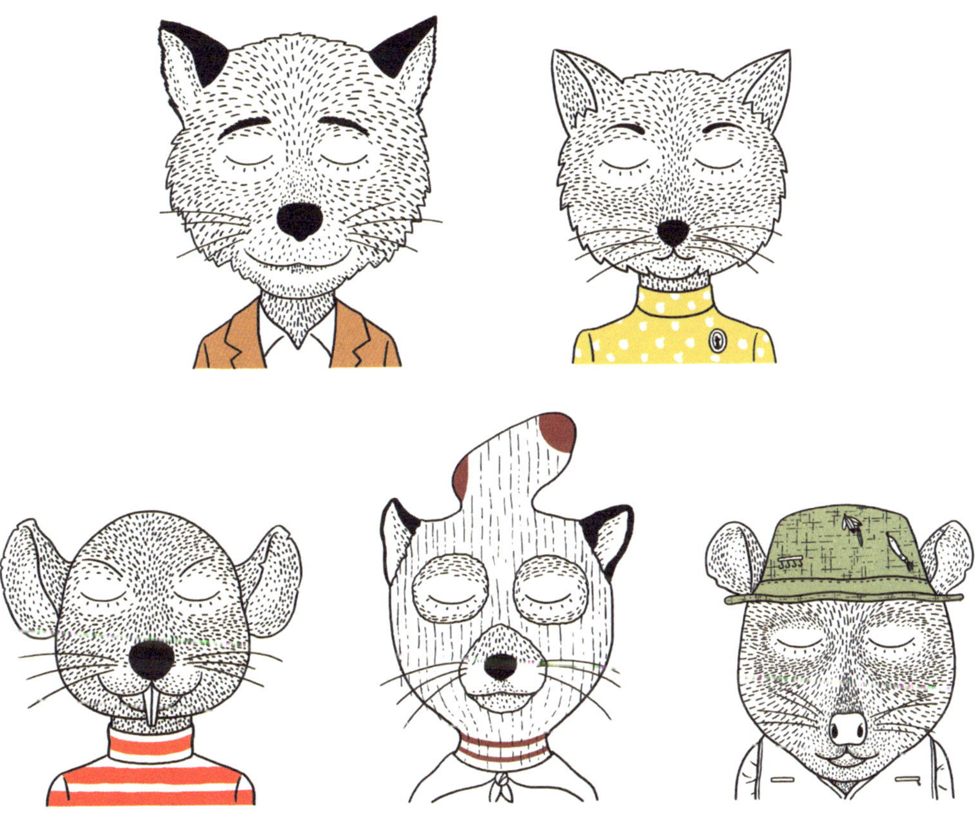

We're all different. But there's something kind of fantastic about that, isn't there?

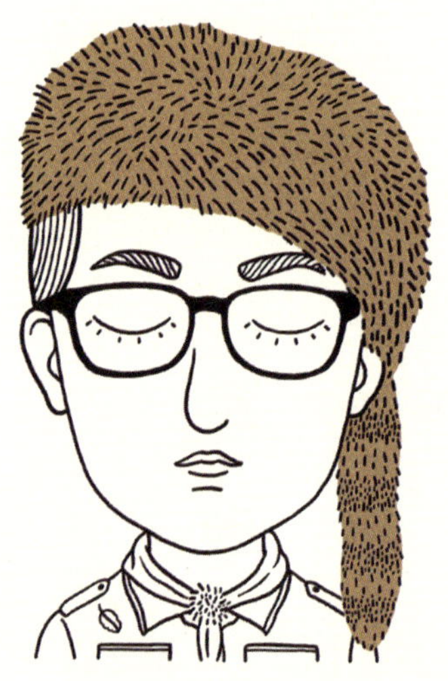

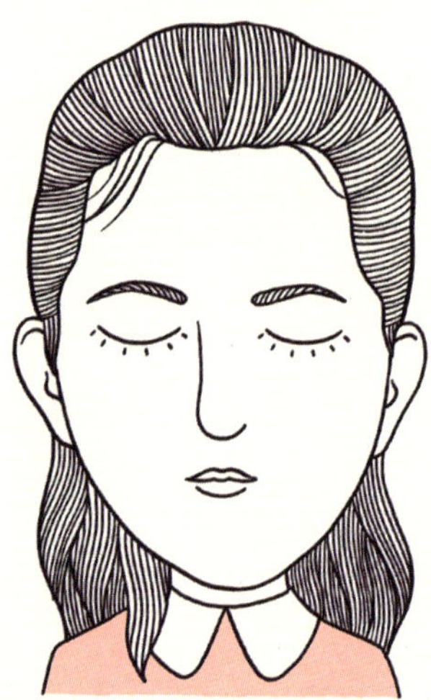

I love you but you have no idea what you are talking about

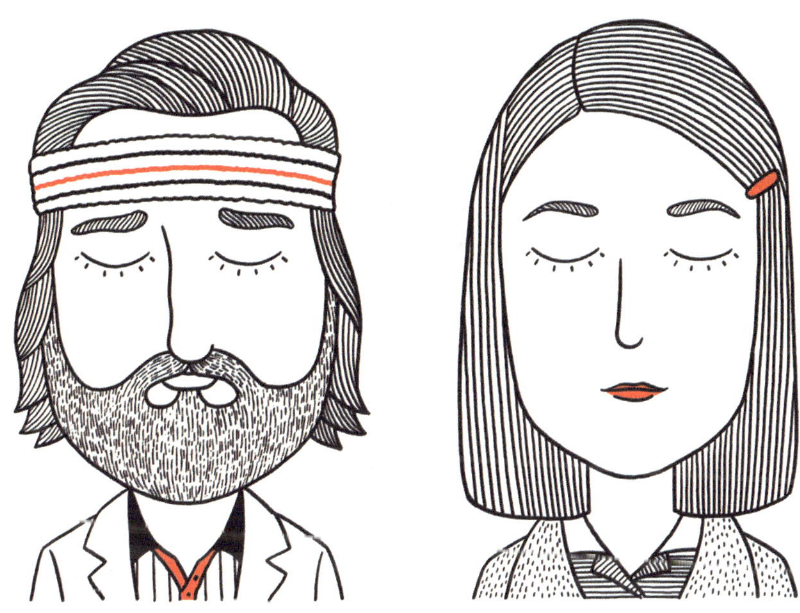

I think we're just going to have to be secretly
in love with each other and leave it at that.

The Royal Tenenbaums

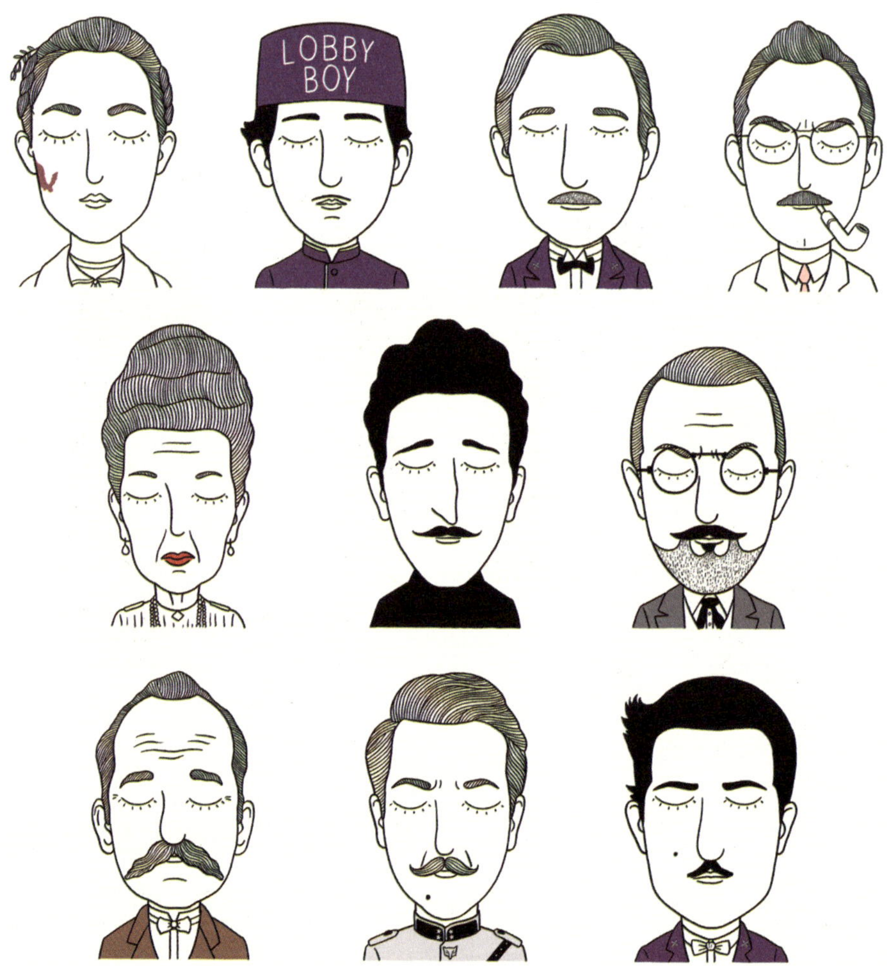

There are still faint glimmers of civilization left in this barbaric slaughterhouse that was once known as humanity

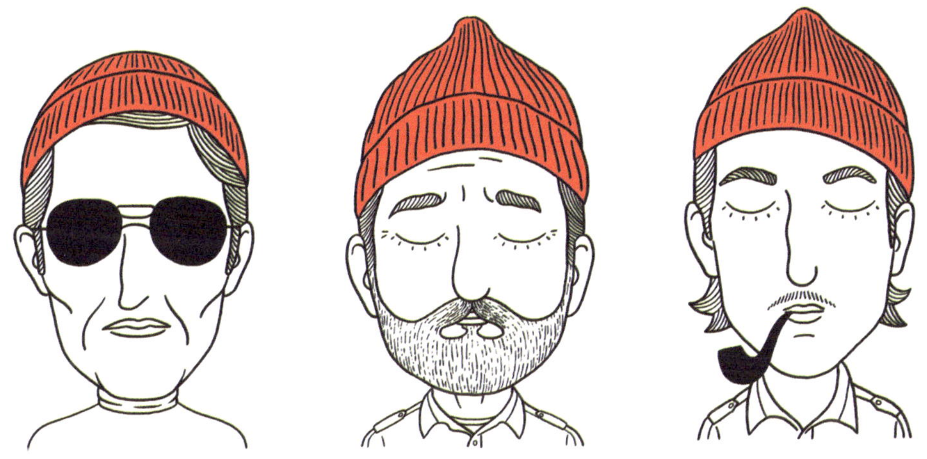

This is an adventure.

The Life Acquatic with Steve Zissou

MARÍA HESSE

www.mariahesse.es
Instagram: @mariahesse
Facebook: @mariahesse

"EACH FILM IS A UNIVERSE OF A DIFFERENT COLOUR"

María Hesse (Huelva, 1982). She became an illustrator at the tender age of 6. She still did not know, but her teacher and her mother did. A few years later, after completing her studies in Special Education, she grabbed her pencils jumped headlong into the illustration world as a professional.

She has been working with the Edelvives publishing house for three years, creating textbooks. She has also illustrated for *Jot Down* magazine, *Maasâi Magazine* and the children's section of the Seville Cathedral magazine.

María has published *Ole Sevilla!* (Ed. Kokoro Multimedia), *En busca de Nicolás* (Ed. En Huida), *Armadura de papel de plata* and *La pandilla de Mago* (Ed. Autores Premiados), *Frida Kahlo. Una biografía* (Editorial Lumen) and *Pride and Prejudice* (Alfaguara).

In addition to her publications, she has made posters for various festivals such as the "I Festival de Cultura Feminista de La Tribu" and "Nocturama 2017".

The work of Maria Hesse has been exhibited in various exhibitions and features a personal focus where sensitivity and women are the main protagonists.

María Hesse (Huelva, 1982). Se convirtió en ilustradora a la tierna edad de 6 años, ella aún no lo sabía, pero su profesora y su madre sí. Unos buenos años después, tras acabar sus estudios en Educación Especial, agarró los lápices y se lanzó a la piscina de la ilustración de manera profesional.

Lleva trabajando tres años con la editorial Edelvives en la realización de libros de texto y también ha ilustrado para la revista *Jot Down*, *Maasâi Magazine* y la sección infantil de la revista de la Catedral de Sevilla.

María ha publicado *Ole Sevilla!* (Ed. Kokoro Multimedia), *En busca de Nicolás* (Ed. En Huida), *Armadura de papel de plata* y *La pandilla de Mago* (Ed. Autores Premiados), *Frida Kahlo. Una biografía* (Editorial Lumen) y *Orgullo y Prejuicio* (Alfaguara).

Además del trabajo editorial, ha realizado carteles para diversos festivales como el "I Festival de Cultura Feminista de La Tribu" o "Nocturama 2017".

La obra de María Hesse ha sido expuesta en diversas exposiciones y cuenta con un trabajo personal donde la sensibilidad y la mujer son las grandes protagonistas.

Moonrise Kingdom (right page)

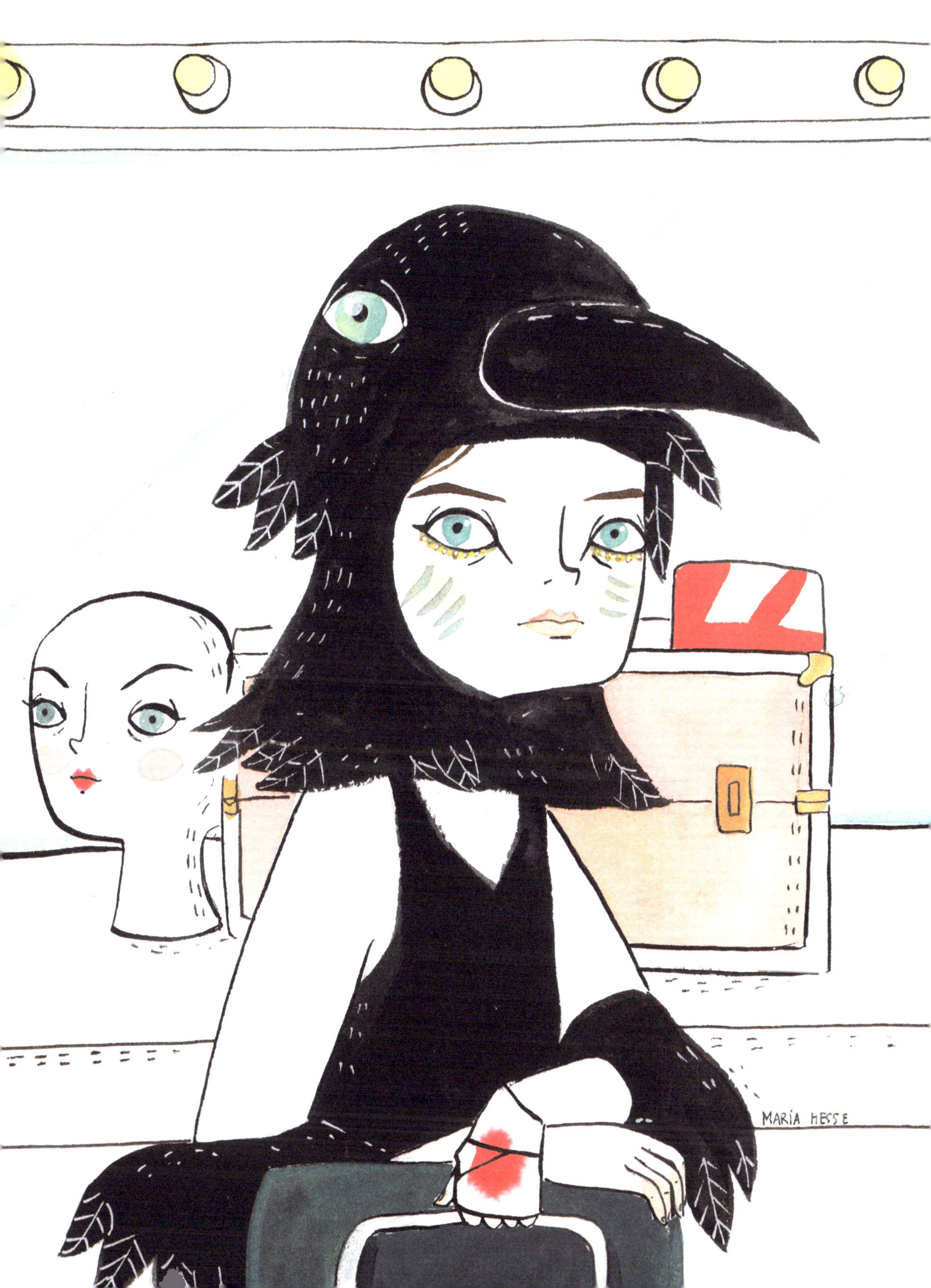
MARÍA HESSE

ANDRES LOZANO

www.andres-lozano.com
www.behance.net/andreslm
Instagram: @andreslozanom
Twitter: @AndresLNews
Facebook: @AndresLozanoIllustration

"I CAN'T WATCH A WES ANDERSON MOVIE WITHOUT WANTING TO STOP THE FILM EVERY 5 MINUTES TO ABSORB ALL THE DETAILS, COMPOSITIONS AND COLORS"

Andrés Lozano is a Spanish illustrator born in Madrid in 1992, he studied design at Universidad Complutense and now is based in London.

He is inspired by nature, architecture, franco-belgian comics and film noir.

His work uses overlayed colors, textures and strong line. His practice spans from commercial illustration (Shop Magazine or Imax) to editorial (The New York Times, Entertainment Weekly, The Wall Street Journal...) and children books, having published a series of 6 books with the UK based "Wide Eyed Books".

Besides illustration he likes painting, making music and cooking.

Andrés Lozano es un ilustrador español nacido en Madrid en 1992, estudió diseño en la Universidad Complutense y ahora vive en Londres.

Su inspiración viene de la naturaleza, la arquitectura, los comics franco-belgas y el cine negro.

En su obra se emplean colores superpuestos, texturas y líneas firmes. Su práctica abarca desde la ilustración comercial (Shop Magazine o Imax) hasta lo editorial (The New York Times, Entertainment Weekly, The Wall Street Journal...) y los libros infantiles, habiendo publicado una serie de 6 libros con la editorial "Wide Eyed", situada en el Reino Unido.

Además de la ilustración, le gusta pintar, componer y cocinar.

Fantastic Mr. Fox (right page)

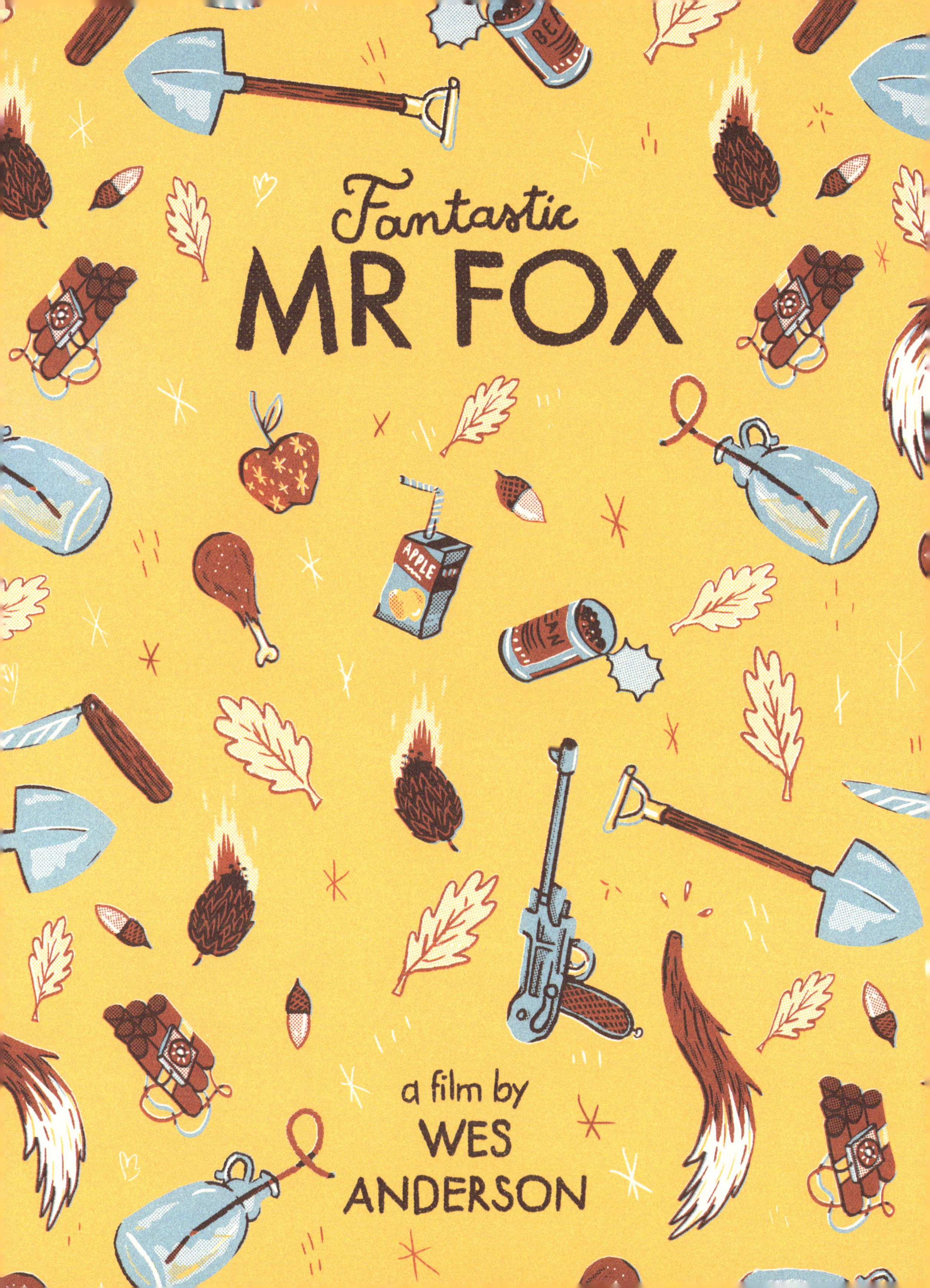
Fantastic
MR FOX
a film by
WES
ANDERSON
APPLE

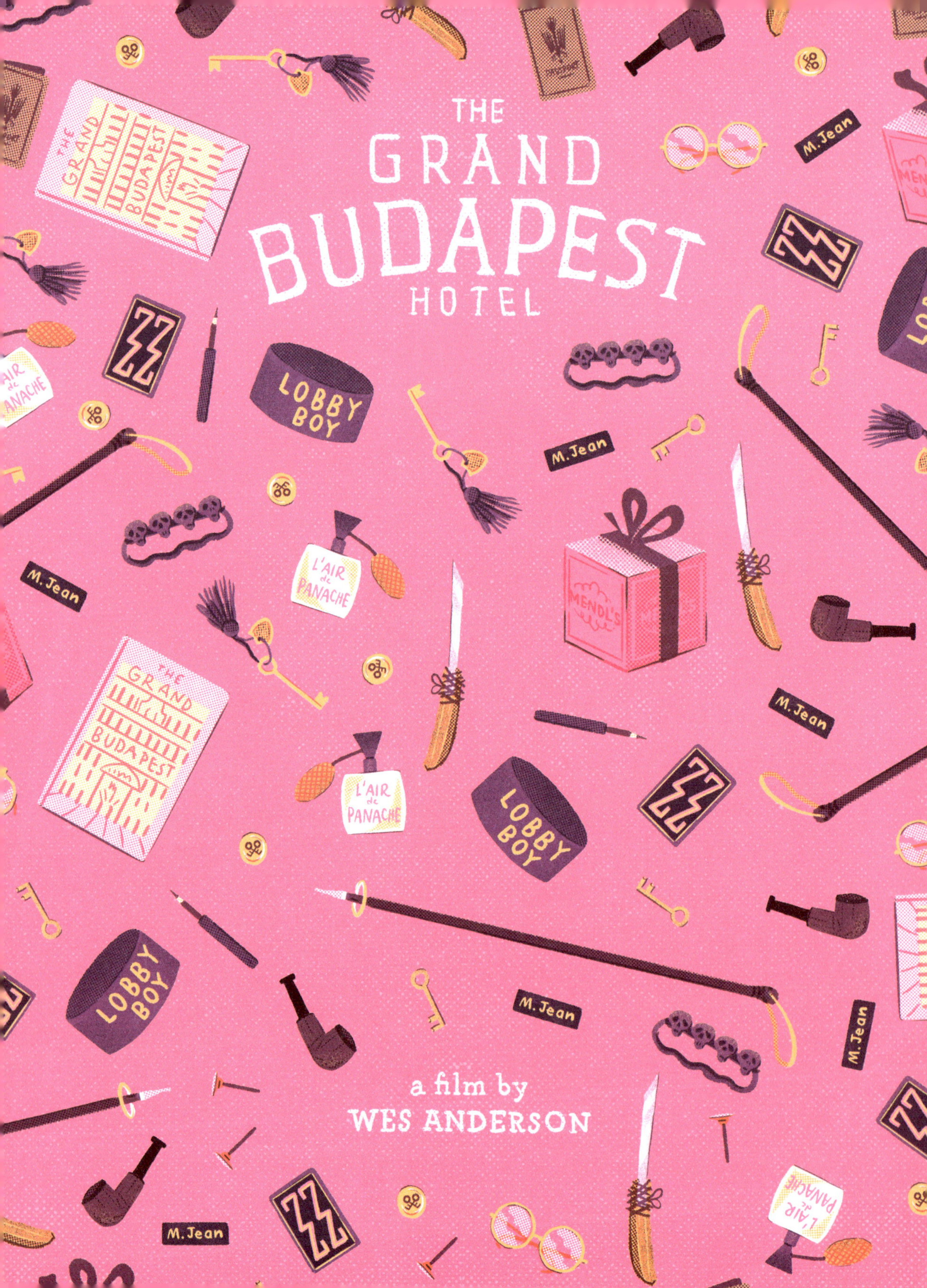
THE
GRAND
BUDAPEST
HOTEL
a film by
WES ANDERSON

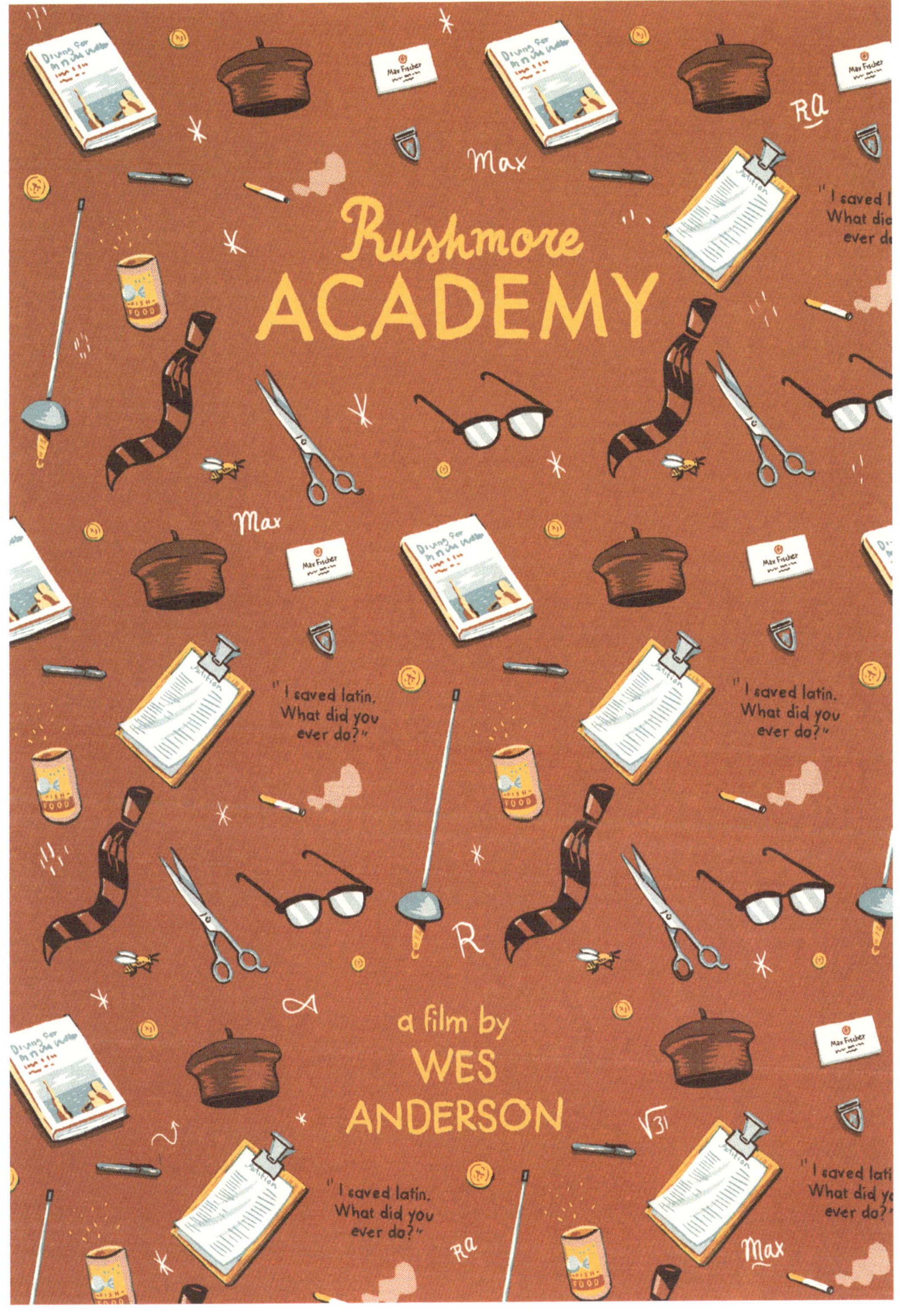

Rushmore Academy
The Grand Budapest Hotel (left page)

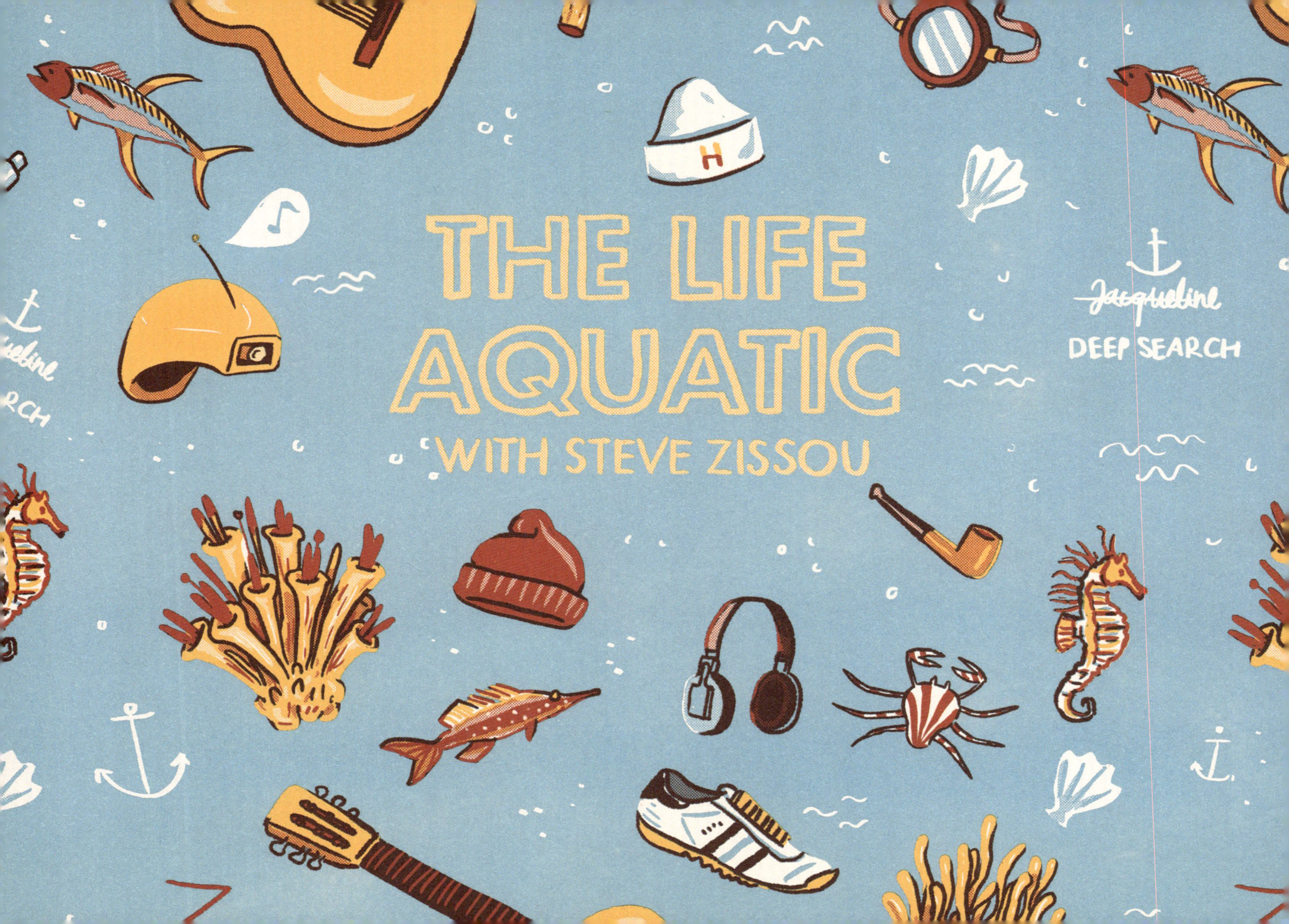
THE LIFE AQUATIC
WITH STEVE ZISSOU
Jacqueline
DEEP SEARCH

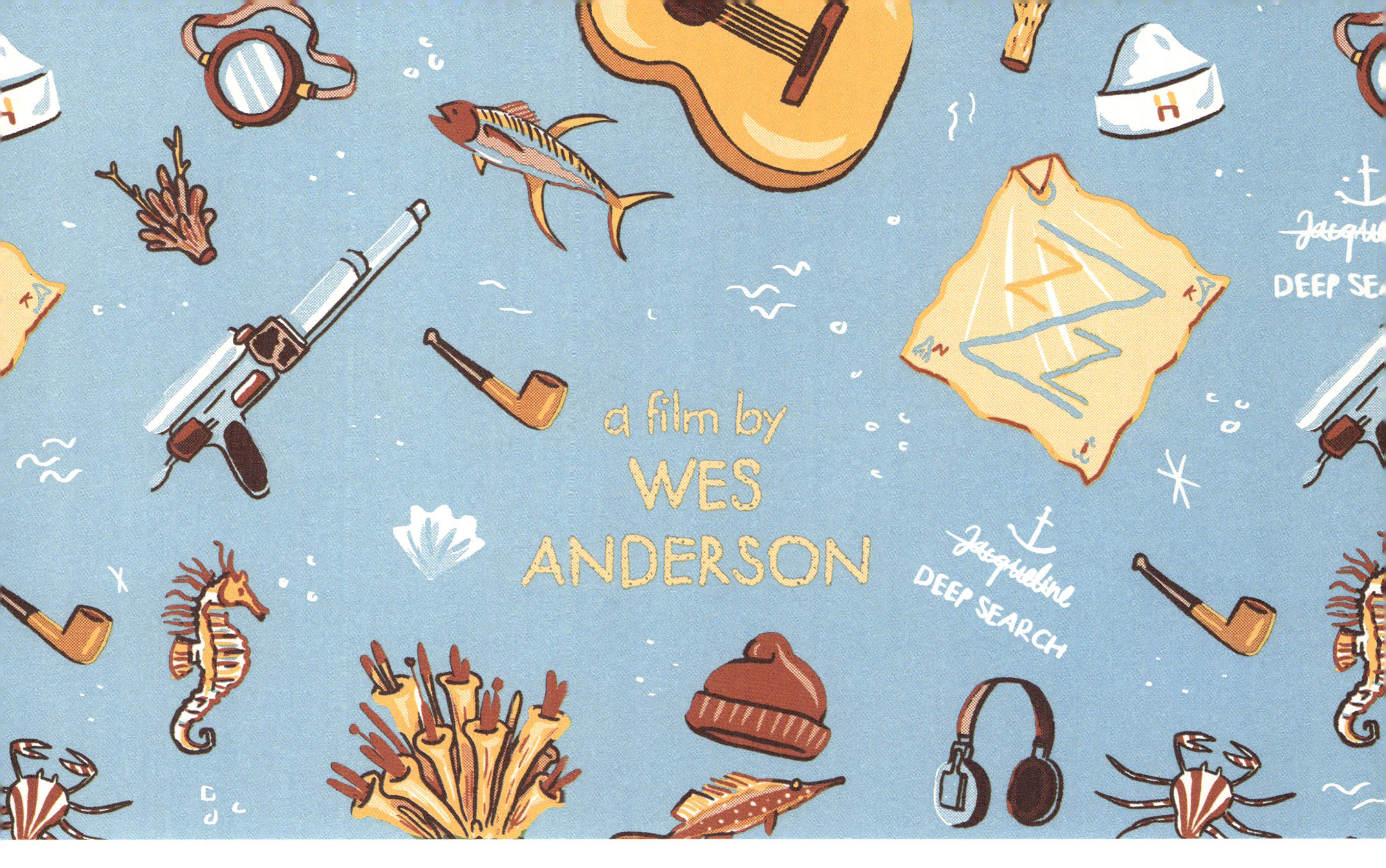

The Life Acquatic with Steve Zissou

ALEX DE MARCOS

www.mundopiruuu.com
Instagram: @mundopiruuu
Facebook: @mundopiruuu
Twitter: @mundopiruuu

"WES ANDERSON'S FILMS ARE WHAT I LIKE TO CALL ANTI-CLOUDS. NO MATTER HOW BAD YOUR DAY IS, GOING TO BED AFTER WATCHING ONE OF HIS MOVIES IS ALWAYS A GOOD IDEA AND WILL CLEAR AWAY THE CLOUDS. I THINK I'VE SEEN *THE LIFE AQUATIC* MORE THAN 18 TIMES"

Alex de Marcos, creator of Mundopiruuu, was born in Madrid on Halloween night of 85.

"He writes drawings" ever since he was a little boy and scribbled monkeys on the margins of school activity sheets. He is involved in all areas of illustration: from publishing to advertising for agencies around the world. He regularly collaborates with major international brands such as Nike, Oysho, Movistar, Levi's and Ron Barceló. In 2011 he received the prestigious Bronze and Gold awards in illustration from ADCI (Art Director Club Italiano) for his campaigns for the Milan Metro and the ROC brand.

He likes uncomplicated people—which is not to say simple people—who do great things with very little, and strolling in search of adventures with Brownie (his dog). His inspiration is LOVE with capital letters. In fact he draws for love and his favourite phrase is "do what you love and you'll get what you want".

Alex de Marcos, creador de Mundopiruuu, nació en Madrid la noche de Halloween del 85.

«Escribe dibujos» desde que era pequeño y garabateaba monos en los márgenes de las fichas del cole. Se dedica a todos losámbitos de la ilustración: desde el editorial hasta la publicidad para agencias de todo el mundo. Colabora habitualmente con grandes marcas internacionales como Nike, Oysho, Movistar, Levi's o Ron Barceló. En 2011 recibió los prestigiosos galardones de Bronce y Oro en ilustración del ADCI (Art director Club Italiano) con las campañas para el Metro de Milán y la marca ROC.

Le gustan las personas sencillas, que no simples, que hacen grandes cosas con poco, y pasear en busca de aventuras con Brownie (su perro). Su inspiración es el AMOR con letras mayúsculas, de hecho dibuja por amor y su frase favorita es «el que hace lo que ama consigue lo que quiere».

Margot (right page)

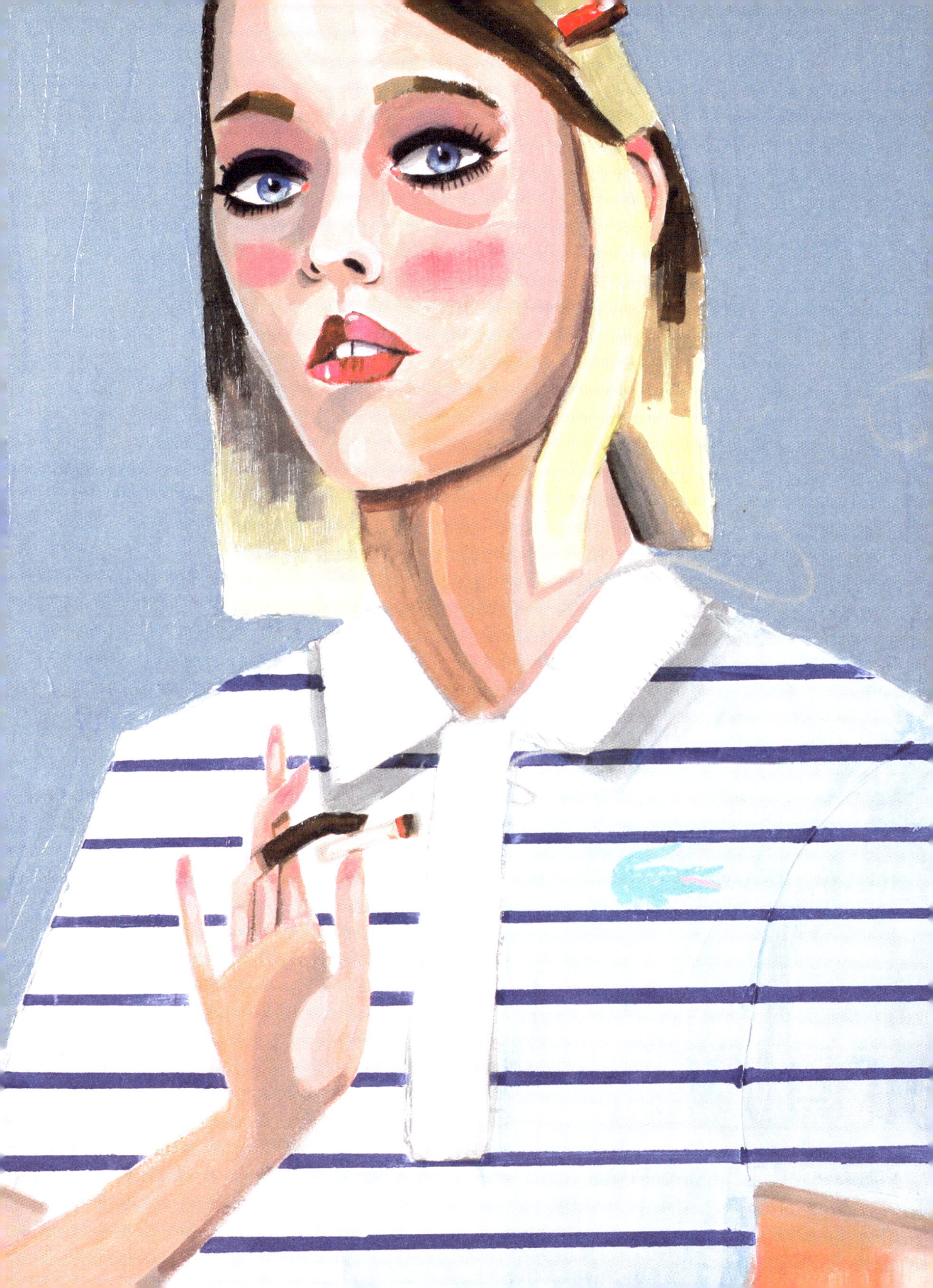

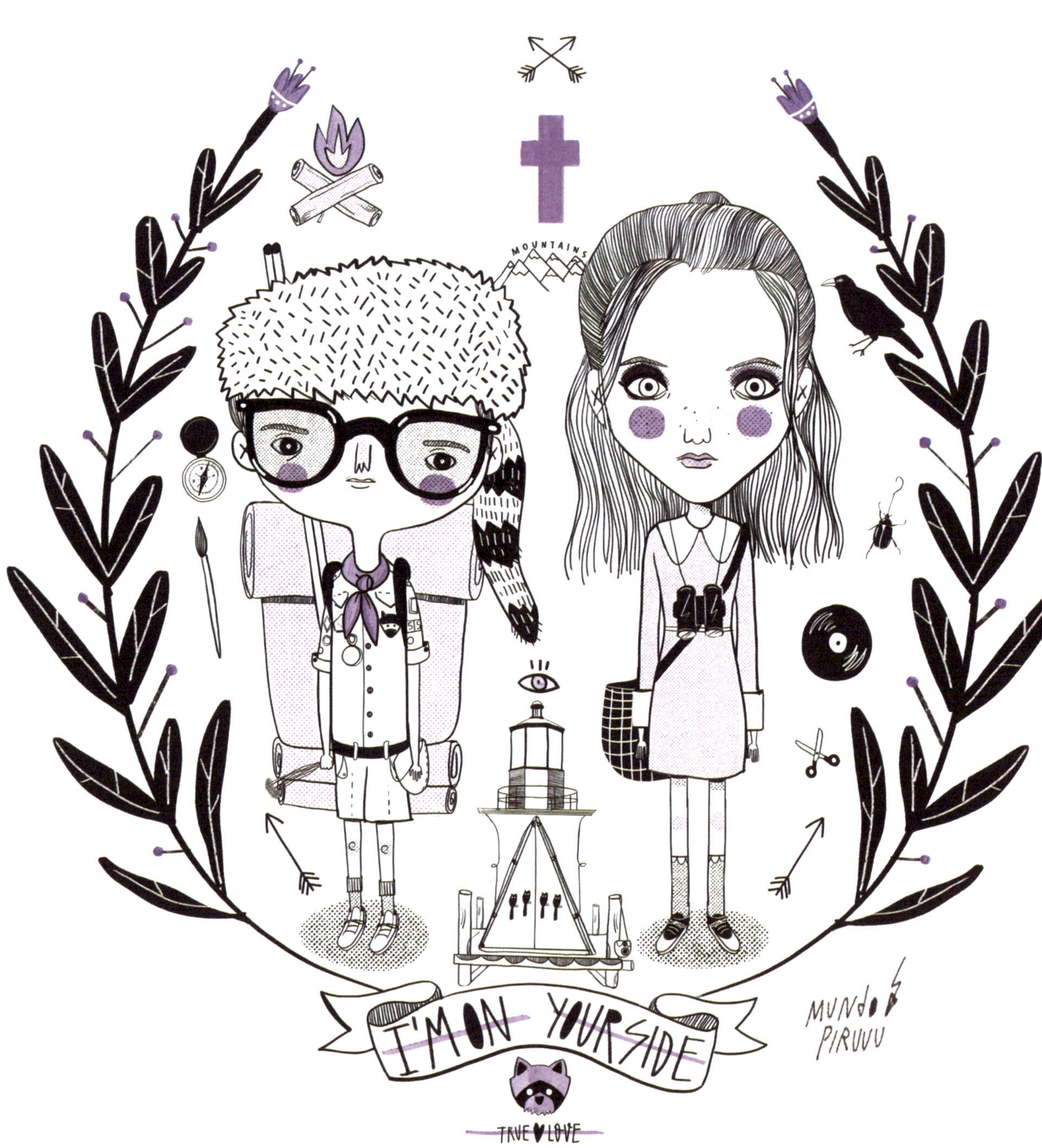
MOUNTAINS
I'M ON YOUR SIDE
TRUE LOVE
MUNDO PIRUUU

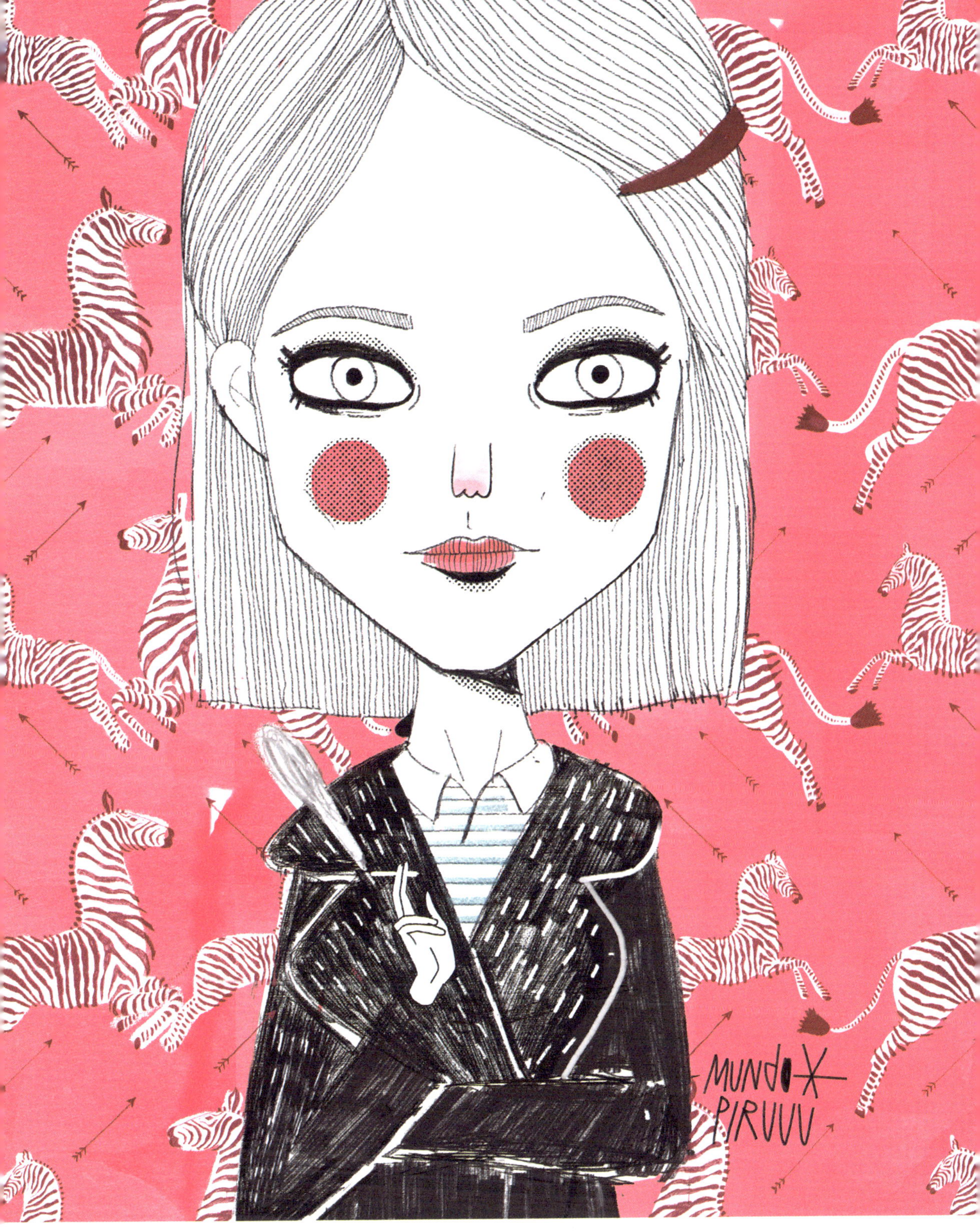

Margot

PATRICK CONCEPCIÓN

www.concepcionstudios.com
Instagram: @concepcion_studios
facebook.com/concepcionstudios

"ANDERSON'S VIVID COLOR PALETTES SUMMON A WARM FEELING OF NOSTALGIA"

Patrick Concepción is the founder and Art Director of Concepción Studios, a studio that focuses on art direction and graphics for the entertainment industry, located in Morgan Hill, California. He served as the Art Director of one of the largest music merchandising companies in the world, Bravado International Group in Los Angeles, before leaving to establish Concepción Studios in 2006. Throughout his career he has reveled in designing for Lady Gaga, Paul McCartney and MUSE. Concepción Studios has earned international recognition with works published in The New Yorker, Rolling Stone, TIME, PRINT Magazine, and Gestalten along with album art aired on the Tonight Show, CONAN, and Jimmy Kimmel Live.

Patrick Concepción es el fundador y Director Artístico de los Estudios Concepción, los cuales se centran en la dirección artística y en los gráficos para la industria del espectáculo y se encuentran en Morgan Hill, California. Ejerció como Director de Arte de una de las compañías de merchandising musicales más grandes del mundo, el grupo Bravado International en Los Ángeles, antes de dejarlo para posteriormente fundar los Estudios Concepción en 2006. A lo largo de su carrera ha disfrutado diseñando para Lady Gaga, Paul McCartney y MUSE. Los Estudios Concepción han adquirido reconocimiento internacional con obras publicadas en The New Yorker, Rolling Stone, TIME, la revista PRINT y Gestalten junto con la carátula del álbum emitida en los programas nocturnos de Tonight Show, CONAN y Jimmy Kimmel Live.

Sam and Suzy (right page) / Offset lithograph / 12 inches x 18 inches
Exhibited at Spoke Art Gallery in New York City for the "Bad Dads: An Art Show Tribute to the Films of Wes Anderson"

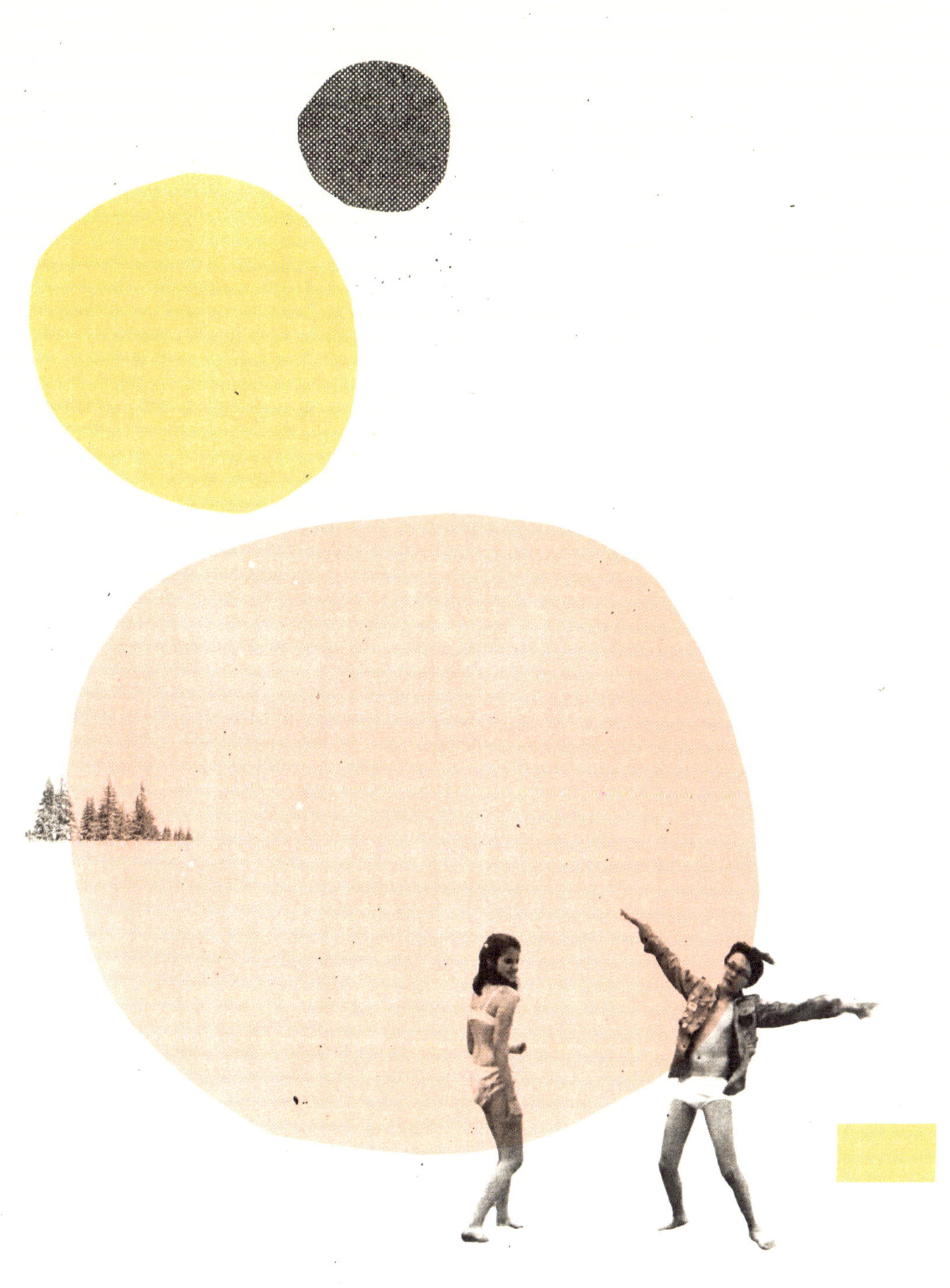

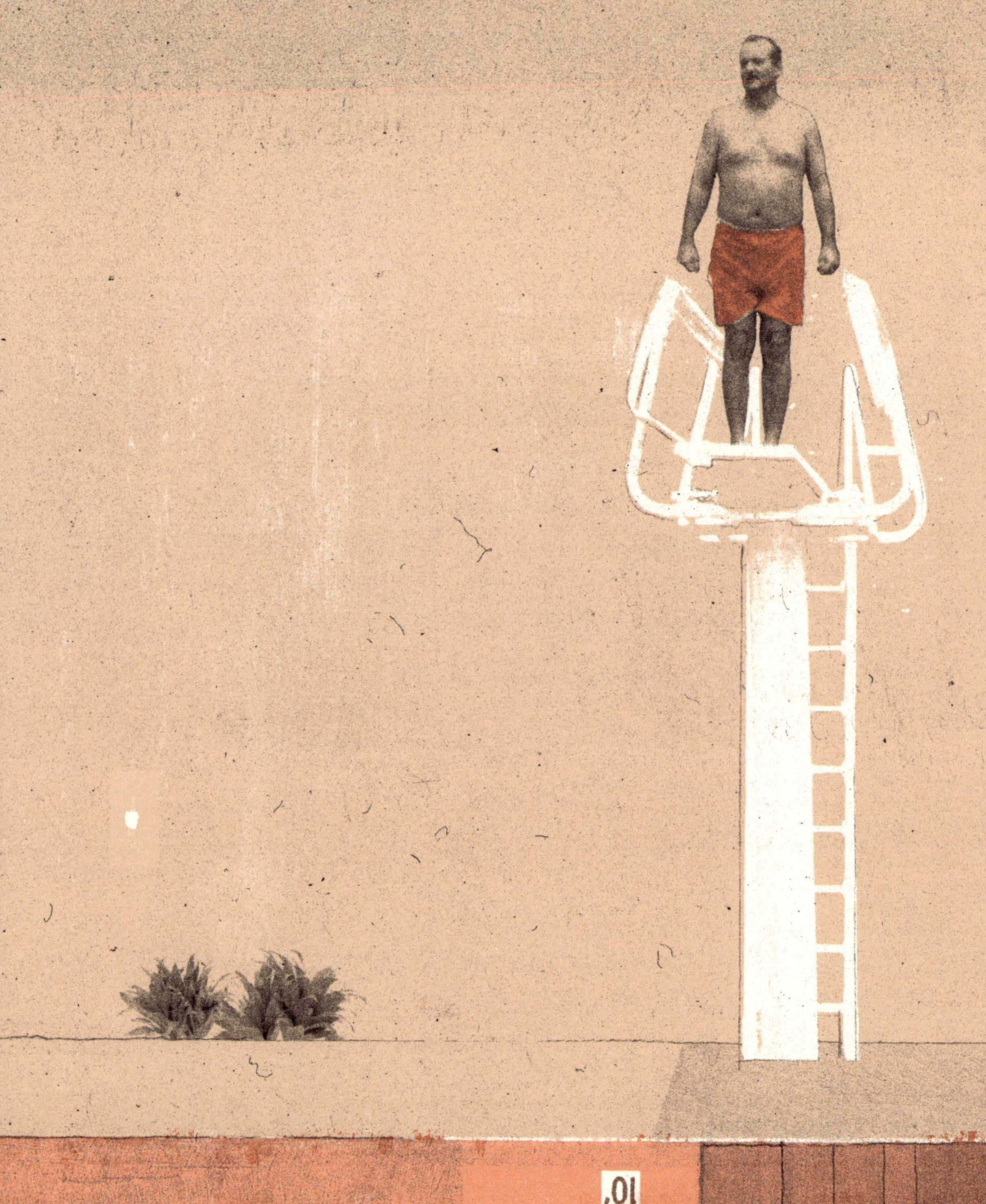
.01

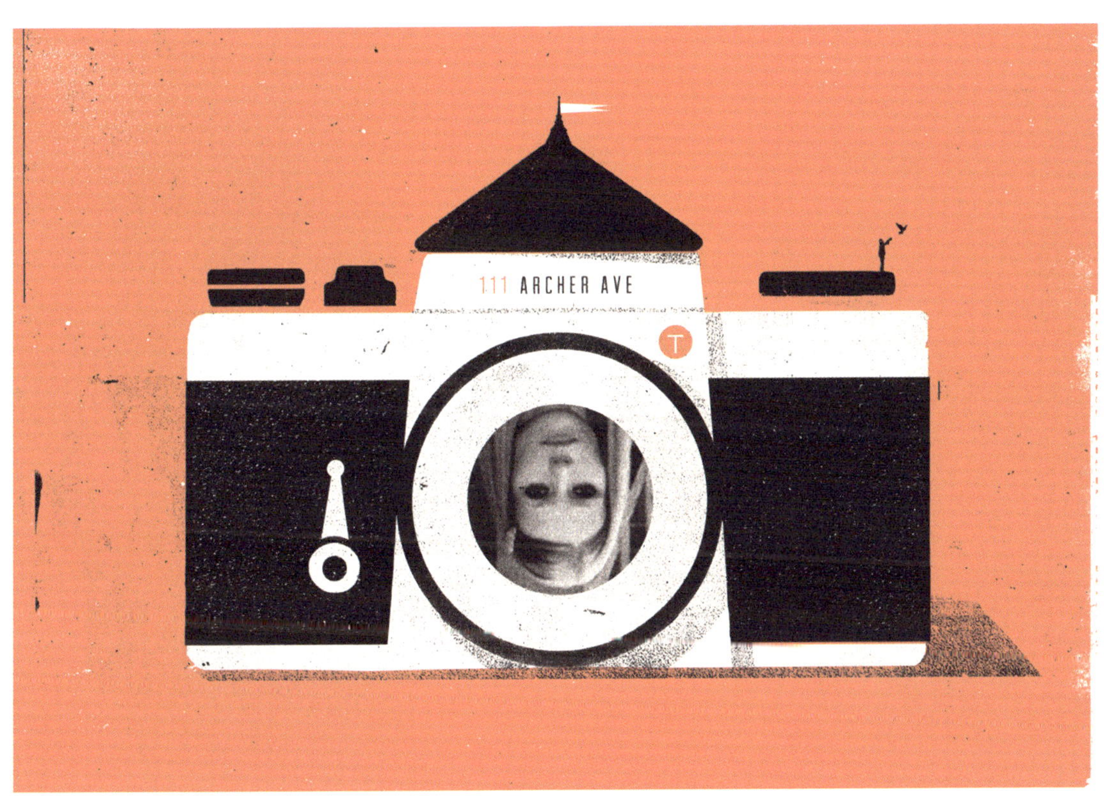

Margot Tenenbaum / Screenprint / 500 millimeters x 700 millimeters
Exhibited at Somerset House in London for Film4's Summer Screen
Herman's High Dive (left page) / Screenprint / 20 inches x 30 inches
Exhibited at Spoke Art Gallery in New York City for the "Bad Dads: An Art Show Tribute to the Films of Wes Anderson"

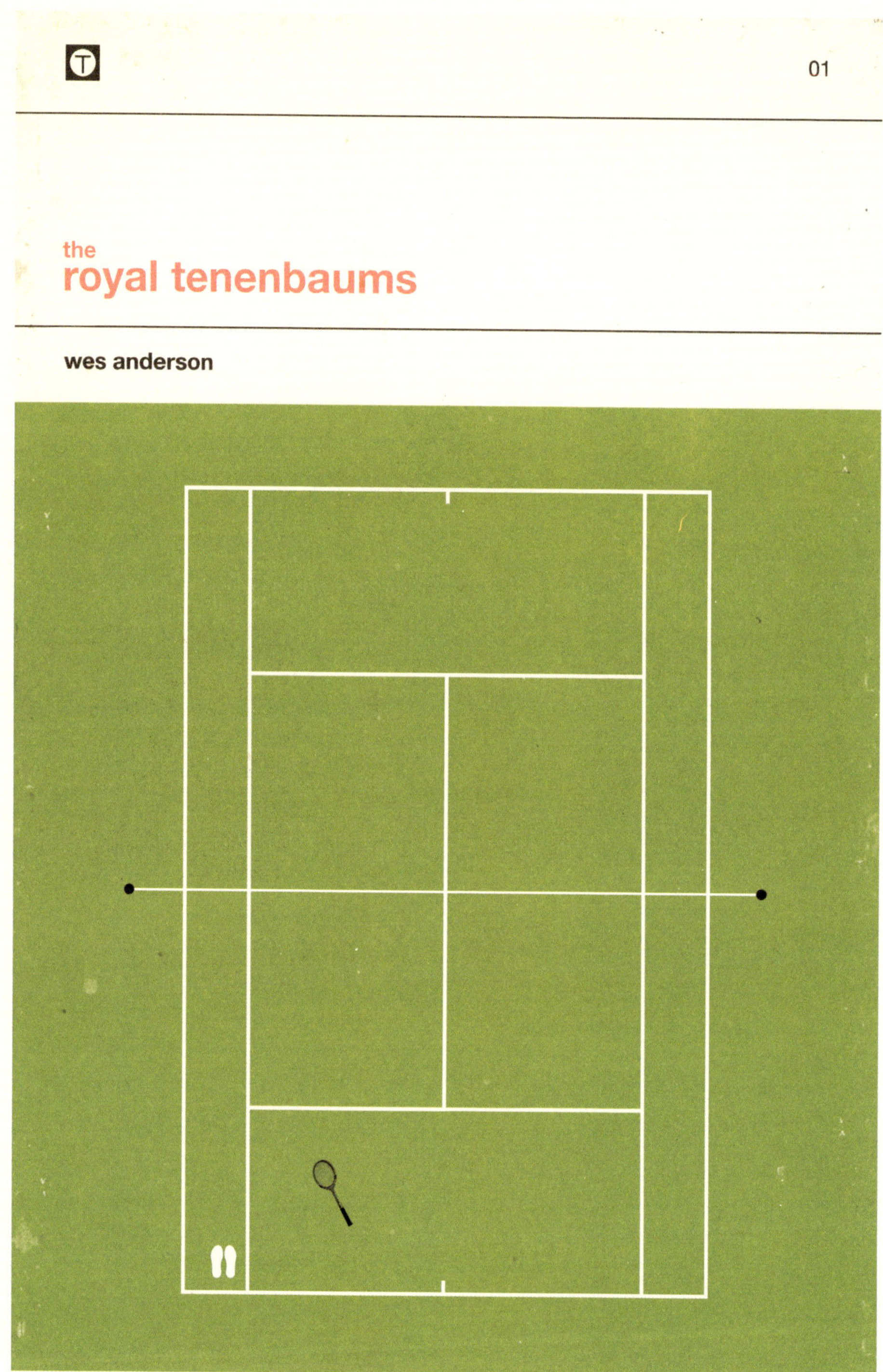

The Life Aquatic / Offset lithograph / 12 inches x 18 inches
Exhibited at Spoke Art Gallery in New York City for the "Bad Dads: An Art Show Tribute to the Films of Wes Anderson"

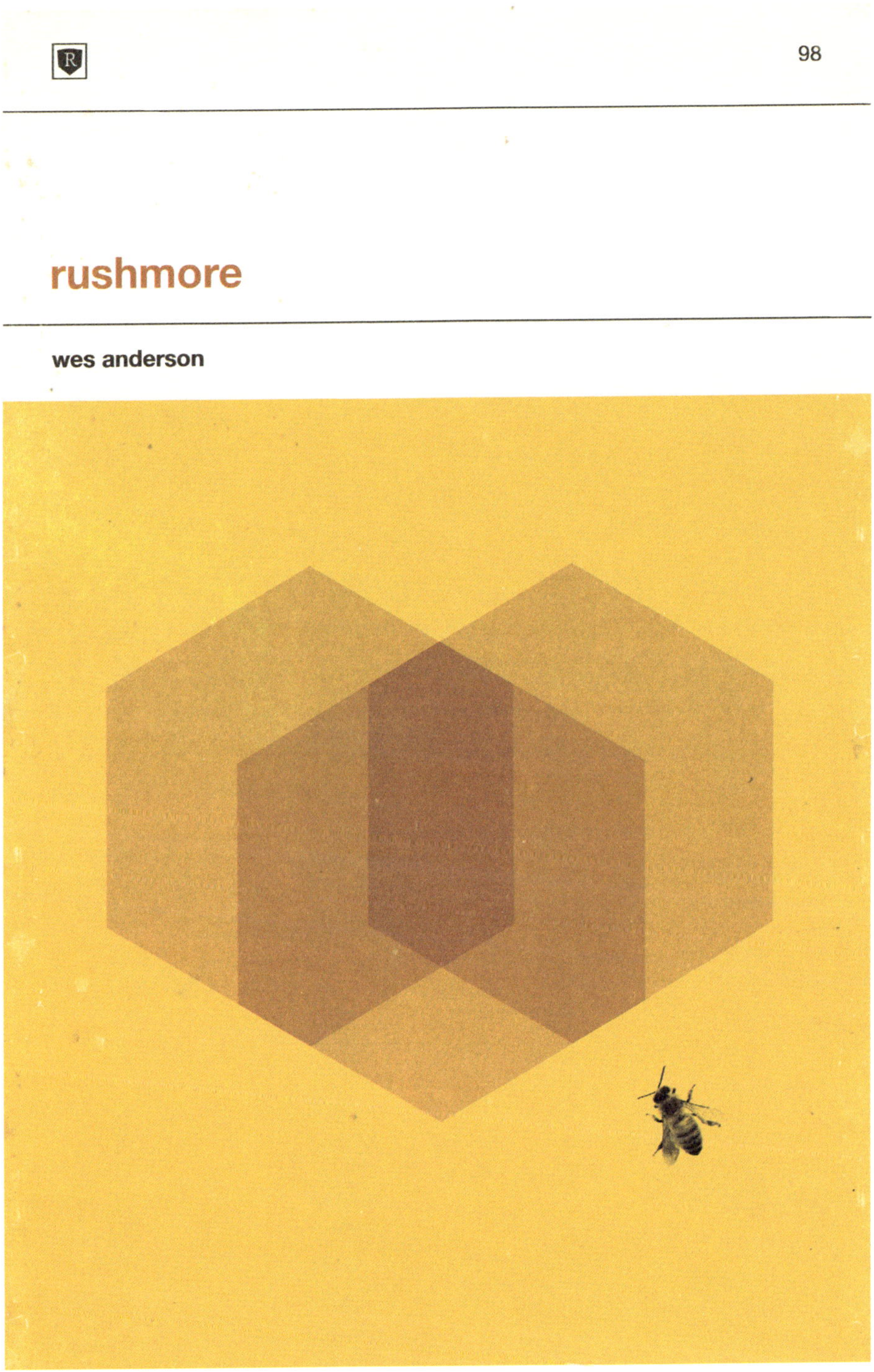

98

rushmore

wes anderson

Rushmore / Offset lithograph / 12 inches x 18 inches
Exhibited at Spoke Art Gallery in New York City for the "Bad Dads: An Art Show Tribute to the Films of Wes Anderson"

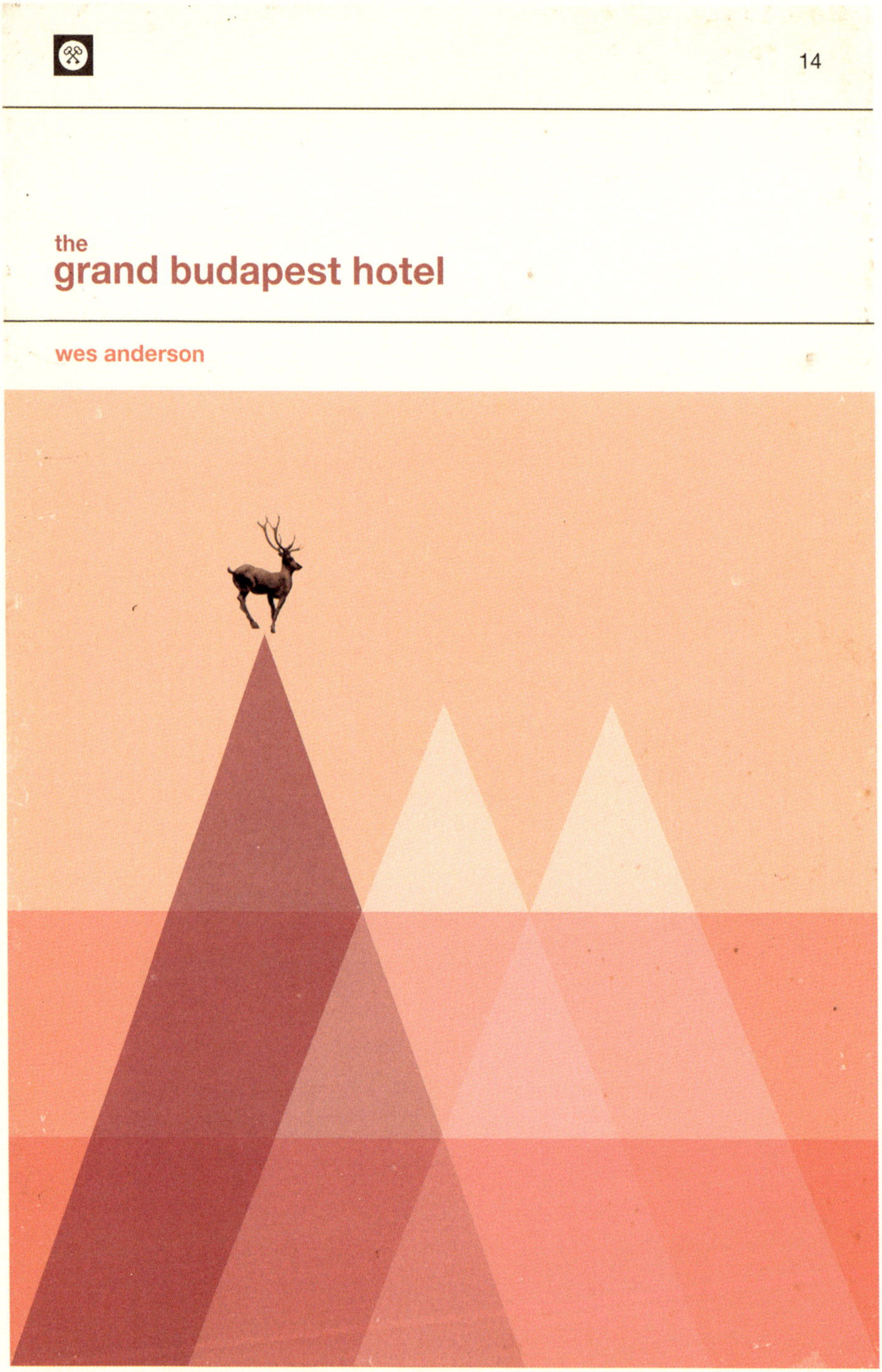

14

the
grand budapest hotel

wes anderson

The Grand Budapest Hotel / Offset lithograph / 12 inches x 18 inches
Exhibited at Spoke Art Gallery in New York City for the "Bad Dads: An Art Show Tribute to the Films of Wes Anderson"

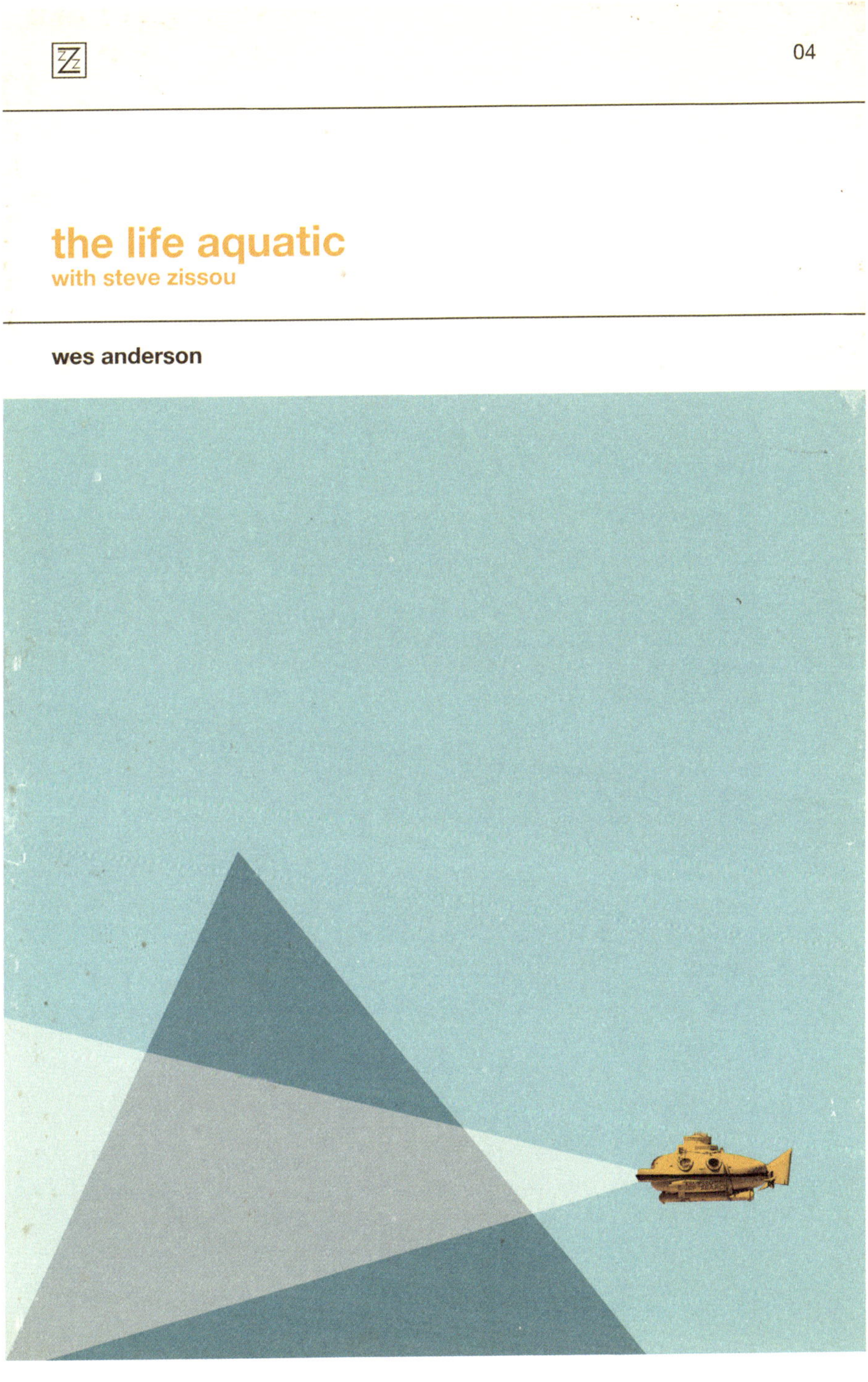

04

the life aquatic

with steve zissou

wes anderson

The Life Aquatic / Offset lithograph / 12 inches x 18 inches
Exhibited at Spoke Art Gallery in New York City for the "Bad Dads: An Art Show Tribute to the Films of Wes Anderson"

JOSHUA BUDICH

www.joshuabudich.com
Instagram: @jbudich
Facebook: @jbudich

"EVERYBODY FEELS LONELY AND TRAPPED SOMETIMES"

Joshua Budich is an independent illustrator working for numerous galleries, including Gallery 1988, Spoke Art and Hero Complex Gallery, movie studios, and media outlets around the globe. Inspired by a love for the pop culture of his youth, his primary focus is on screenprints that celebrate popular movies (Star Wars, Star Trek, The Big Lebowski), television series (LOST, MARVEL's Agents of S.H.I.E.L.D.), animated shows (The Simpsons, My Neighbor Totoro, AKIRA) and more.

Budich graduated from the University of Maryland Baltimore County with a Bachelor of Fine Arts (Imaging and Digital Arts) in 2000. He enjoys cooking with his wife, drawing with his son, and reading to his daughter.

He lives in the Baltimore/District of Columbia area with his wife and their two children.

Joshua Budich es un ilustrador independiente que trabaja para numerosas galerías, incluyendo la Gallery 1988, la Spoke Art y la Hero Complex, así como para estudios cinematográficos y medios de comunicación en todo el mundo. Inspirado por el amor a la cultura pop de su juventud, su objetivo principal son las serigrafías que homenajean las películas populares (Star Wars, Star Trek, El Gran Lebowski), series de televisión (PERDIDOS o los Agentes de S.H.I.E.L.D, de MARVEL), programas de animación (Los Simpsons, Mi vecino Totoro, AKIRA) y mucho más.

Budich se graduó de la Universidad de Maryland, en el Condado de Baltimore, con una Licenciatura en Bellas Artes (procesamiento de imágenes y artes digitales) en 2000. Le gusta cocinar con su esposa, dibujar con su hijo y leerle libros a su hija.

Vive en Baltimore/Distrito de la zona de Columbia con su mujer y sus dos hijos.

Fantastic Mr Fox (right page)
Joshua Budich (SPOKE Art, "Bad Dads - A Tribute to Wes Anderson")

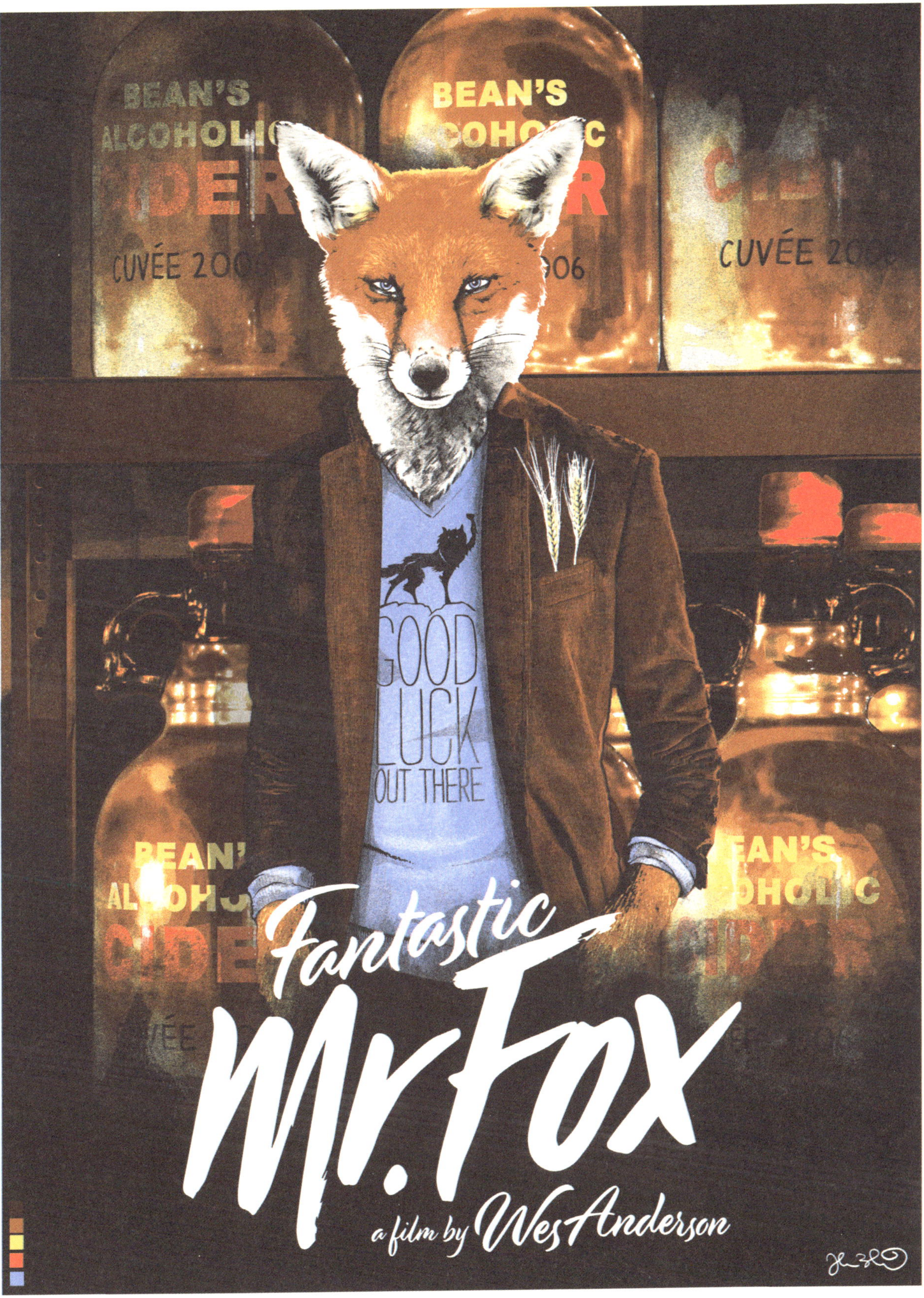

GOOD LUCK OUT THERE

Fantastic Mr. Fox

a film by Wes Anderson

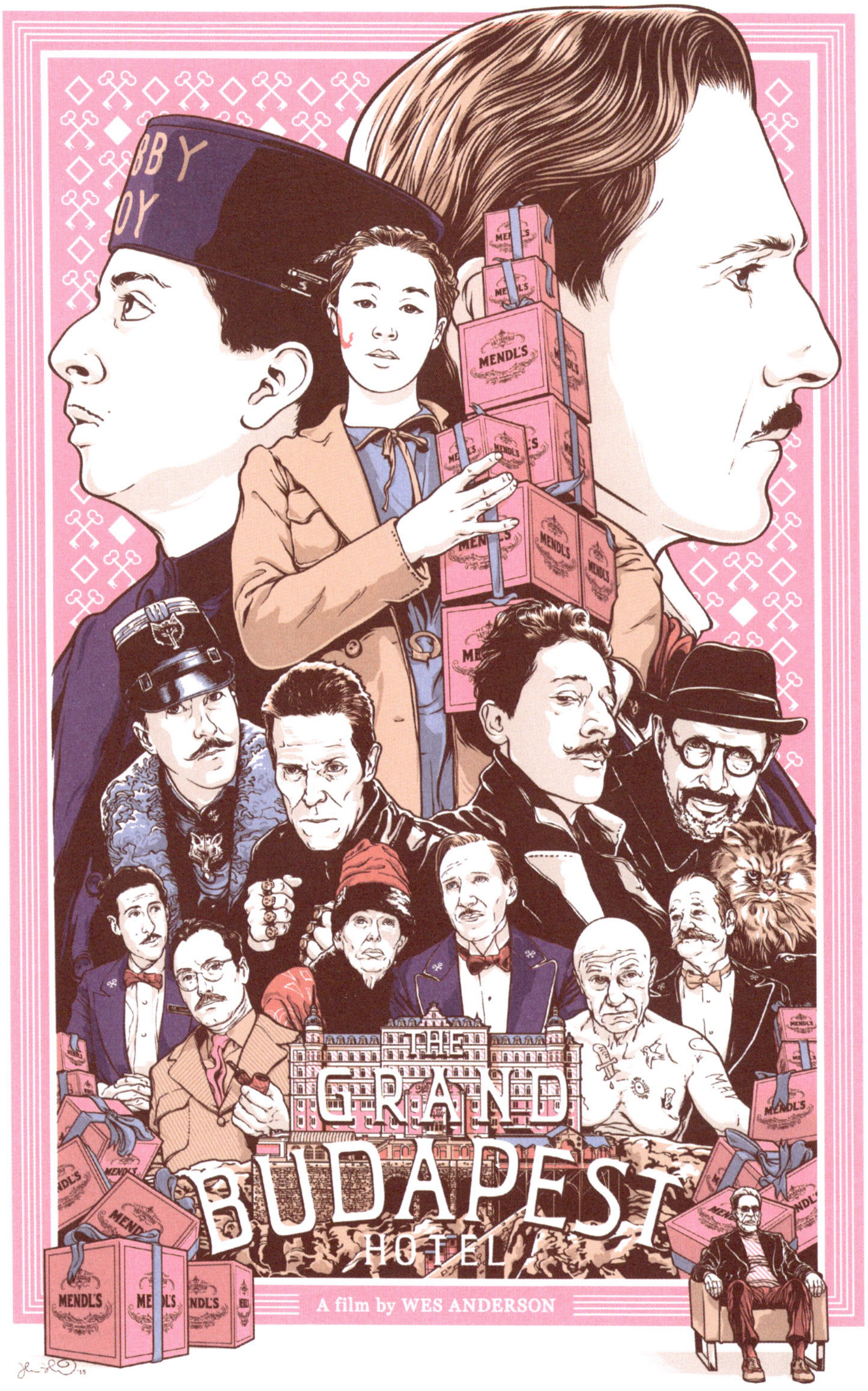

The Grand Budapest Hotel - Joshua Budich (SPOKE Art, "Bad Dads - A Tribute to Wes Anderson")

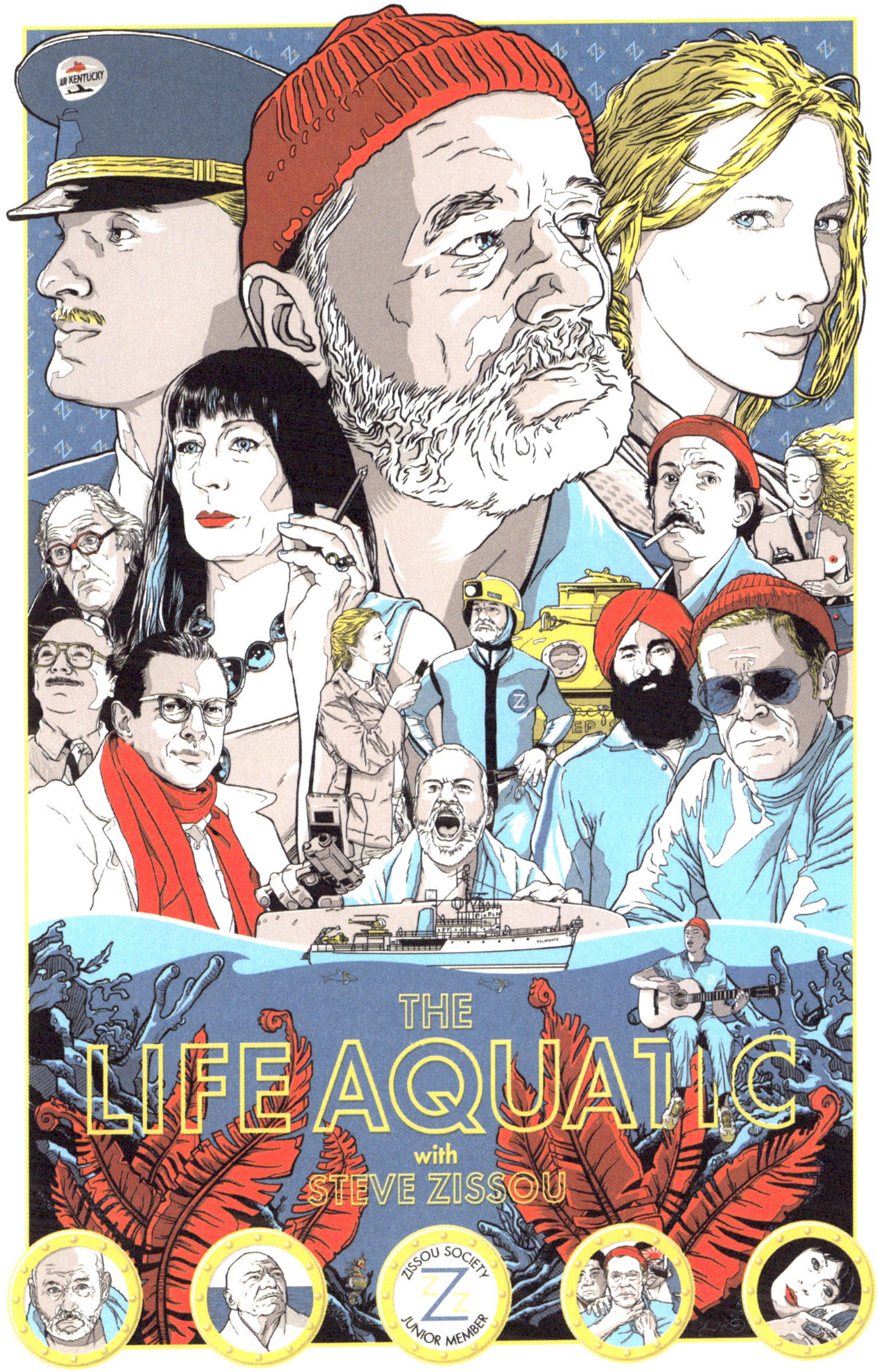

The Life Aquatic - Joshua Budich (SPOKE Art, "Bad Dads - A Tribute to Wes Anderson")

AITOR SARAIBA

www.aitorsaraiba.com
Instagram: @aitorsaraiba
facebook: Aitor Saraiba

"FOR ME, HIS FILMS ARE LIKE GOING BACK TO SEEING THE WORLD LIKE I SAW IT WHEN I WAS 11"

Aitor Saraiba writes, draws, walks, listens to Heavy Metal, reads Nicanor Parra and Borges and messes around doing nothing whenever he can.
He is the author of several books including *El hijo del Legionario*, *Nada más importa* and *Cómo ser valiente, justo, feliz y otras cosas en la vida*.
His works—ranging from drawing to photography and ceramics—have been exhibited here and there, from Mexico to Tokyo, across the African continent... making several stops in Europe.

Aitor Saraiba escribe, dibuja, pasea, escucha Heavy Metal lee a Nicanor Parra y Borges y pierde el tiempo siempre que puede.
Autor de varios libros entre los que habría que destacar *El hijo del Legionario*, *Nada más importa* y *Cómo ser valiente, justo, feliz y otras cosas en la vida*.
Sus obras que van del dibujo, a la fotografía o la cerámica se han expuesto por aquí y por allá, desde México hasta Tokio, pasando por el continente africano y haciendo varias paradas en Europa.

Moonrise Kingdom (right page)

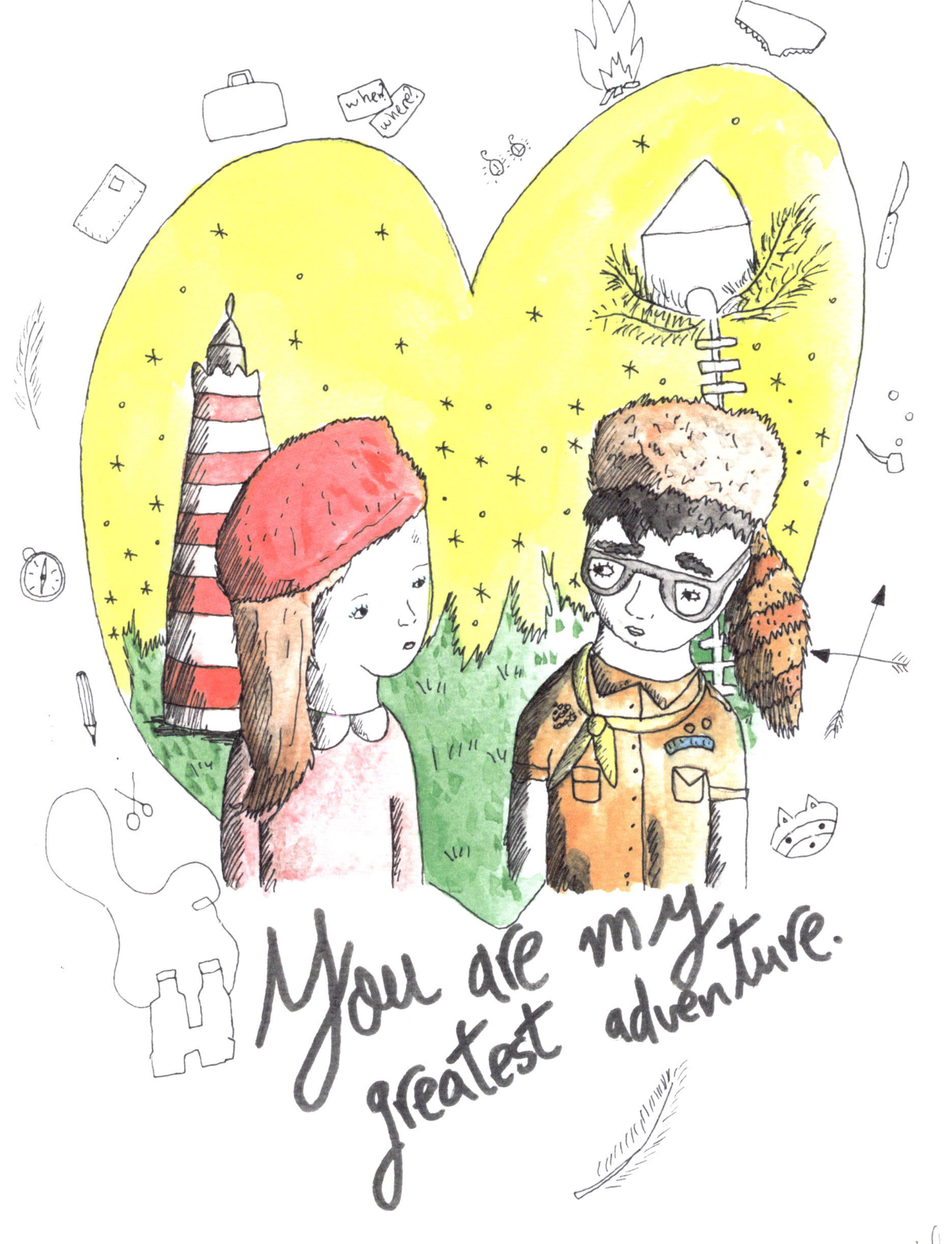

a. savaila
2016

SALOME PAPADOPOULLOS

www.salomepapadopoullos.co.uk
Instagram: @salomepapa
Facebook: Salome Papadopoullos Illustration

"THE COLOURS, COMPOSITION AND CHARACTERS OF WES ANDERSON'S FILMS ARE AN ENDLESS SOURCE OF INSPIRATION"

Salome is a freelance artist and illustrator from London. In 2015 Salome graduated from Middlesex University with a BA in Illustration. Since then she has exhibited work in 'The Art Life' exhibition, celebrating the works of David Lynch at The Electric Cinema in Birmingham, The Secret 7" at Sonos Studios raising money for Amnesty International and was shortlisted for the Penguin Design Awards in 2015. Working solidly from her home in London, Salome has been building a portfolio with a variety of clients from magazines to skateboard brands. Inspired by her affinity with music and cinema Salome's work is colourful and whimsical, often featuring women and specialising in portraiture she uses her work to touch on serious issues too.

Salome es una artista e ilustradora freelance de Londres. En 2015, Salome se graduó por la Universidad de Middlesex con un Grado en Bellas Artes en la especialidad de Ilustración. Desde entonces, ha expuesto su obra en la exposición 'The Art Life', homenajeando las obras de David Lynch en el Electric Cinema de Birmingham, el proyecto Secret 7" de los Estudios Sonos, recaudando fondos para Amnistía Internacional y, además, estuvo nominada a los Premios Pingüino de Diseño en 2015. Trabajando concienzudamente desde su casa en Londres, Salome ha ido creándose una cartera con gran variedad de clientes que abarcan desde revistas a marcas de monopatín. Inspirada por su afinidad con la música y el cine, la obra de Salome es colorida y caprichosa, a menudo representando mujeres y especializándose en el retrato, utiliza su obra para abordar también temas serios.

The Grand Budapest Hotel (right page)

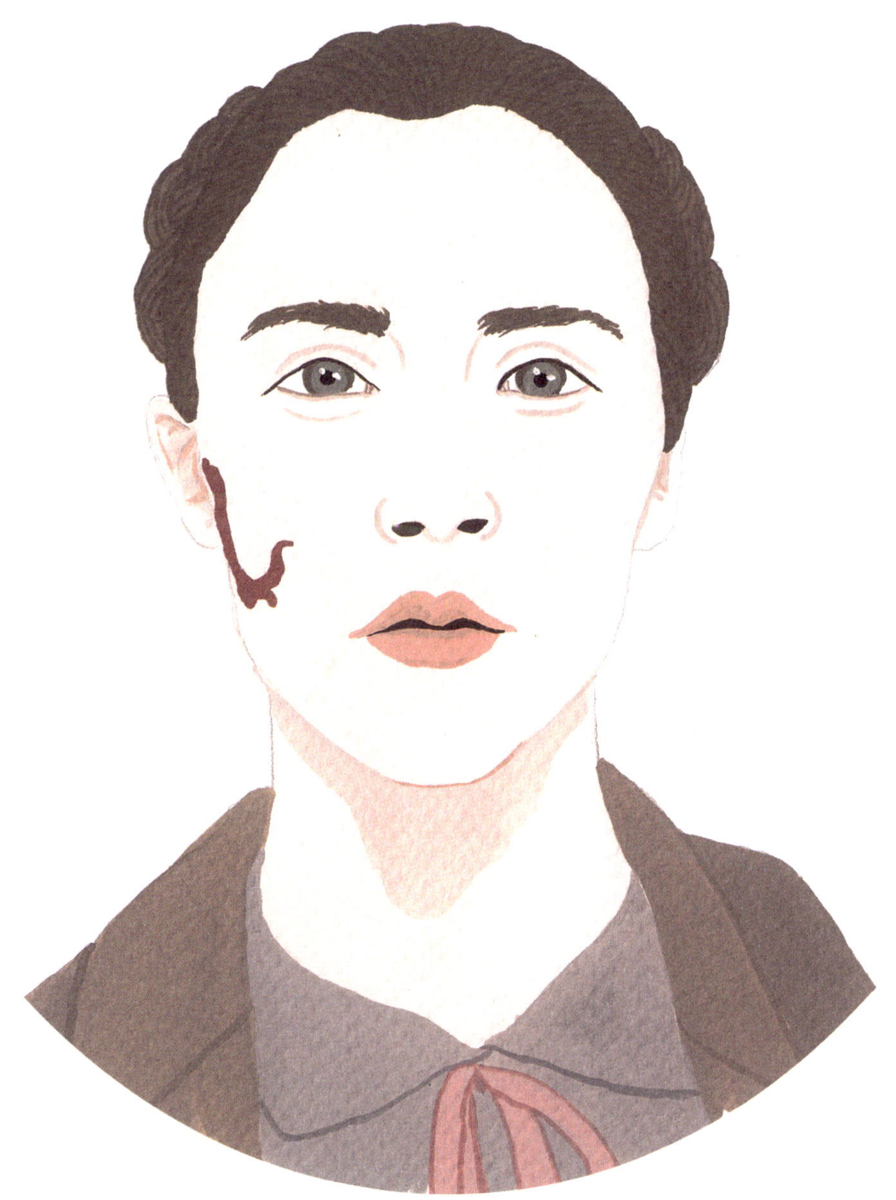

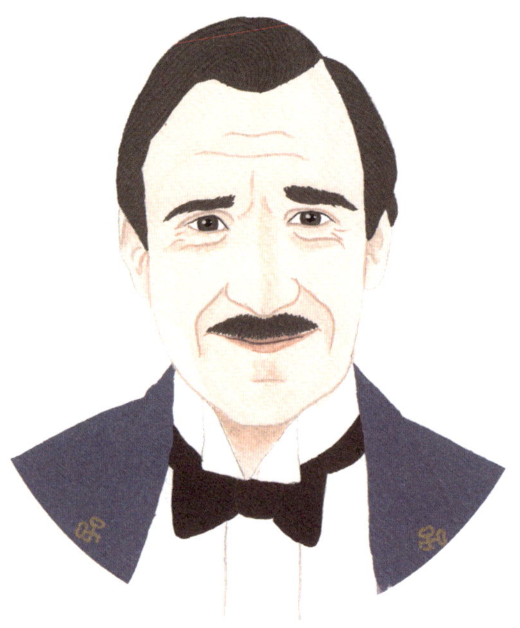

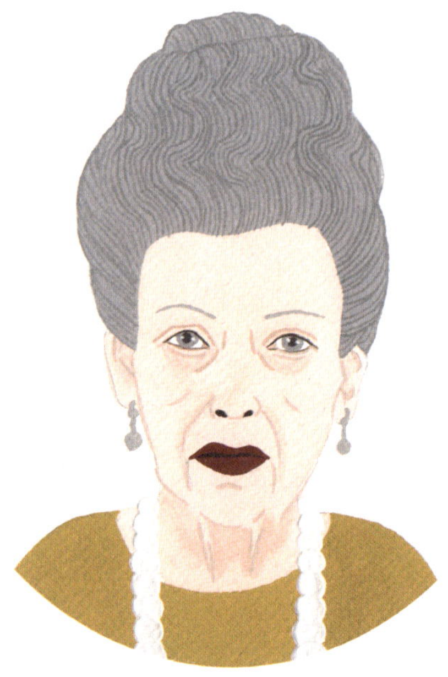

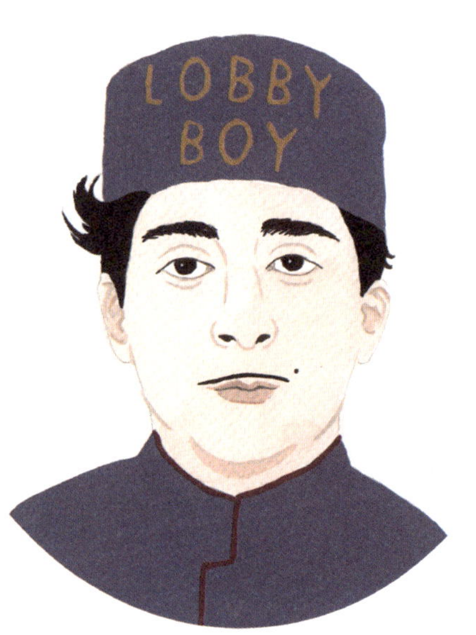

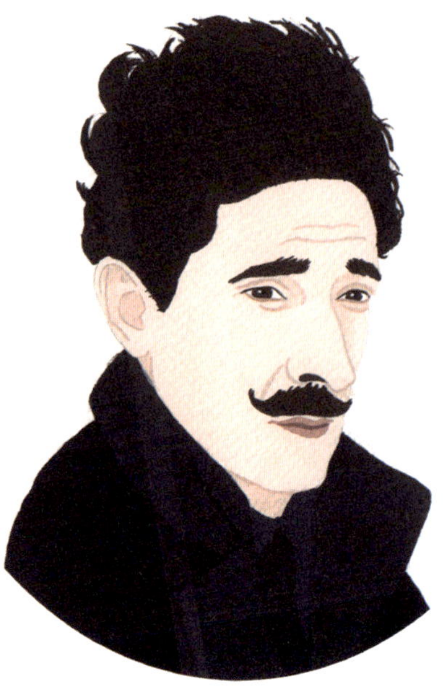

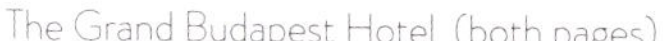
The Grand Budapest Hotel (both pages)

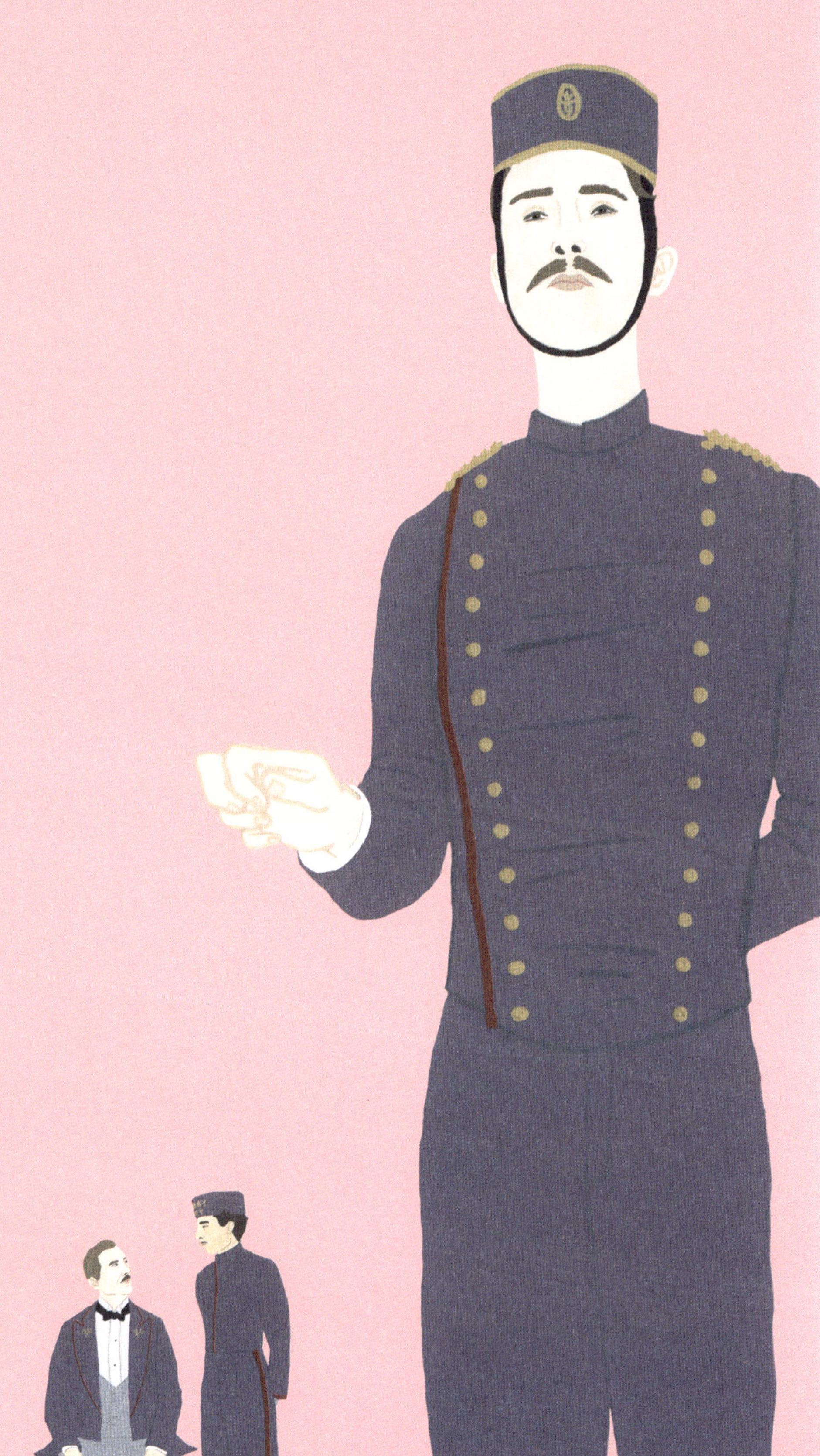
HE
RAND
UDAPEST
OTEL
ILM BY
S ANDERSON
H FIENNES
EN BRODY
EM DEFOE
LAW
MURRAY
ARD NORTON
RSE RONAN
SWINTON
N WILSON

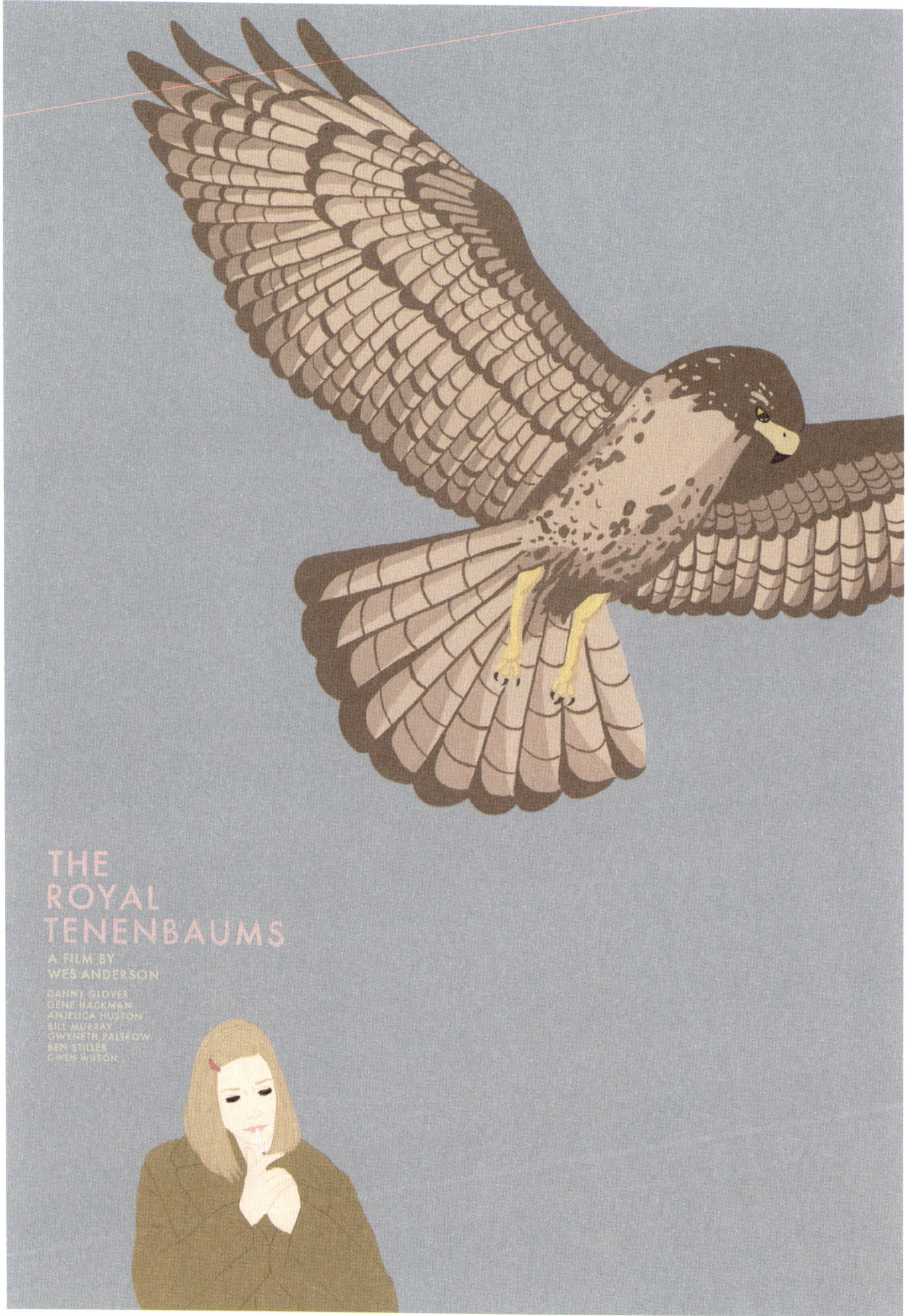

The Royal Tenenbaums

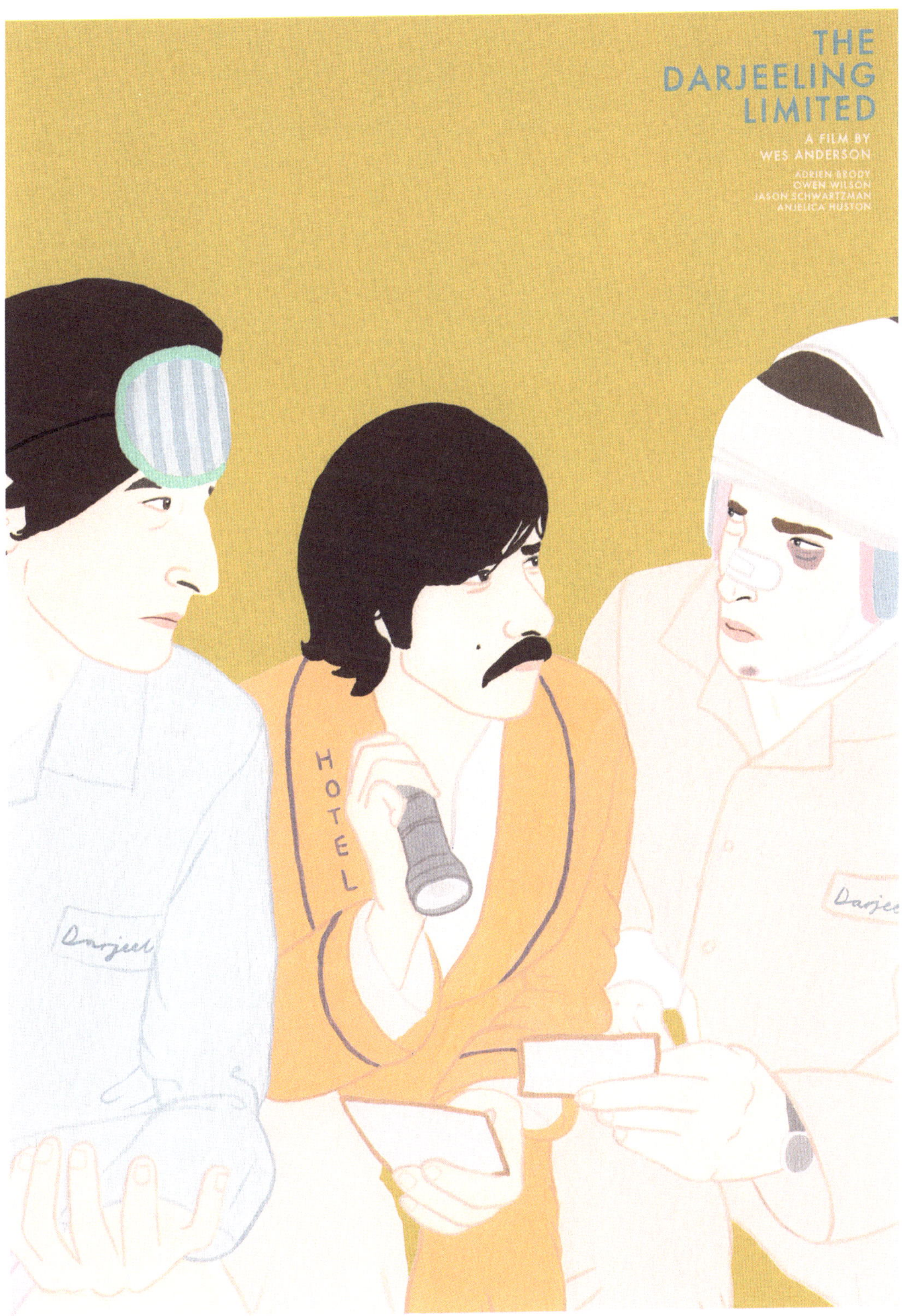

The Darjeeling Limited

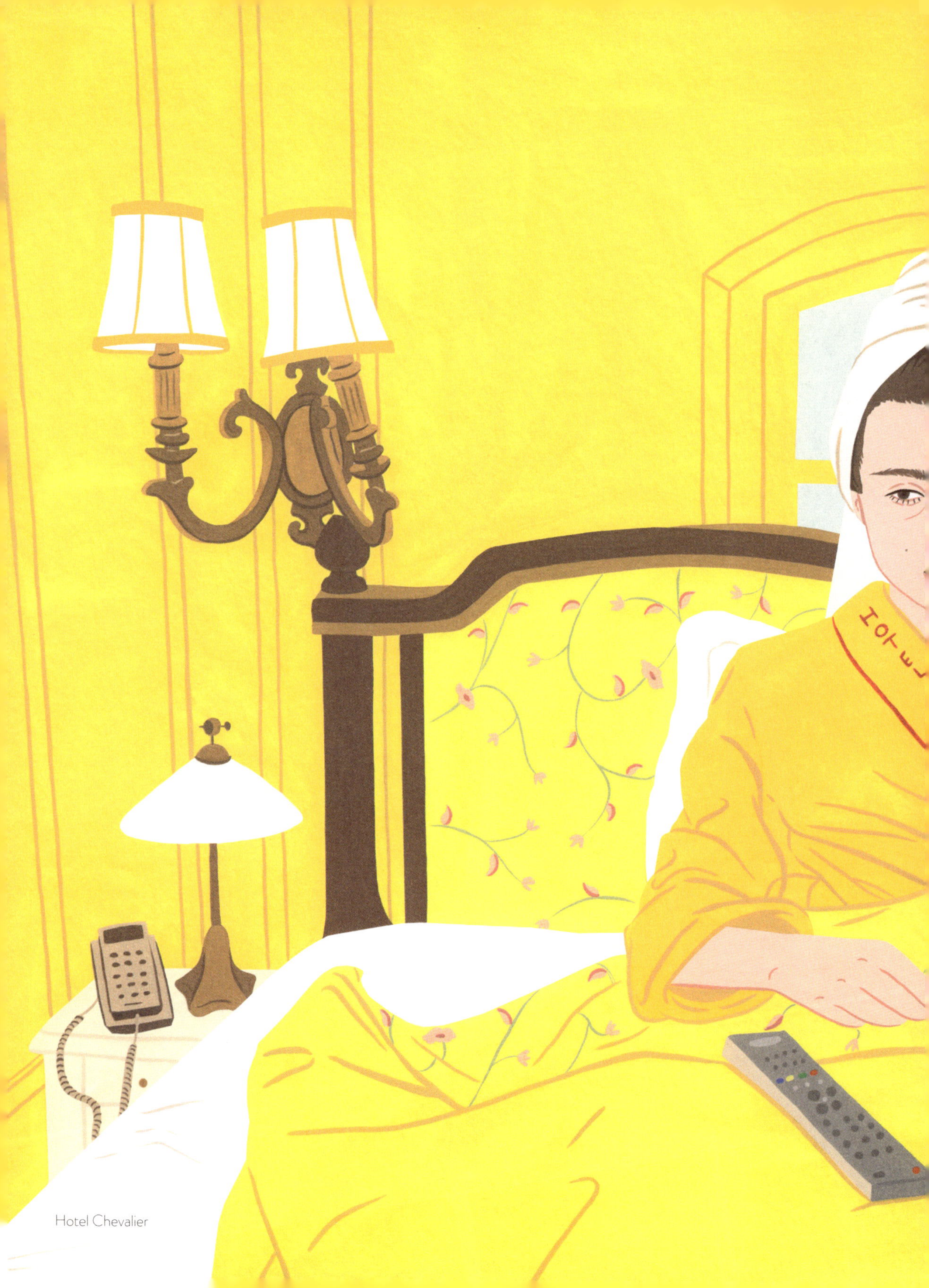

Hotel Chevalier

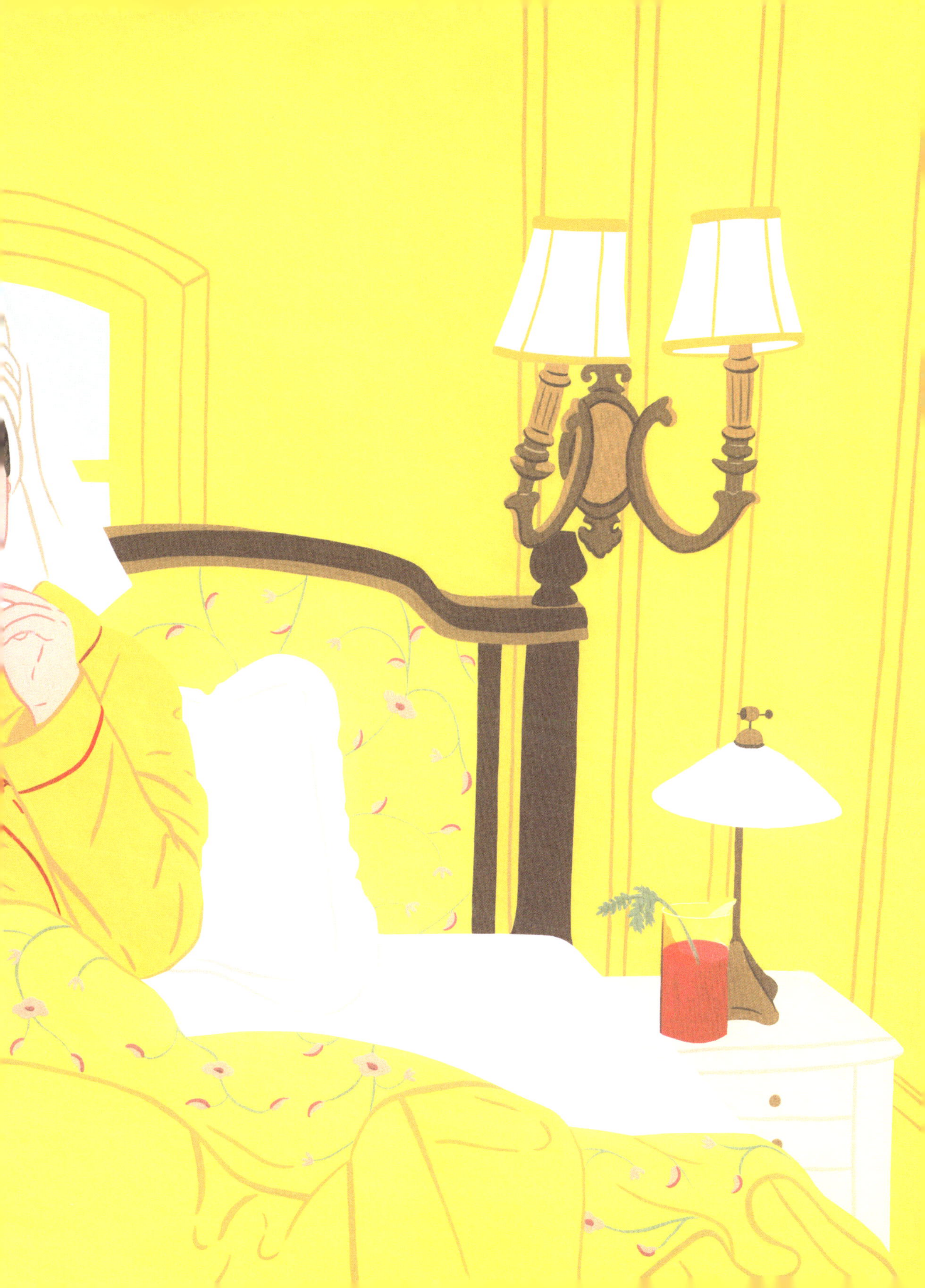

TODD SLATER

www. toddslater.net
Instagram: @toddslaterart
Twitter: @ToddSlaterART
Facebook: @ToddSlaterART

"WHAT I REALLY APPRECIATE ABOUT WES IS THAT EVERY FRAME, EVERY STILL IMAGE, IS CONSIDERED AND THOUGHTFUL. AS A VISUAL ARTIST I CAN THINK OF NOTHING MORE INSPIRING THAN THIS APPROACH TO ART AND CRAFT"

"Todd Slater is as prolific as he is piercingly inventive. In a decade since graduating from art school, and now operating out of a converted garage studio on the outskirts of Austin, Texas, he has created hundreds of dazzling posters featuring the music industry's hottest acts—including The Black Keys, Jack White, Avett Brothers, and the Arctic Monkeys to mention just a few. Todd draws his inspiration directly from each artist's music, translating the sounds into gut instincts for graphics, and he has an acute sense for the vibes that drive color selection and design schemes."

Bio courtesy of Guitar Center

"Todd Slater es tan prolífico como penetrantemente inventivo. Hace una década que se graduó en la escuela de arte, actualmente trabaja en un garaje convertido en estudio a las afueras de Austin, Texas, ha creado centenares de carteles deslumbrantes que representan los eventos más polémicos de la industria musical; incluyendo los Black Keys, Jack White, los Avett Brothers y los Arctic Monkeys, entre otros. Todd obtiene su inspiración directamente de la música de cada artista, traduciendo los sonidos en instintos viscerales para los gráficos, y tiene un sentido agudo para las vibraciones que conducen la selección del color y los esquemas del diseño."

Texto de Guitar Center.

Rushmore Academy (right page)

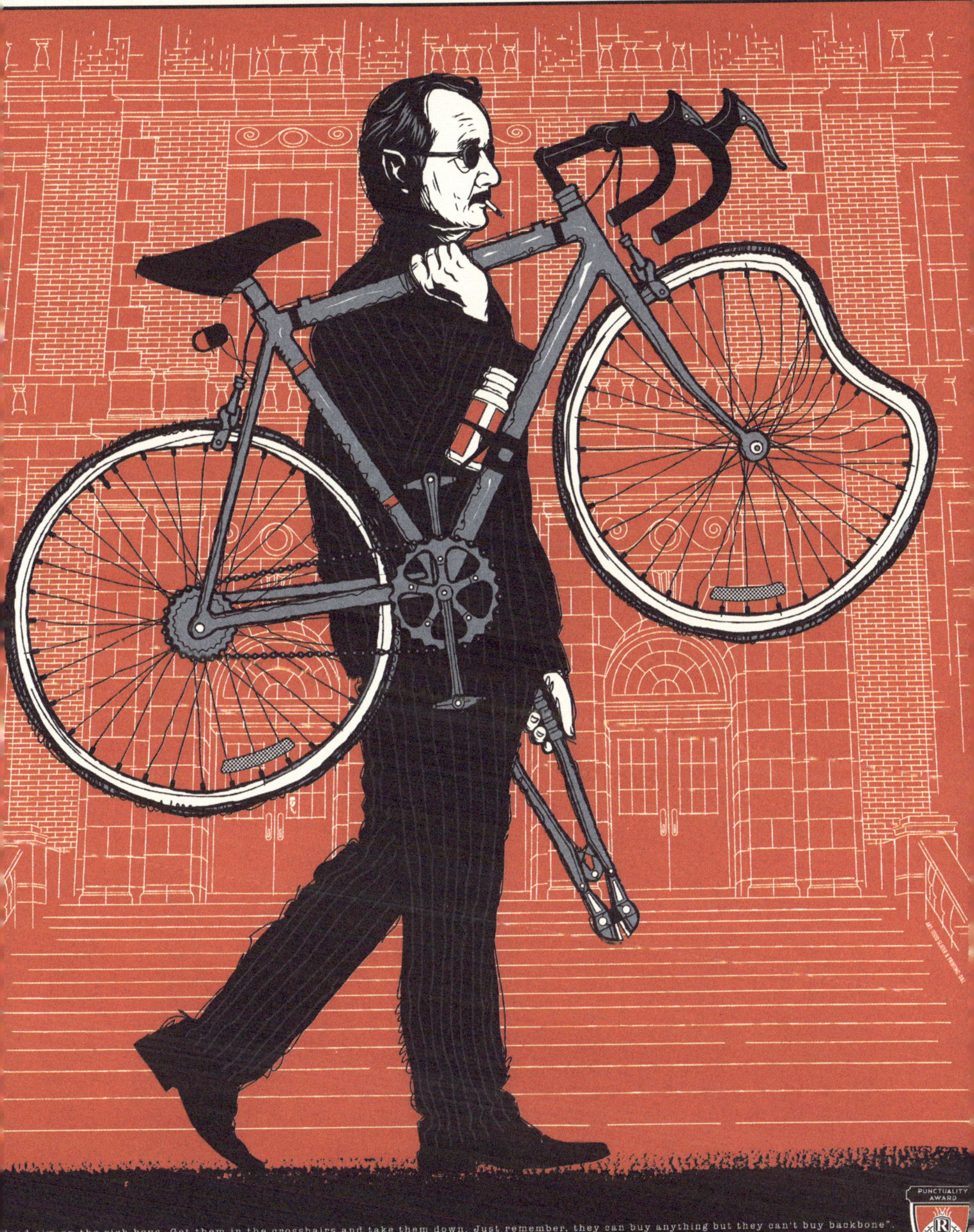
ART: TODD SLATER & PRINTING:
dead aim on the rich boys. Get them in the crosshairs and take them down. Just remember, they can buy anything but they can't buy backbone".
PUNCTUALITY AWARD
R

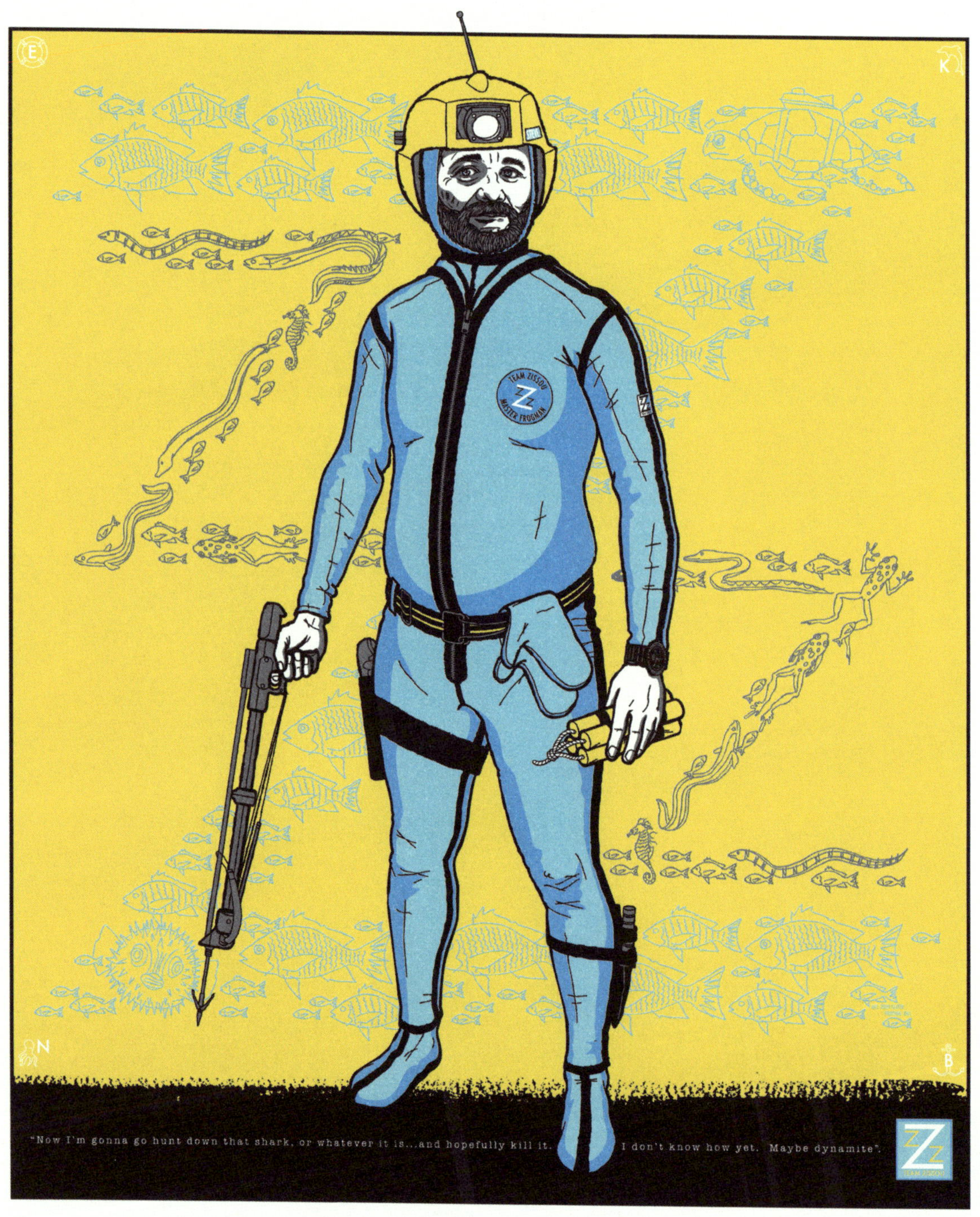

The Life Aquatic
The Royal Tenenbaums (right page)

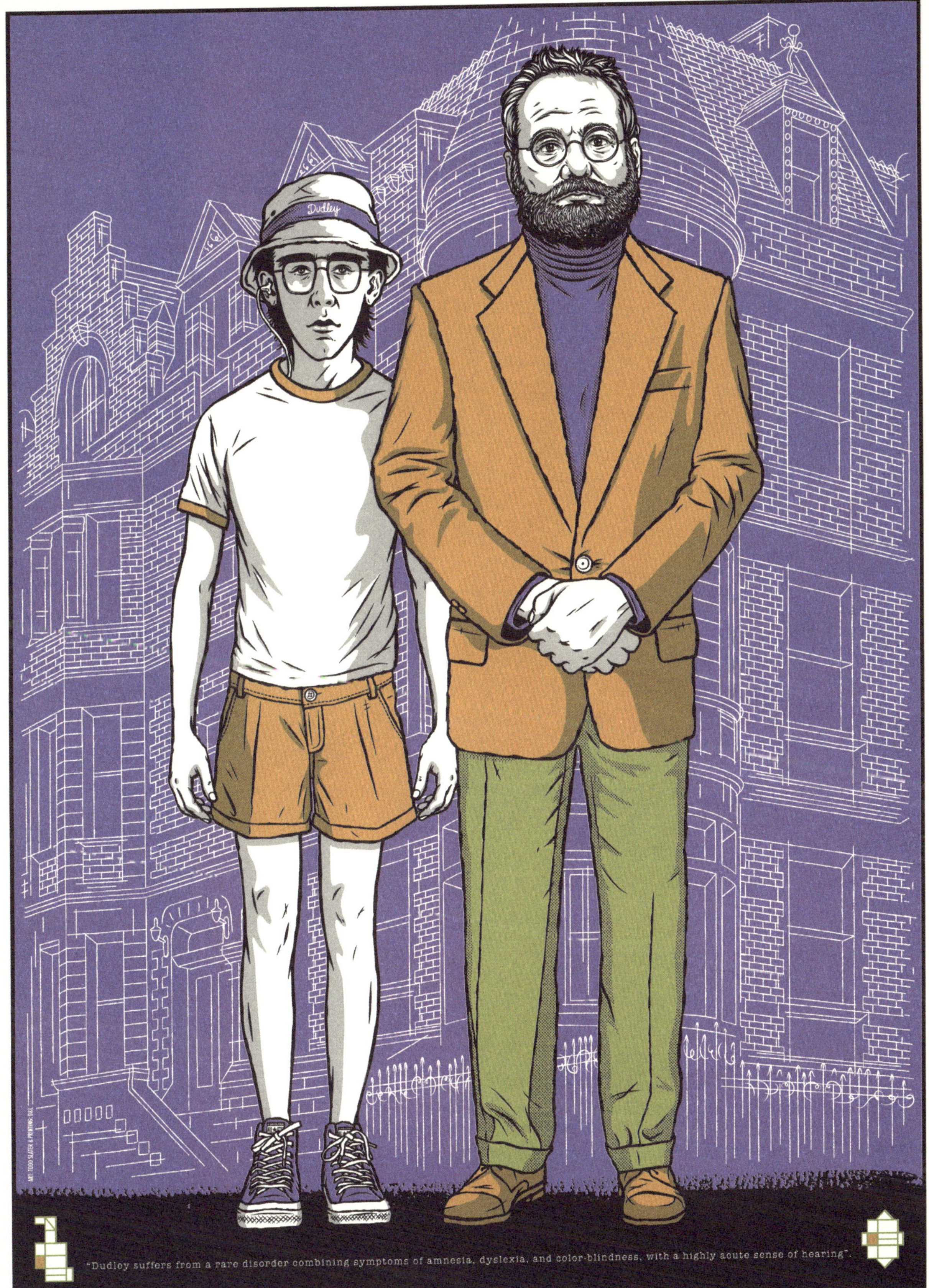
Dudley
ART: TODD SLATER & PRINTING: D&L
"Dudley suffers from a rare disorder combining symptoms of amnesia, dyslexia, and color-blindness, with a highly acute sense of hearing".

BEN BIONDO

www.benbiondo.com
www.circanoon.com
Instagram: @benbiondo

"HIS ATTENTION TO EVERY DESIGN ELEMENT AND VISUAL DETAIL IN HIS FILMS - HIS ARTISTRY IS UNPARALLELED"

Ben Biondo is a designer and maker of things originally from Grand Rapids, MI currently living in Southern California. Ping-Pong, KME, Surfing, Carbonated H20, my AE-1, Scandanavian Desing (as of late), Tumblr and good times with comrades are a few things he enjoys. His advice: Never Not Have Fun. Always be making things.

Ben Biondo es un diseñador y creador de cosas originario de Grand Rapids (Míchigan) que actualmente vive al sur de California. Algunas cosas de las que disfruta son el Ping-Pong, el KME, el surf, el agua con gas, su cámara AE-1, el diseño escandinavo (en los últimos tiempos), la plataforma Tumblr y pasar buenos ratos con los compañeros. Su consejo: Prohibido no divertirse. Siempre hay que estar haciendo algo.

The Darjeeling Limited (right page)

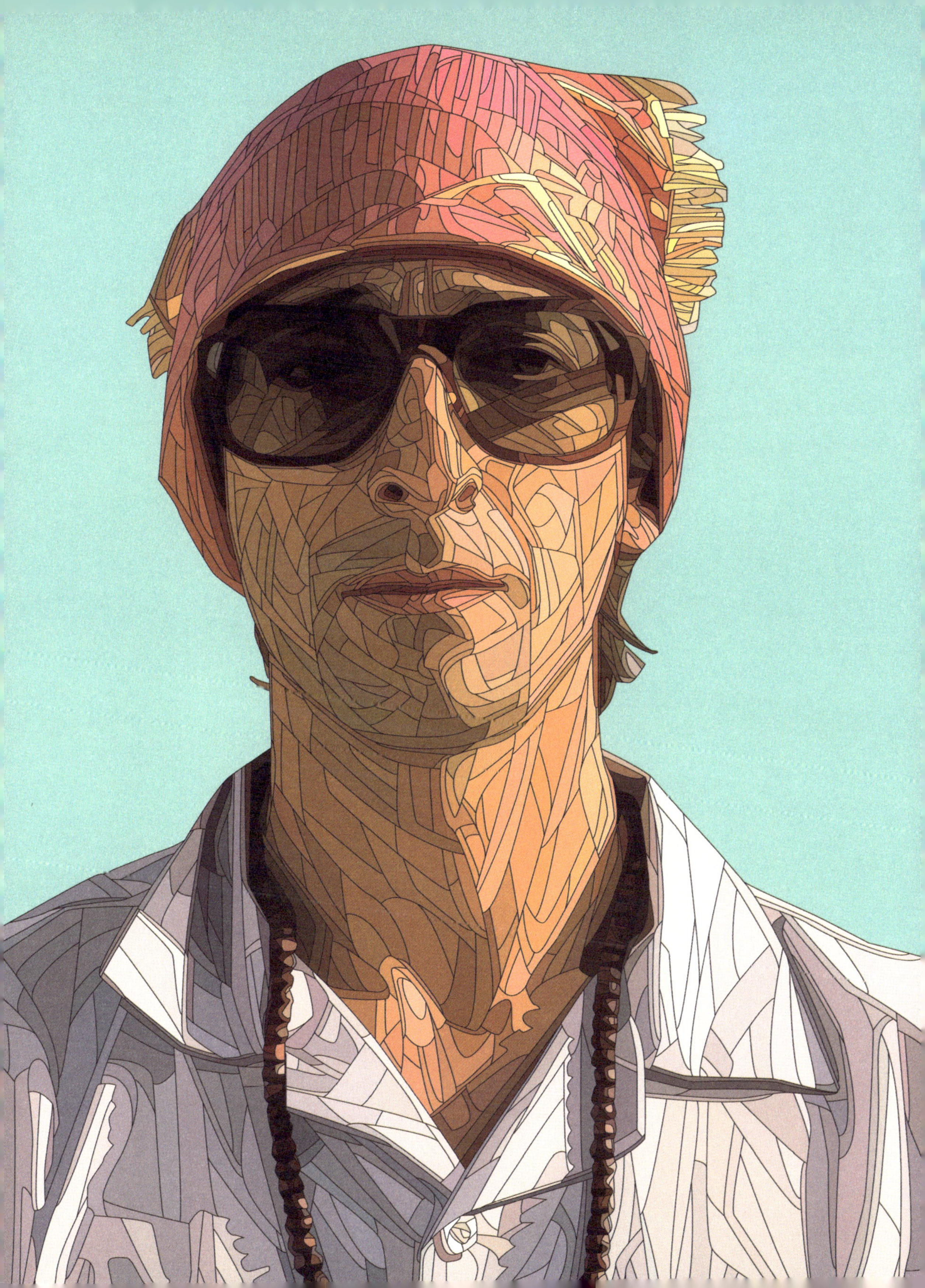

OWEN WILSON
DIGNAN

LUKE WILSON
ANTHONY ADAMS

NED DOWD
DR. NICHOLS

SHEA FOWLER
GRACE

WES ANDERSON'S
BOTTLE ROCKET

WITH DIGNAN

SYNOPSIS

AMONGST OTHER THINGS

Bottle Rocket focuses on a group of young Texans aspiring to become master thieves. Upon his release from a mental hospital following a nervous breakdown, the direction less Anthony joins his friend Dignan. Their leader is Dignan, who seems far less sane than the former is an upbeat, and quite naive charmer who convinces his friends Anthony and Bob Mapplethorpe to enter the crime business. Dignan has hatched a very hare-brained scheme for what seems like an as-of-yet-unspecified crime spree. After their first heist, a bizarrely-executed robbery of a local bookstore, the trio goes on the lam, taking up residence in a border hotel where Anthony falls in love with a maid played by Lumi Cavazos. When the three buddies decide that what they really need is to return to the real world, they hook up with a master con-man who sends them on a daring, quite ill-concieved mission that makes Bottle Rocket one wild ride.

RELEASE DATE:
02.21.1996

RUNTIME:
91 MINUTES

BUDGET:
$7,000,000

OPENING WEEKEND:
$124,118
At 28 screens in the US on 02.21.1996

LANGUAGE:
English

FILMING LOCATIONS:
Dallas , Fort Worth, & Hillsboro Texas, St. Mark's School (10600 Preston Road, Dallas)

PRODUCTION COMPANIES:
Colombia Pictures Corp. and Gracie Films

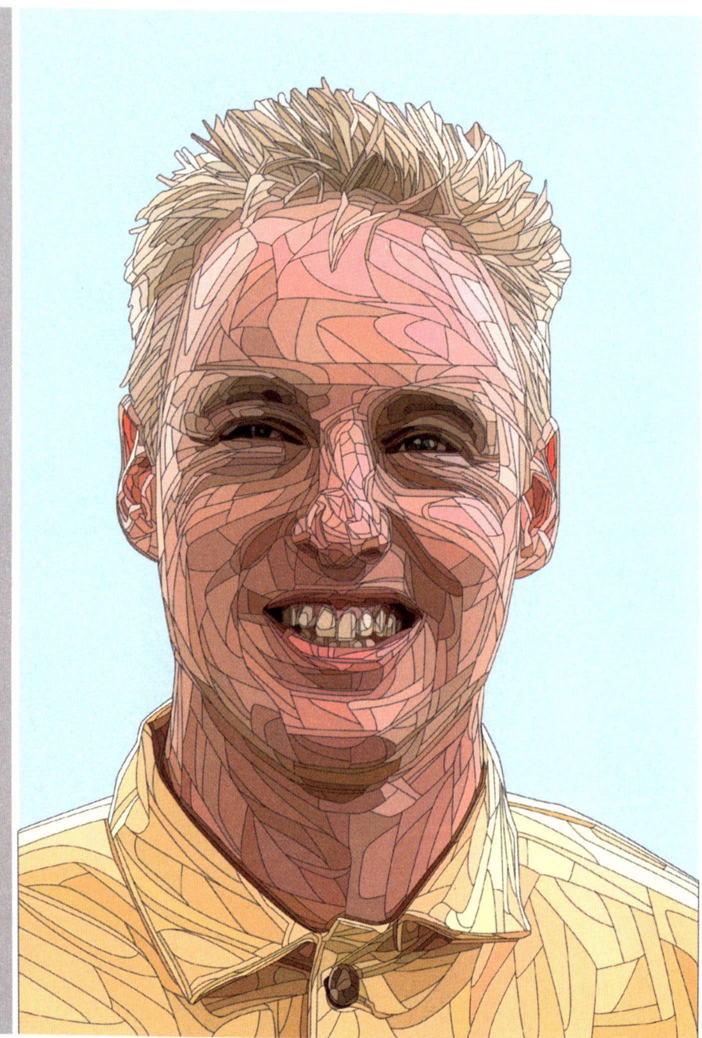

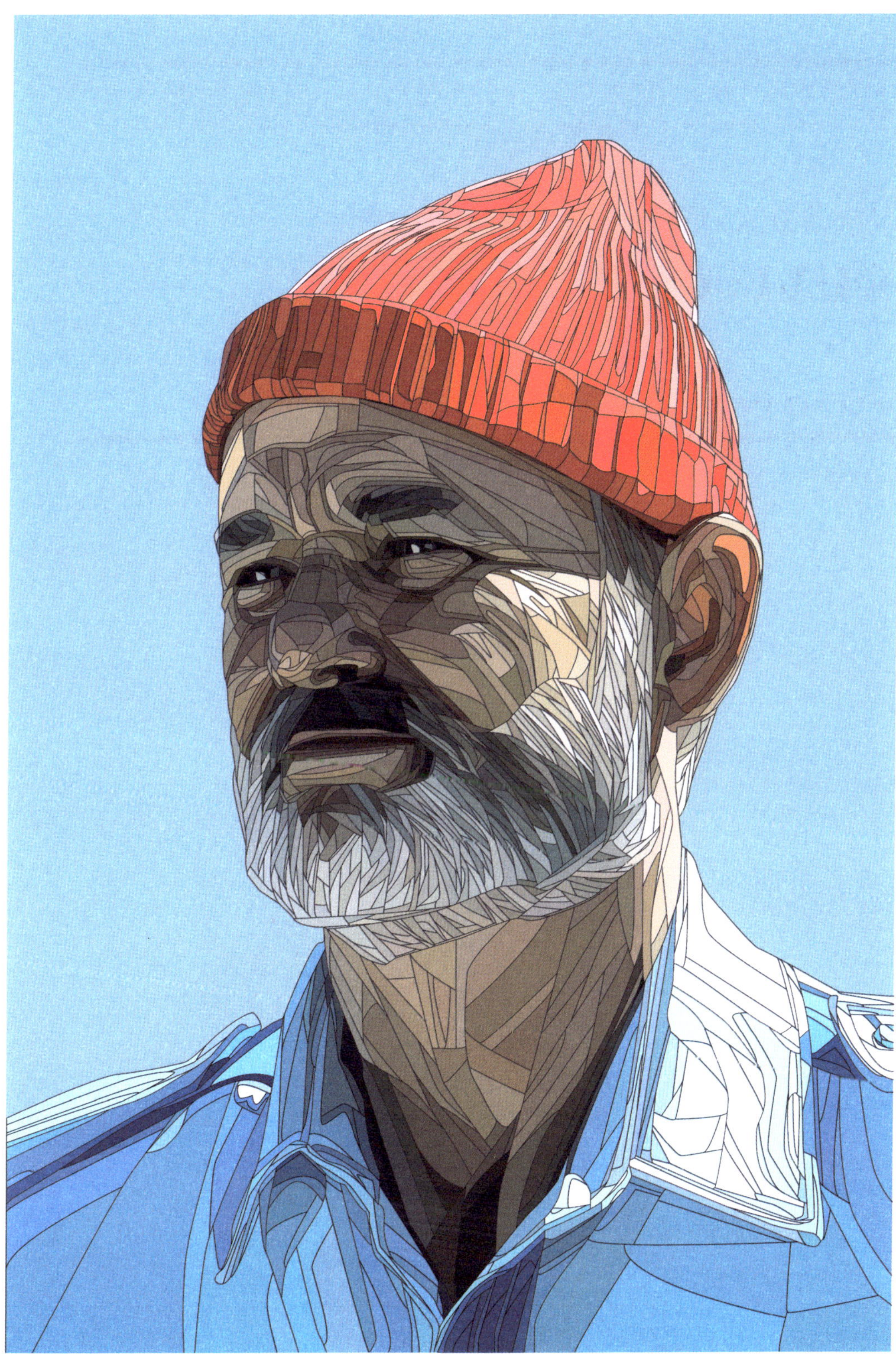

The Life Aquatic - with Steve Zissou

JASON SCHWARTZMAN
MAX FISCHER

BILL MURRAY
HERMAN BLUME

OLIVIA WILLIAMS
ROSEMARY CROSS

SEYMOUR CASSEL
BERT FISCHER

WES ANDERSON'S RUSHMORE

WITH MAX FISCHER

SYNOPSIS
AMONGST OTHER THINGS

Max Fischer is a very precocious 15 year old whose reason for living is his attendance at Rushmore, a private school where he's not doing well in any of his classes, but where he's the king of extracurricular activities - from being in the beekeeping society to writing and producing plays, there's very little after school he doesn't do. His life begins to change when he finds out he's on academic probation. On top of that he stumbles into love with Miss Cross, a pretty teacher of the elementary school at Rushmore. Added to the mix is his friendship with Herman Blume, a very wealthy industrialist and father to two boys who attend Rushmore, and who also finds himself attracted to Miss Cross. Max's fate becomes inextricably tied to this odd love triangle, and how he sets about resolving it by going to extreme and peculiar extents to prove his love for a woman who is not only to old for him, but does not share the same love interest.

RELEASE DATE:
02.05.1999

RUNTIME:
93 MINUTES

BUDGET:
$20,000,000

OPENING WEEKEND:
$43,666
At 02 screen in the US on 12.01.1999

LANGUAGE:
English

FILMING LOCATIONS:
Bay Town & Houston Texas, Kinkade School (201 Kinkade School Drive), Lamar High School (Westheimer Road), North Shore High School (13501 Hollypark Drive), North Street Houston & St. John's School

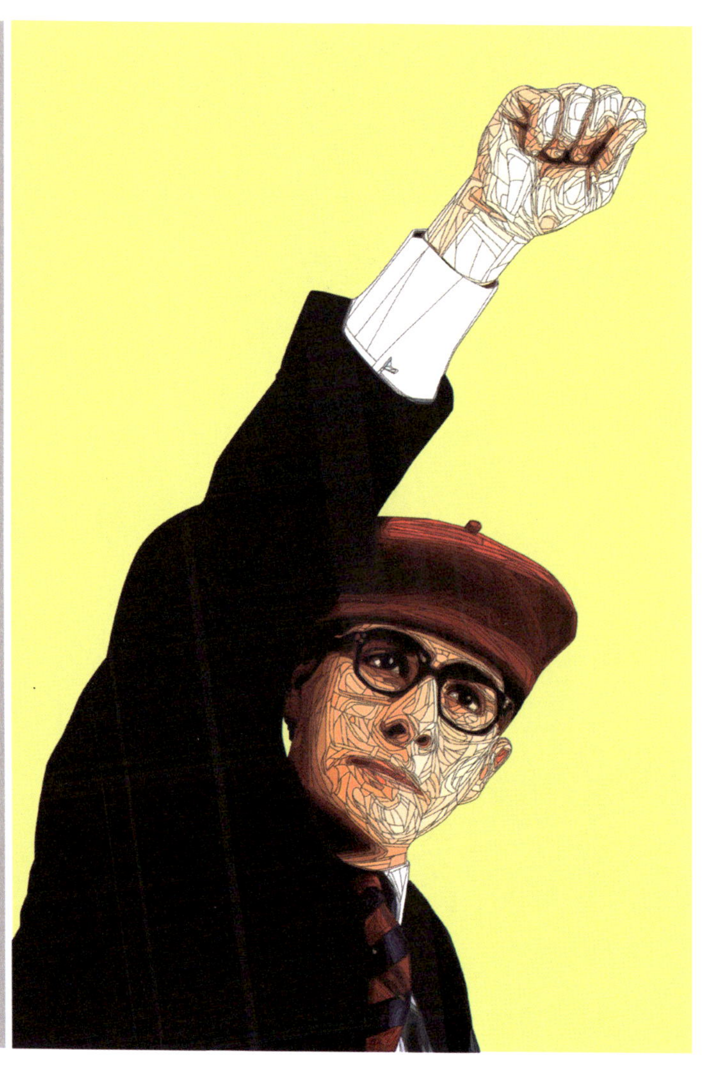

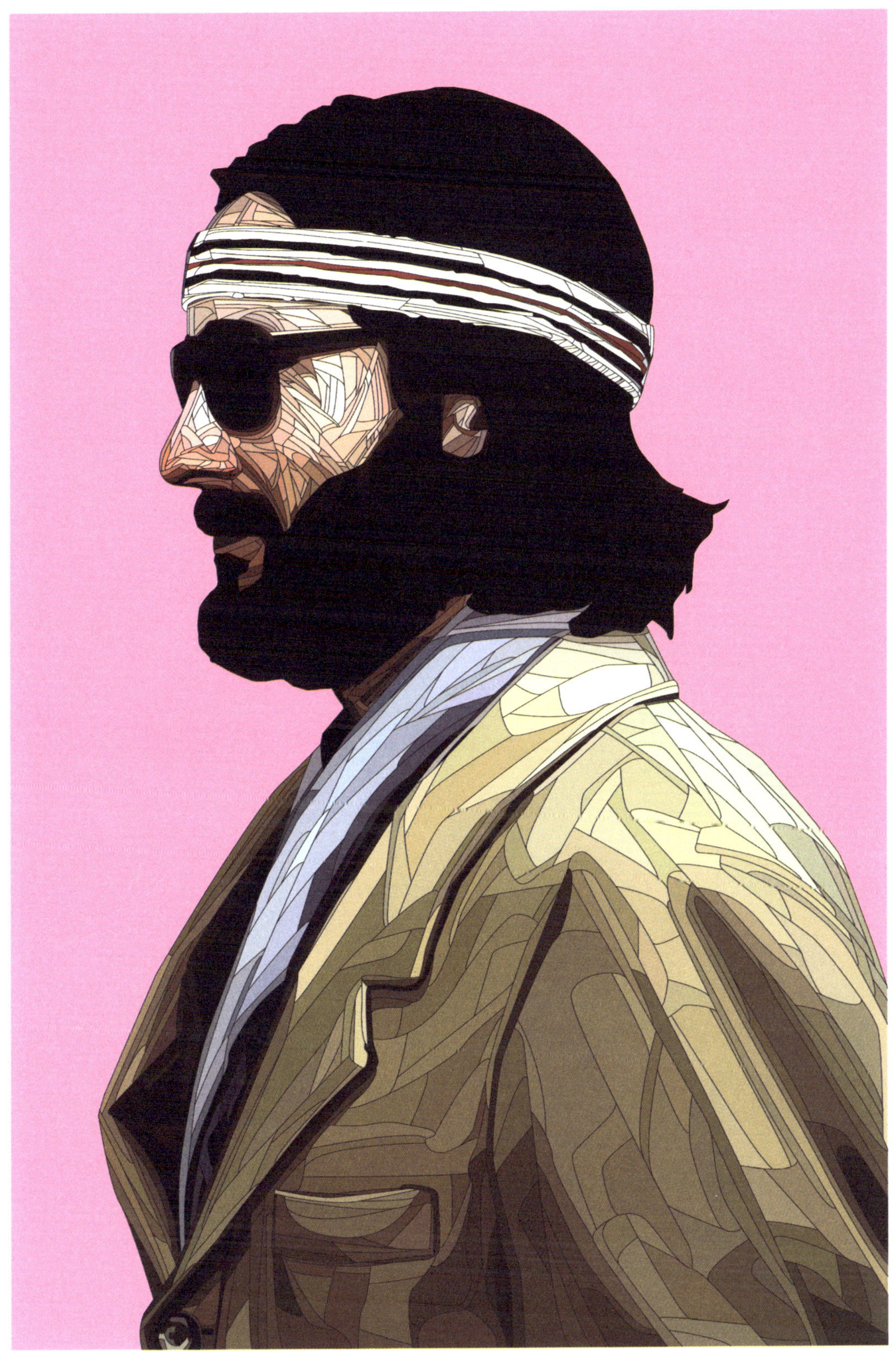

The Royal Tenenbaums

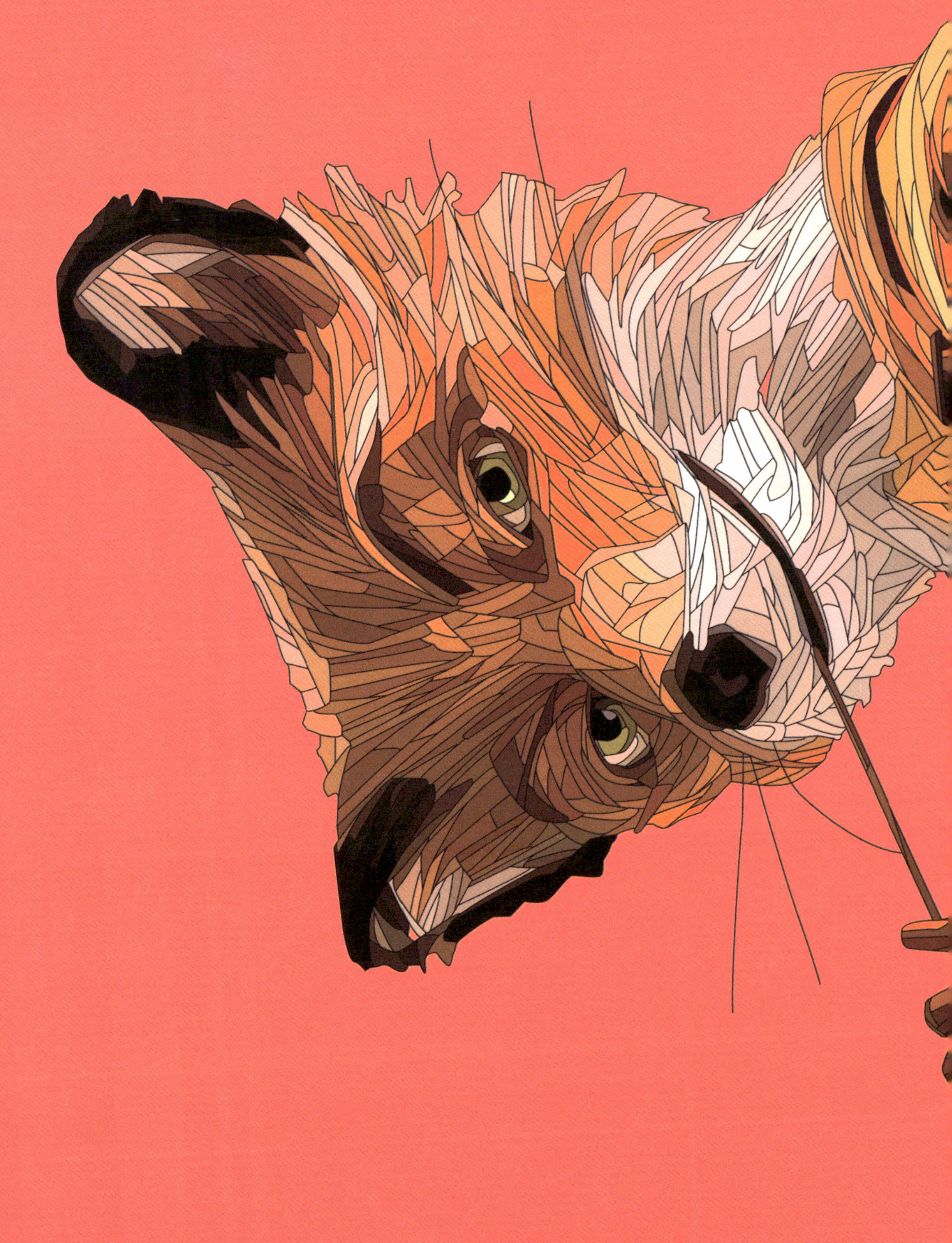

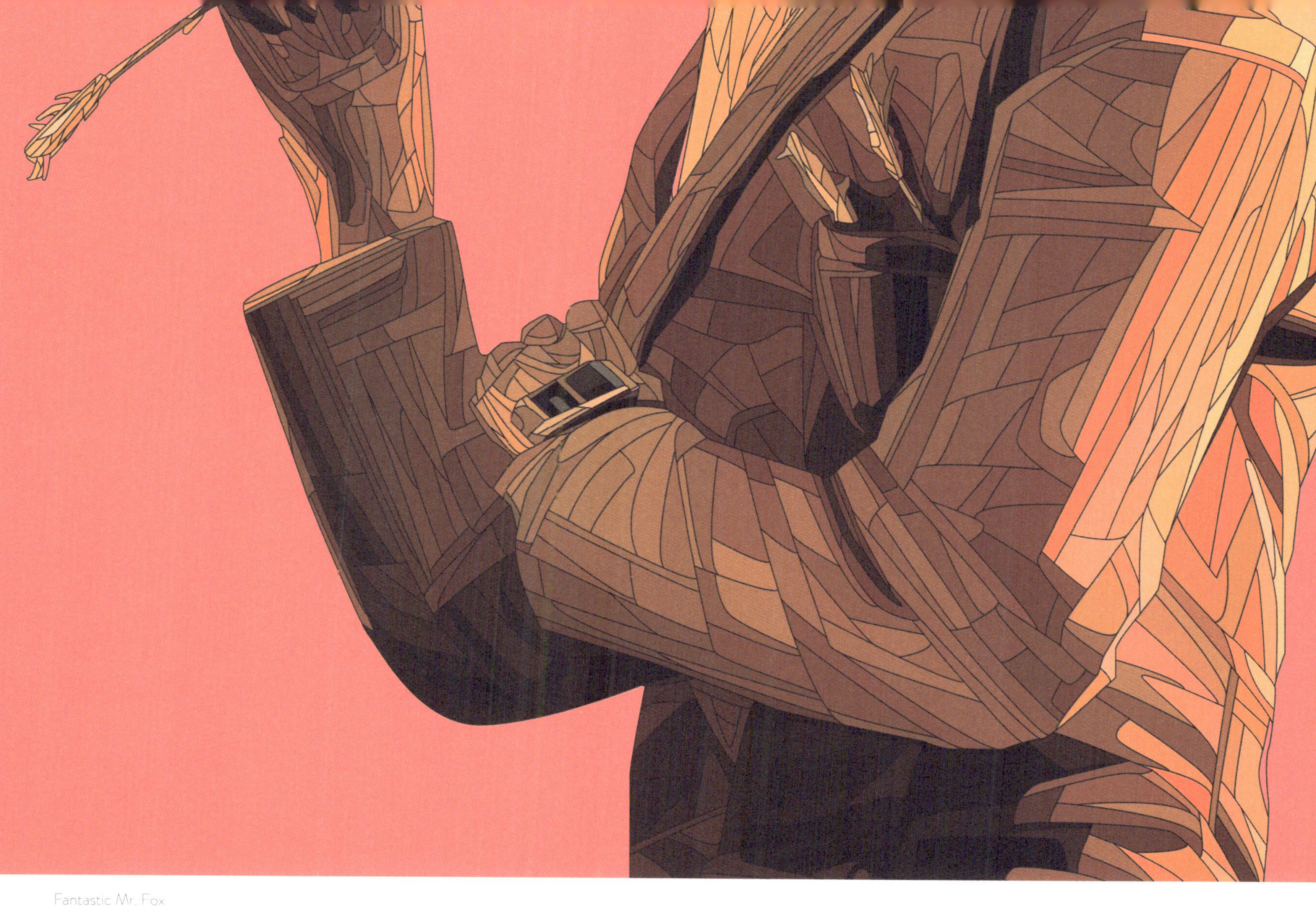

Fantastic Mr. Fox

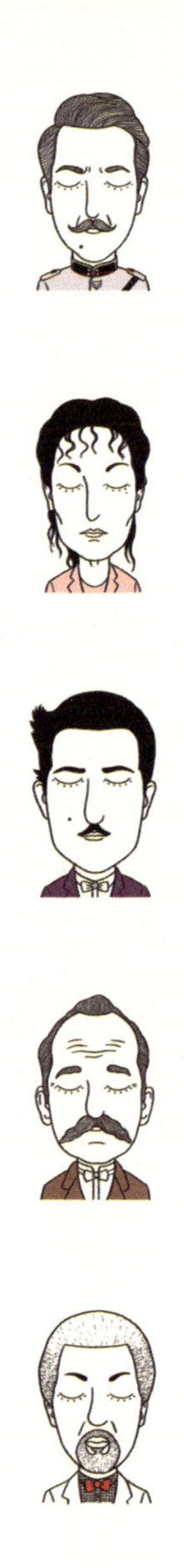
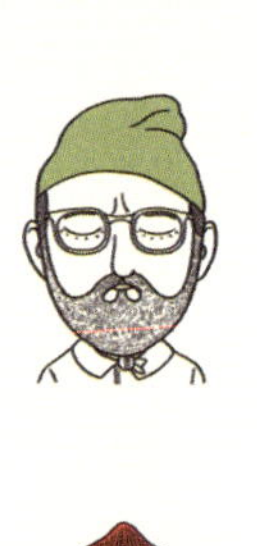
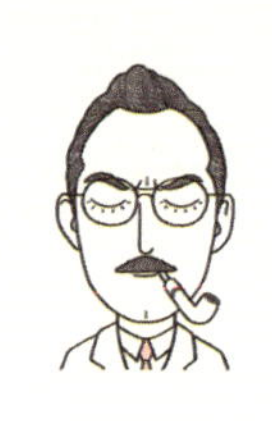
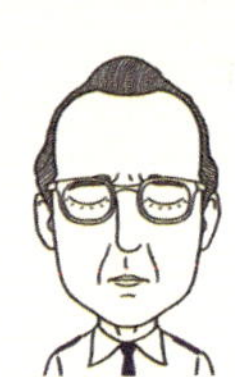
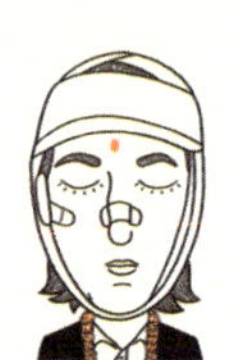
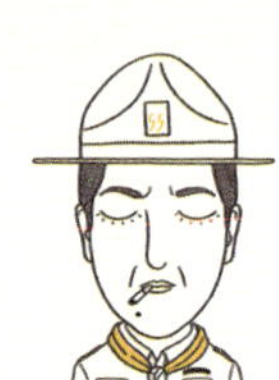
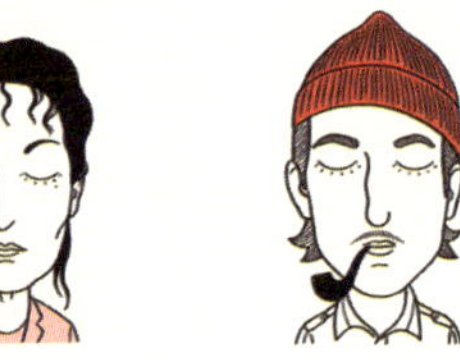
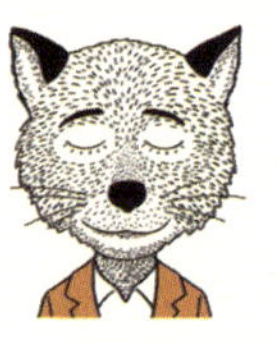
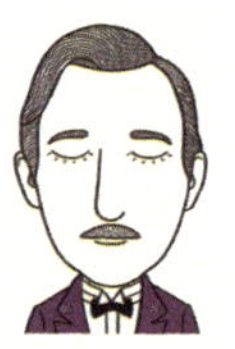
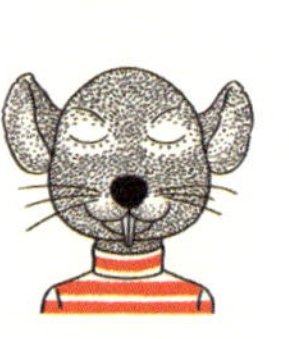
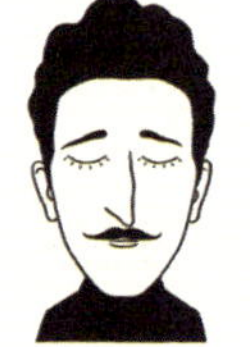
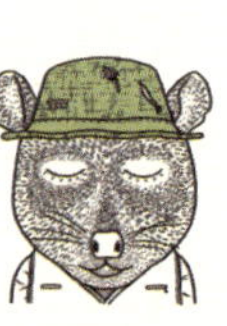
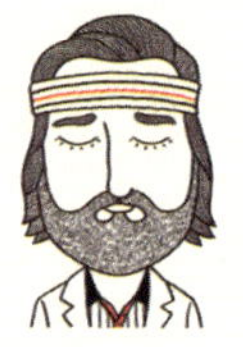
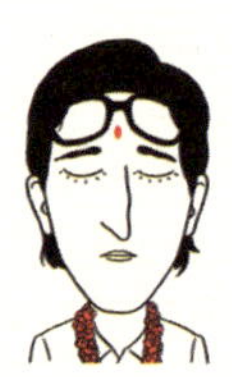
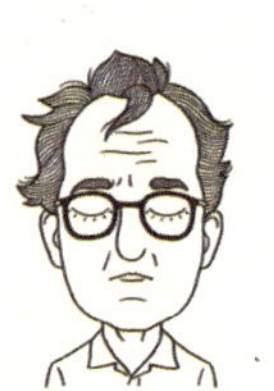
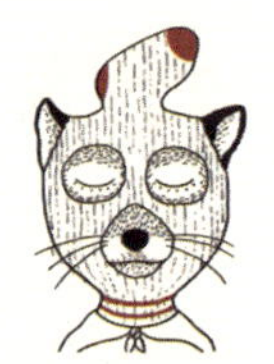
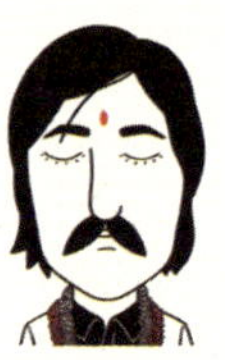
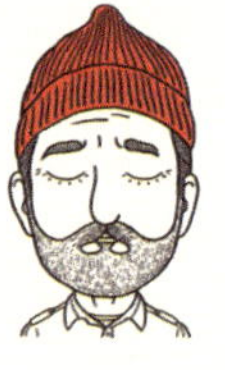
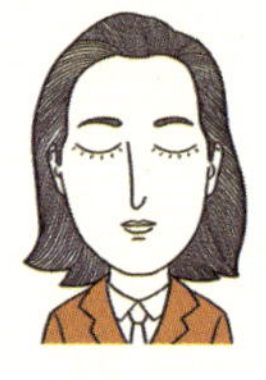
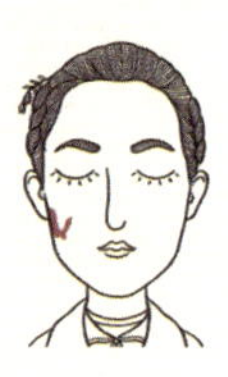
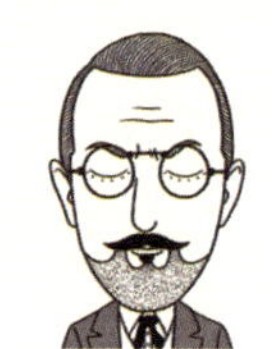
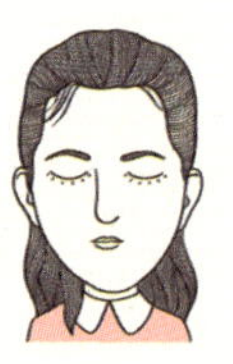
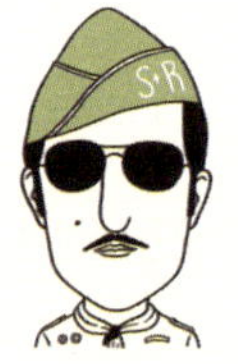
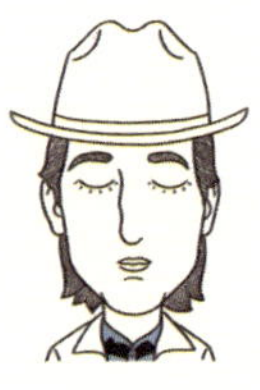
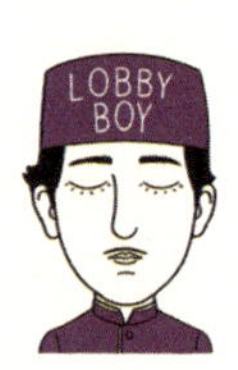
LOBBY
BOY
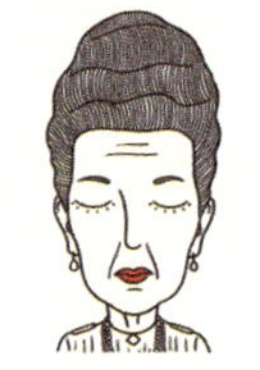
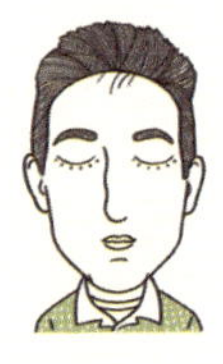
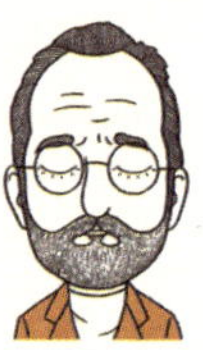
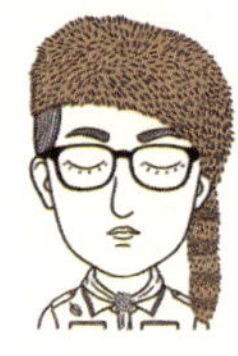
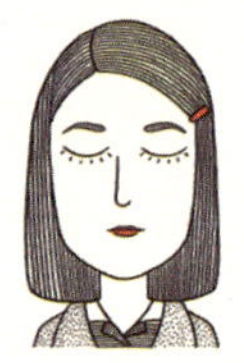
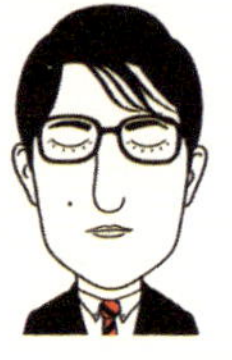
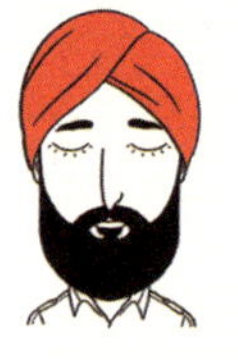
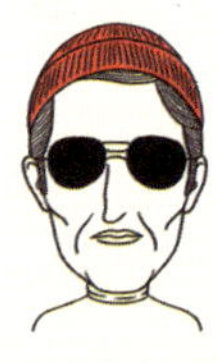
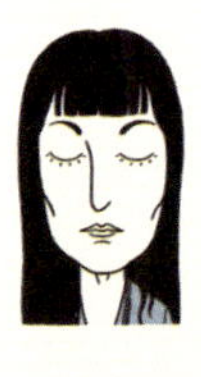
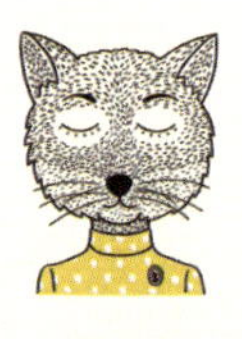
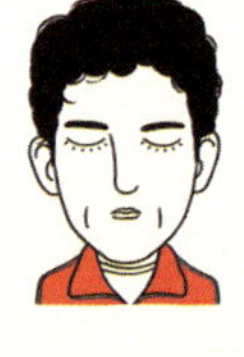
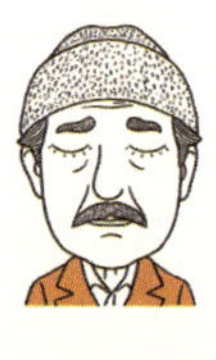
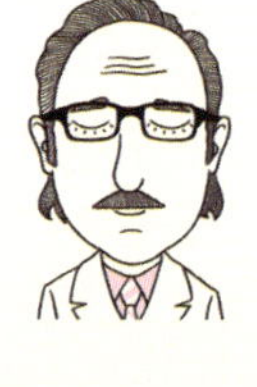